Chinese Labor in a Korean Factory

Chinese Labor in a Korean Factory

CLASS, ETHNICITY, AND PRODUCTIVITY
ON THE SHOP FLOOR IN
GLOBALIZING CHINA

Jaesok Kim

STANFORD UNIVERSITY PRESS
STANFORD, CALIFORNIA

Stanford University Press
Stanford, California

Printed in the United States of America on acid-free, archival-quality paper

Library of Congress Cataloging-in-Publication Data

Kim, Jaesok, author.
  Chinese labor in a Korean factory : class, ethnicity, and productivity on the shop floor in globalizing China / Jaesok Kim.
      pages cm
  Includes bibliographical references and index.
  ISBN 978-0-8047-8454-2 (cloth : alk. paper)
    1. Corporations, South Korean—China—Qingdao—Sociological aspects.
2. International business enterprises—China—Qingdao—Sociological aspects.
3. Clothing factories—China—Qingdao—Case studies. 4. Sweatshops—China—Qingdao—Case studies. 5. Industrial relations—China—Qingdao—Case studies.
6. Labor and globalization—China—Qingdao—Case studies. 7. Business anthropology—China—Qingdao—Case studies. I. Title.
HD2910.Z8Q365   2013
331.7'687095114—dc23
                                                                    2012034936

ISBN 978-0-8047-8612-6 (electronic)

To my parents

Contents

Figures and Tables

Acknowledgments

This book would not have been possible without the help of many people. First of all, I am deeply indebted to the people of Nawon Apparel, a multinational garment factory in a dull-colored industrial area in the northern part of Qingdao. I owe a special debt of gratitude to the many workers of the factory. Without their willingness to let me work with them and ask questions about daily work routines on the shop floor, this book would not have been possible. Though I cannot acknowledge their contributions by name, I appreciate their frankness and hospitality. I am also grateful to the managers of the factory for their assistance with my research, especially for their unusual generosity in allowing me to live in the factory for a long time. My description of the people in the factory, however, does not carry all their experiences—both good and bad—that I observed through my interactions with them. Responsibility for the interpretations of all the experiences presented here, including any errors, lies solely with me.

Many people have helped me shape and complete this project. James (Woody) Watson, my advisor at Harvard, has consistently given his attention and advice to my research and writing projects. Without his encouragement and guidance, my work on the project would have been much delayed. Michael Herzfeld, Arthur Kleinman, and Rubie Watson have been unflagging in their support for this project and my academic life. My colleagues at Penn, especially Adriana Petryna, Robert Preucel, Deborah Thomas, and Greg Urban, encouraged me to finish this project. I also owe a debt to my professors at Seoul National University who shared their experiences and knowledge with me, particularly Professors Kwang-ok Kim, Myung-Seok Oh, and Hahn-Sok Wang. Yuhua Guo at Qinghua University also gave me tremendous support at the early stage of my research. My friends at Harvard, Zongze Hu, Ahmed Kanna, Maple Raza, Ramyar Rossoukh, Fei Wu, and Amy Young, provided insightful comments and lasting comradeship on my project. A special word of thanks goes to Ahmed, who read early drafts of the chapters.

Last but not least, I thank my family back in South Korea. My parents, Doogon Kim and Myungja Kim, have in so many ways helped and encouraged me. My sister, Soo-a, has shared the role of her absent younger brother since I moved to the United States to continue my academic career. I also thank my wife's parents, who thoroughly understand this project. They offered support indispensable for conducting successful fieldwork. To Seoyeon Choi, my wife and an anthropologist, my debt is beyond mere words. She provided me with invaluable assistance by reading my manuscript and making many insightful comments on revisions. My daughter, Yoon-Jae, gave me a strong motivation to complete this book. All other members of my family have traveled this long road right by my side, supporting my difficult project in their own important ways.

Chinese Labor in a Korean Factory

Introduction

We will make Qingdao the most investment-friendly
place for Korean enterprises.

—C H O N G   Y Ü , vice-mayor of Qingdao, March 2006

Chengyang is not a part of Qingdao but a part of Seoul.[1]

—J U N G , manager of Nawon Korea, September 2002

Globalization is usually perceived as a progressive shift from bounded, local, and homogeneous forms of modernity to an ungrounded, flexible, and fluid postmodernity (Harvey 1991; Appadurai 1996). The urban landscape of China clearly shows the increasing intensity of transnational and global flows of people, media images, ideas, and capital. When I arrived in the northern Chinese city of Qingdao on a late summer day in 2002, the first scene that caught my eye was the colorful electric signs in English. Many of them advertized Hollywood movies running in local theaters, as well as branches of multinational corporations (MNCs), including chain stores such as Wal-Mart, Carrefour, and JUSTCO, fast-food restaurants such as McDonald's and KFC. The signs indicate that Qingdao is a key consumer market of MNCs: Qingdao is the wealthiest city in Shandong province and also is ranked tenth out of China's top twenty wealthiest cities (KPMG 2006).

However, the dazzling scene of thriving consumerism created by foreign corporations is misleading because the service industry is not the main interest of foreign direct investment in the region. Instead of in the tertiary industrial sector, foreign corporations made about four-fifths of their investment in the manufacturing sector. Foreign MNCs accounted for more than half of the total value of the city's exports, and foreign corporations' exports have been growing by more than 10 percent each year (SDBS 2008). In fact, since the Chinese government named a district of Qingdao a Special Economic and Technology Development Zone, the city has transformed itself into the province's center of manufacturing. The city has attracted a large amount of foreign direct investment (FDI), reaching US$2.6 billion in 2008 and growing by more than 10 percent each year since then (SDBS 2009). As a result, Qingdao was named as one of the most favored Chinese cities by the world's top corporations, as almost 130 corporations on the Fortune 500 list have invested in the city (KPMG 2007).

Although the large and growing number of MNCs indicates that Qingdao is an ideal city for their overseas business, it does not mean that MNCs operate in China without difficulties. MNCs, as creatures of late industrial capitalism, relocate incessantly from one location to another pursuing better business conditions that guarantee them higher profits (Bartlett and Ghoshal 1991). Although their investment decisions are based on economic calculations of profit and loss, the actual movement of a corporation is not purely economic; it includes the transfer of the local culture of the place where the corporation is originally located. Workers and government officials of the host country are also embedded in their own local cultures. Here I define the term "culture" in a particular way, as notions of time and punctuality, ideas of discipline, norms of desirable personhood, beliefs in legitimate workshop authority, and expected standards of bodily cleanliness. In fact, "culture" was the most commonly used term in the multinational factory that I researched, where a small group of expatriate Korean managers supervised more than seven hundred Chinese workers. On the shop floor of this factory, for example, I frequently heard Han-Chinese workers complaining about Korean managers' "excessive fretfulness"[2] to keep production deadlines, while the Korean managers expressed their frustration with the "sluggish" work speed of the workers. Interestingly, both the workers and the managers explained their complaints about the other party in terms of "cultural" differences that allegedly exist between China and (South) Korea. The vague idea of cultural difference contributes to establishing a distinctive factory management in which the Korean managers assumed an authoritarian and paternalist role in "properly" disciplining and caring for untrained Chinese workers.

The mounting pressure from the global market complicates the situation of the multinational workplace. The global market, by its nature, constantly requires MNCs to shorten lead time and reduce production costs. The continuing pressure from the market often pushes management toward a higher level of globalization, which in this case requires the rationalization of shop-floor organization and increased labor productivity. My study shows how the mandate of the global market to increase productivity and cut production costs brought constant changes to a multinational factory, prompting the foreign management to adopt different managerial strategies and methods of labor discipline. At the level of the shop floor, management's demands translated into faster work speed, tightened labor surveillance, and poorer work conditions, thus eventually creating local workers' grievances against the foreign management. The same mandate perpetuates the tense relationship between foreign managers and local labor as it blinds management to local cultural ideas about proper levels of labor discipline and acceptable methods of shop-floor control.

NAWON APPAREL

I conducted my fieldwork at Nawon Apparel (Nawon), a multinational garment corporation located in the city of Qingdao. Major fieldwork was conducted from 2002 to 2003. After the fieldwork, I conducted follow-up research to 2006 and interviewed Nawon's managers and workers. Nawon was a medium-sized garment manufacturing corporation. In 2003, it employed about seven hundred employees, including Korean expatriate managers, Korean-Chinese interpreters, and Han-Chinese workers. Management hired Korean-Chinese—one of the fifty-five ethnic minorities in China—for its local assistants of business, considering their bilingualism in Korean and Chinese and their Korean cultural background to be of great value. Han-Chinese, the absolute ethnic majority of China, represented about 90 percent of the workforce at Nawon and numbered more than six hundred. Most Han-Chinese workers were young and unmarried women from rural backgrounds, which reflected management's belief that women are more docile than men and its belief in the usefulness of women's "nimble fingers" in labor-intensive garment production.

Nawon Korea, the corporate headquarters of Nawon, was located in Seoul, South Korea. Established in 1993 as an exclusively Korean-invested enterprise, Nawon was one of the few among the eighty Korean-invested garment factories in the greater Qingdao area that had continuously operated for more than ten years (KOFOTI 2003). This corporation operated as a typical contract manufacturer that makes and ships products under contract to foreign buyers. In 2002, the corporation exported 68 percent of its manufactured products to Japan and the rest to the United States (Personnel Department, Nawon Korea 2003).

Korean-invested corporations were the most numerous group of MNCs in Qingdao. Thanks to its geographical proximity to Korea and low labor costs, Qingdao has been the largest investment destination for Korean corporations in China since 1992. In 2003, Korean enterprises accounted for 23.5 percent of foreign trade (US$4.2 billion) and 45.4 percent of total foreign investment (US$1.8 billion) in the region (SDBS 2003, 2005; Kong 2005; SDBFT 2005).[3] In 2003, almost seven thousand Korean-invested corporations were located in the city, and about forty thousand Korean nationals lived in and around the city (*Qingdao ribao* 2003; Jang 2003). Many Koreans took great pride in their dominant economic status in Qingdao. Some of them even regarded the district of Chengyang, where more than fourteen hundred Korean MNCs operated and over thirteen thousand Koreans lived, not as a part of Qingdao but as a part of Seoul (interview with Koreans, December 2002, March, April 2003; Moon 2002). Several Korean newspapers have described Qingdao as leased territory controlled by Korea and have even compared Qingdao with Dalian—an export-oriented harbor city in Liaoning Province—which was formerly a bridgehead of imperialist Japan during the World War II and is heavily under the influence of Japanese MNCs (Cho 2004; Bonyeong Lee 2005a).

The personnel composition of Nawon in June 2002 seems to demonstrate the factory's successful localization. Localization, a term common in Korean business administration literature, is often measured by the ratio between the number of Koreans and that of "indigenous" people among managerial staff, where a high ratio of the indigenous people indicates a high level of localization (Shanghai Asset Inc. 2005; Shin 1993). Successful localization, then, indicates management's effective control of local labor even with a small number of foreign managers. At Nawon, only three Korean managers supervised around seven hundred Chinese employees, including sixteen Korean-Chinese interpreters,[4] twenty-six Han-Chinese managerial staff, and over six hundred rank-and-file workers of Han-Chinese ethnicity. Compared with a nearby Korean garment factory where nine Korean managers struggled to control about three hundred Chinese workers, the small number of Korean managerial staff in the factory indicates that the management at Nawon controlled the shop floor effectively. In fact, the factory experienced virtually no labor disputes during its decade-long operation in China, while many nearby garment factories, both foreign-invested and Chinese-owned, suffered from frequent labor disputes, which mostly resulted from excessive overtime and delayed payment of wages. The situation at Nawon was even more extraordinary because the workers of the factory also had to put in endless overtime, often longer than those of the other factories.

What explains the relatively stable labor-management relationship at Nawon? How could the relatively small foreign managerial staff control such a large number of Chinese workers without difficulty? The history of the evolving factory regime of the corporation may explain the more than a decade-long absence of major labor disputes. Just as industrial workers are not created overnight but produced in prolonged struggles over restructuring of working habits (Thompson 1966: 9), the factory regime at Nawon is in fact an end result of long-term, occasionally intense, daily interactions between foreign management and local people. In the context, my ethnographic study investigates how Nawon's foreign management ensured the uninterrupted operation of the factory by creating specific forms of power relations and ideologies on the shop floor. My study also analyzes how the Chinese workers reacted to management's effort to mold them into "model" industrial workers. The corporation, which had boasted of its exceptional record of "no labor disputes," encountered an unexpected workers' strike in 2002. I look into the historical process through which the workers gradually changed from submissive subjects of labor control to active organizers of resistance. This change eventually set a limit on management's call for a higher level of globalization.

The foreign management's authoritarian labor control and its attitudes toward local labor resulted from collective misrecognition. It is misrecognition, because the managers at Nawon misunderstood the workers they encountered on the everyday shop floor, based on their limited personal experience and knowledge of China and Chinese workers. It is collective, because the misrecognition involved not an individual manager but the entire group of the Korean expatriate managers. Such misrecognition is a local effect of globalization. Globalization, the ever-intensifying transnational flows of capital, people, ideas, and cultural objects, is often believed to improve people's understanding of different "cultures" and thus promote their tolerance of cultural others (Lane 2006: 89–90). However, especially during the early period of globalization, intensifying transnational flows often bring about misrecognitions, which makes the people involved misunderstand objects, ideas, or people they encounter. At Nawon, the Korean managers' initial perception of the Han-Chinese workers clearly reveals collective misrecognition. The managers viewed the Han-Chinese workers in their late teens as heavily affected by the radical Communism of the Maoist period, even though the workers had not experienced even a single moment of radical Communism. As we shall see, management's misrecognition of Chinese workers brought a particular political effect, which in this case determined its methods of labor surveillance and discipline.

MULTINATIONAL CORPORATIONS AND SUPERIORITY OF THE WEST

Much of the literature on globalization assumes the agencies of the global are located in the West. For example, David Harvey argues that key technological advances in the West such as the railroad, the telegraph, and the automobile, by bringing disparate places into a world market as global producers and consumers, have served to make the world a smaller place (Harvey 1991: 229–32). Mokyr (1990) points to British technological advances in industrial sectors such as textiles and steel as the key factors that account for the Industrial Revolution and the subsequent globalization. Explanations of Western technological prowess are closely related to the search for the philosophical, cultural, or moral backgrounds that made technological development possible only in the West. Max Weber insisted that medieval cities of the West had been the places of origin of the modern concepts of individualism, rationality, and freedom (Weber 1968 [1956]: 1226–50), which eventually influenced the development of capitalism in the West (Weber 2001 [1930]). He contrasted the civilizations of the non-Western world with the "true" civilization of the West, which created and retained the values and ideas of legality, urban autonomy/freedom, and communal obligations (Weber 1986 [1921]). Following Weber, many scholars also have argued that some values and ideas indigenous to the West contributed to technological achievements and, later, to the emergence of capitalism and the Industrial Revolution. They commonly have praised the West for its role in establishing a unique set of laws that protect private property and contracts (Hansen and Prescott 2002; Lucas 2002; North and Weingast 1989) and creating cultural norms such as hard work, frugality, and educational discipline (Clark 2007).

In the West-centered model of capitalism and globalization, the non-Western world inevitably assumes less important and peripheral roles, such as consumers of Western products or providers of raw materials. The model also assumes that the non-Western world remained less developed because it lacked the societal structures and cultural values that helped the West to take the lead in the Industrial Revolution and globalization. Countries like China and Japan may have been not much different from the European countries in terms of the "commodification of goods, land, and labor, market-driven growth" (Pomeranz 2000: 107), but the material achievement of the non-Western world did not lead to an industrial revolution and thus failed to grant the non-Western world the agency of globalization. This, it has been argued, was because it adhered to hereditary societal statuses and privileges, and thus lacked social mobility and dynamics (Braudel 1992 [1979]: 581–601). Following this logic, the non-Western world can be best described as a provider of raw materials to the Western countries who helped the latter to rapidly expand their industry without driving up the cost of raw materials. This is the role of the non-Western world in the so-called first great globalization shock (O'Rourke and Williamson 2002), the fast growth of productivity that coincided with the development of new transport technologies and the unprecedented expansion of world trade during the nineteenth century.

The workplace of many MNCs shows how the historical idea of Western-led globalization and the belief in the prowess of the West is reproduced in present times, enhanced by the unequal power relationship between foreign managers and local employees. In the workplace, management—most from the Western countries that are economically more developed than the host country—has tended to view its local employees as inferior subjects. The managerial practices of many MNCs reflect the foreign management's belief in the universal or "global" validity of its Western cultural values and norms, considered superior to those of the local employees. For example, Fuller (2009) reports that in a Japanese subsidiary of a U.S.-based company, the expatriate American managers developed contrasting cultural distinctions between themselves and its Japanese employees. The managers assigned to themselves desirable or "global" traits such as vision, creativity, directness, and risk-taking, which in fact reflected a certain version of the ideal personality thriving in the United States. In contrast, they put Japanese employees on the opposite side of the desirable traits and considered them uncreative, overly submissive, excessively reserved, and conservative (Fuller 2009: 97–98). Klubock (1996) shows another corporate version of the West-centered globalization in the guise of "global" management by looking at a Chilean copper mine owned and operated by an American firm. In the Chilean mine, the management designed corporate regulations and benefits programs based on contrasting cultural traits between the United States and Chile. In the programs, the Chilean miners appeared to have undesirable cultural traits (unruly, violent, promiscuous, and overly masculine), in contrast to desirable American traits (law-abiding, peaceful, and monogamous). The "universal" values imposed on the Chilean mining community, however, originated from the particular values of white-collar, middle-class American society.

Western management's view of local employees as inferior subjects is also expressed in terms of a time difference between the two. It has been reported that, in many MNCs, foreign managers consider themselves belonging to a more advanced stage than that of the local workers on an evolutionary scale of historical change (Chae 2003; Peterson 1992). Their denial of local employees' coevalness (Fabian 1983) imposes the identity of "others" on the workers in the sense that they *still* live in the past. This denial has a remarkably powerful effect, which reinforces foreign management's feeling of superiority over local workers. It reinforces the managers' assumed attitude of "enlighteners" toward local labor, justifying their paternalist treatment of the workers.

Management's denial of local employees' coevalness contributes to racialized cultural distinctions between the Western management and the non-Western, "local" employees. This suggests that the corporate hierarchy between Western management and non-Western labor is hard to change, to the extent that management firmly believes in its ultimate cultural superiority over non-Western labor and maintains its superior position in the workplace. Local employees can be promoted to a certain level if they transform themselves by conforming to strict corporate regulations and worker-training programs. Their promotions, however, are limited because Western management often puts a racialized glass ceiling in the corporate ladder. Management believes that the ability of local employees to change is fundamentally limited, because they are deeply embedded in "local," non-Western cultural traditions that are inferior to those of management. The relationship between Western management and non-Western employees can even be compared to that between parents and children. The metaphor exemplifies management's supposition that non-Western employees are maturing but are still in an adolescent stage of development (Fuller 2009: 78).

GLOBALIZATION IN A NON-WESTERN MULTINATIONAL CORPORATION

The situation at Nawon shows how the non-Western origin of this multinational corporation made its management strive to make their alleged superiority to the local employees obvious and apparent. In the factory, for example, management created a highly rigid hierarchical distinction between foreign management and local employees, based on their understanding of local employees as "backward" subjects. The rigid distinctions seem unusual because the management came from a non-Western country, South Korea, which had been regarded as one of the peripheral countries in the global commodity chain.[5] Until the late 1980s, many foreign MNCs had considered South Korea an ideal place for maximizing their profits, taking advantage of its low labor costs and relatively high-quality labor. Since the late 1980s, however, South Korea quickly transformed itself from an ideal destination of foreign MNCs into the headquarters of Korean MNCs, as many Korean corporations began to relocate their production facilities to other countries. Nawon was the Chinese subsidiary of Nawon Korea, one of the South Korean corporations that had transformed themselves into MNCs. The presence of Nawon demonstrated that Nawon Korea successfully moved upward in the global chain of commodity production, changing itself from a subcontract factory to an intermediary corporation that directly dealt with international buyers and placed orders with subcontract factories.

Nawon Korea's successful transformation into an MNC, as well as the rapid macro-level economic development of South Korea during the 1970s and 1980s, led the Korean managers of the corporation to firmly believe in the Korean management's superiority to the Chinese employees. The managers asserted that the successful growth and transformation of many South Korean corporations was possible mainly because, by faithfully following "global" standards, they kept their corporate organization and practices efficient and rational. Nawon's management located the origin of "global" standards in the West, identifying them as advanced production technologies, highly efficient managerial practices, and the rationalized organization characteristic of Western MNCs. Nawon's corporate charter, written in 1993, declared that every operation of the corporation should be based on "the advanced managerial practices and production technologies" of Nawon Korea, which, again, located its corporate model in the West. Just like the foreign managers from the West, the management at Nawon believed that their advanced practices and technologies entitled them to control and discipline the "backward and undisciplined" Chinese workers who were bound to their recent past of radical Maoism and deep-rooted "peasant nature."

The fragility inherent in the Korean managers' feeling of superiority over the Chinese workers made them more attentive to securing the distinctions between "global" management and local labor. Foreign management from the West maintains its superiority over local labor since the economic and social gap between the two is too wide to be easily closed. The situation at Nawon was different, because the foreign managers there felt the gap between their country of origin, South Korea, and China was not wide enough to maintain their superiority. The Korean managers often felt their superior status over local labor was far from secure. This feeling arose both from the historical collective memory of the "China threat" to Korea and from the rapidly developing Chinese economy. To establish their superiority over the Chinese labor that was not immediately acknowledged, the managers worked diligently to make the space and organization of the factory reflect an inviolable hierarchical difference between Koreans and Chinese. For example, they assigned the core part of the factory space to themselves, while putting the Han-Chinese workers in factory dormitories located just outside the factory space. My study shows that the discrimination against the Chinese workers created new differences between Koreans and Chinese and maintained the sense of cultural superiority among the Korean managers. I especially show the various methods that management devised to maintain its superiority over the local Chinese labor, and management's arbitrary understanding of the cultural differences between Koreans and Chinese that contributed to the production of those methods.

The non-Western origin of the management at Nawon also affected the actual operations of the factory. Contrary to their initial expectations, the Korean managers realized the limited effect of "universal" or Western methods of labor control. In their effort to overcome this difficulty, they began to incorporate alternative methods of labor discipline and managerial practices into the existing "universal" ones. The alternative methods and practices clearly bore non-Western characteristics in that they had been formulated through the Korean historical experiences of the Cold War, oppressive military government, and authoritarian work culture as a result of the military regime. The foreign management from South Korea initially tried to *de*emphasize their Korean background, while highlighting the universal or Western principles of high efficiency and advanced industrialism. Management, however, eventually decided to actively incorporate its managerial experience in Korea to resolve problems caused by "Communist" Chinese labor. Furthermore, management enhanced its authoritarian and paternalist control of Chinese workers by exploiting elements of their culture, such as the Han-Chinese workers' feeling of filial obligation and their basic trust in "humane" management.

THE CHANGING MEANINGS OF NATION, NATIONALITY, AND ETHNICITY

The presence of multinational factories added new meanings to existing ethnic differences and changed the power relationship among ethnic groups in China. In the country, Han-Chinese are the overwhelming ethnic majority and have occupied the "center" of China in the historical, social, and geographical senses. In contrast, most Korean-Chinese live in a marginal area of northeast China and have little political leverage over central politics, which is dominated by Han-Chinese. At Nawon, however, the dominant status of Han-Chinese was completely overturned. In the factory, a small number of Korean-Chinese occupied most intermediary managerial staff positions, while the majority of Han-Chinese employees took on the heavy burden of sweatshop labor on the shop floor as rank-and-file workers.

The managerial status of Korean-Chinese is significantly different from general patterns of interethnic division of labor. According to a common pattern, minority groups are usually overrepresented in marginal or low-paid jobs, owing to economic, social, and cultural discrimination (DeAnda 1996). It is also said that immigrants tend to take relatively menial and marginal jobs because they are not familiar with the culture of the host country (Lamphere 1992). These two statements indicate that the social status of a minority group would be worse if its members were recent immigrants to the host country. The social and economic status of Korean-Chinese in China seems to perfectly fit these statements. Most Korean-Chinese are descendents of poor farmers who migrated from Korea during the early twentieth century. In addition, the largest group of Korean-Chinese live in a remote region of northeast China infamous for its relatively slow economic and social development compared with rapidly developing southeast China (Ching Kwan Lee 1999, 2000a, 2000b).

At Nawon, however, Korean-Chinese employees held job positions higher than those of their Han-Chinese counterparts and enjoyed exceptional corporate benefits. The superior status of the Korean-Chinese is another effect of locally embedded globalization, as it resulted from management's strong favoring of Korean-Chinese over Han-Chinese. The management from South Korea considered

Korean-Chinese much more reliable than Han-Chinese, because it believed Korean-Chinese were part of the Korean nation. The Korean identity of Korean-Chinese, management thought, guaranteed that Korean-Chinese would have the "superior" Korean cultural traits such as diligence and obedience, which Han-Chinese generally lacked. The Nawon management heightened the ethnic tension between its Korean-Chinese and Han-Chinese employees and increased their ethnic consciousness by implementing discriminatory policies that heavily favored Korean-Chinese. The Korean-Chinese employees justified their privileged status in the corporation by their belief in an alleged Korean-Chinese ethnic or cultural superiority. This clearly shows that ethnicity can be understood as a vehicle to advance the interests of one ethnic group over others, when multiple groups of people divided by ethnicity compete with one another for limited resources (Glazer and Moynihan 1963: 17). Ethnicity, in this context, might be defined as strife between ethnic groups, in the course of which their members emphasize their identity and exclusiveness (Cohen 1969: 4).

By pointing out management's preconceptions of a different ethnicity and its belief in Korean cultural superiority, I do not mean that the preconceptions and belief are based on some unchanging cultural values and traits. On the contrary, they are the end result of a dynamic process of multiple mediations that include the past and the ongoing changes in the social and the economic environment of the factory. The mediations are also affected by the diverse reactions of the people involved in such changes. My study highlights how the foreign management at Nawon selectively used terms such as "nation," "nationality," and "national culture" to justify its policies that discriminated against Han-Chinese. In the factory, the meanings of the terms were not only arbitrarily constructed but also constantly changing as management modified its view of the "ethnic nature" of Korean-Chinese and Han-Chinese to cope with the rapidly changing economic and political environment of the corporation. Management, for example, gradually changed its negative view of Han-Chinese and more positively evaluated their ethnicity, acknowledging the apparent cost-saving effect of hiring Han-Chinese for intermediary managerial positions. Moreover, the managers from South Korea were never a homogeneous group, as implied by the unifying and homogenizing concept of Korean culture. In fact, there was an internal conflict in Nawon's foreign management, which was caused by an expatriate Korean manager who tried to develop strong ties with Han-Chinese workers while distancing himself from the corporate headquarters in Korea.

GLOBAL-LOCAL COLLABORATION
AND POST-SOCIALISM

The space of a factory often gives us a strong impression that it is a self-contained, hard-to-access place. Concrete walls topped with barbed wire, surveillance cameras, and unkind guards at the factory entrance create and maintain such an impression, making the factory seem a space hardly accessible to people from the outside. Contrary to the common image, however, the shop floor of a multinational factory is closely connected to the larger organizations outside, such as local governments and surrounding communities. On the shop floor of Nawon, I observed the growing collaboration between the global and the local, which contradicts the theory of unilateral globalization that presumes the overwhelming power of the global over the local (Salinas and Paldan 1979; Schiller 1976). My study shows that the global can neither fully encompass the domains of existing local institutions nor colonize the lived experiences of local people. MNCs, as the agents of global capitalism, need the local government's timely support in order to operate smoothly, which eventually results in growing collaboration between the two.

At first glance, the relationship between MNCs and local governments seems to prove the superior status of the global, because local governments have to compromise some key elements of their national sovereignty in order to attract MNCs. Historically, the space of a country has been considered an exclusive territory and the basic requirement for establishing national economies (Brenner 1998; Taylor 1995). It also has been argued that national economies, after their establishment, contribute to maintaining the national territory as a stable container where a "spatial fix" for industrial development can be established (Block 1994; Harvey 1985: 150). In special economic zones (SEZs), however, national governments do not seem to exercise their full sovereign rights. In this particular space, they depart from the grand political principle of unification that subordinates various economic and social practices within a determinate space of national territory (Lefebvre 1991: 281). Governments sometimes even go further and sign away parts of their legal rights such as taxation and corporate supervision in order to guarantee the smooth operation of MNCs.

Government officials make such decisions because they recognize the increasing importance of MNCs in the national economy of production and commodity exchange (Riain 2000). For example, Chinese government officials believed that a large influx of foreign capital could accelerate the development of the national economy and resolve the unemployment problem that had been made worse by the existence of more than 150 million semi-unemployed farmers in the countryside (Choi 2004; He 1998; Xin et al. 2000). To attract transnational capital, the Chinese government set up laws and ordinances that gave preferential treatment to MNCs, including exemptions from income and land taxes and a reimbursement program for value added taxes (VAT). In addition, the central government authorized local governments at different levels to implement their own preferential policies for foreign trade and investment (SCC 1986).[6] The local-level governments' effort to increase foreign investment was expressed in the forms of various benefits. These included an extra reduction in local taxes, low-cost electricity and water, and most importantly, some pro-management policies—both official and unofficial—such as loose customs control and connivance at labor code violations. The benefits meant local officials were voluntarily limiting their own authority as part of their effort to create more favorable conditions for MNCs. The benefits provided by the local officials became the key element of their growing collaboration with the foreign management, as the management responded to the benefits with some "special" gifts to the officials. We can understand the space of an SEZ as a recent invention of national governments as part of their effort to develop the national economy by meeting the MNCs' demand for the free flow of capital and a "flexible" labor market.

The strong presence of MNCs and local governments' partial concession of their territorial rights, however, do not necessarily mean the decline of the power and the functions of the territorial state. Instead, they promote the reconfiguration of the conventional state. It is the states that make efforts to establish and manage SEZs and, through those efforts, state organizations begin to operate as local agents of globalizing capitalism. For example, central governments often transfer parts of their legal authority to local-level governments to allow them to negotiate more efficiently with MNCs. The territorial power of the state, therefore, is not being eroded, but rearticulated in relation to both sub- and supra-state levels (Swyngedouw 1997).

It is not just the state that goes through a reconfiguration. MNCs also give up parts of their rights as agents of global capitalism when they comply with the guidelines of their host countries. In the age of global economy, transnational capital is said to be mobile and "virtual" while labor and states—as the containers of local labor—are not (Burawoy 1985; Shaiken 1990). Globalization thus tends to dis-embed the economy and workplace from their context of a specific locality (Giddens 1991). However, what exactly happens in SEZs departs from the images of free-flowing transnational capital and local governments desperately trying to catch the flow. Instead, the current situation of SEZs demonstrates the growing collaboration between capital and its local partners (Harvey 1982: 398–405; Sassen 2000: 218–19). Ironically, the ever-increasing demand for higher flexibility and effectiveness in globalized production makes it more critical for transnational capital to be successfully embedded in local spaces—although temporarily. This makes an MNC a space where a government's unending desire to grow its "national economy" meets transnational capital's demand for uninterrupted profit.

My research on the Nawon factory in China reveals an unusual instance of the collaboration between the global and the local that was facilitated by the socialist legacy of the patron-client relationship between enterprises and state bureaucracy. During the socialist period of China, the government tightly controlled enterprises through the state ownership of the enterprises and the virtual monopoly of key resources such as production materials, labor, and welfare benefits. The chronic scarcity of production materials during that time encouraged the management of enterprises to establish and maintain close, unofficial connections with the government offices that controlled and distributed the resources (Henderson and Cohen 1984; Walder 1986).[7] Interestingly, the close relationship between enterprises and government officials continues in post-socialist China.[8] In many post-socialist countries, the rapid transition from a socialist to a capitalist system has created an unprecedented degree of social disorder and economic dislocations (Clarke 1992; Harvey 2006; Howell 1994; Humphrey 1995; Pine and Bridger 1998; Plywaczewski and Plywaczewski 2005). In the post-socialist countries, the relative scarcity of transparent rules about proper economic transactions and decision-making procedures has made many corporations depend more on connections, backroom influence, or recommendations from influential government officials than is typical of corporations in other countries (Heintz 2002; Kubicek 2004; Ledeneva 1998). In post-socialist China, enterprises often tend to maintain close relationships with government officials, who still exert broad influence over the economy through their monopoly of political power (Ding 1999, 2000; Solinger 1992; Yang 1989). Chinese officials also support the uninterrupted operations of enterprises, because they believe that economic development has a legitimizing effect on their political regime (Solinger 1995: 127–29, 136; Wank 1995: 57–65). This shows how the socialist practice of the patron-client relationship continues to exist in post-socialist China, as both enterprises and officials find a shared interest in maintaining the relationship.

At Nawon, the persisting patron-client relationship between enterprises and government, a legacy of the socialist past, has made the government officials of the nearby village willing to provide "special" services for the management. The socialist legacy convinced the village officials to accept management's request to jointly control the Chinese employees of the factory by undertaking the supervisory authority over the factory dormitory. My research further shows that the growing reliance of Nawon's management on the local officials' unofficial support eventually created a particular situation on the shop floor where the collaborative relationship between management and local officials gave birth to a powerful mechanism of labor control that operated through a system of local-level surveillance (Chan 1998a; Ching Kwan Lee 1998a).

This unusual mode of global-local collaboration contributes to the understanding of another political situation in post-socialist countries, that is, the trend whereby criminal organizations forge alliances with local government officials and businesses (Shelley 1997; Varese 2001; Voronin 1997). New opportunities for corruption and the temptation of embezzlement in the transition to a market economy, which are galvanized by juridical uncertainties in regulating economic relations, greatly increase corruption in government, especially among local, grassroots-level government officials. In Russia, for example, many acts of corruption go beyond the "simple" forms of abuse of power and merge with the criminal activities of the underworld, causing far-reaching effects on the business of many enterprises (Varese 2001: 53–58). At Nawon, I observed the growing influence of the unofficial alliance between local-level government officials and a village gang, an example of what is called in China the "merger of the black and the white" (Yunxiang Yan 2003: 27). While studies describe this "merger" as a local phenomenon limited to relatively "backward" regions such as rural north China (He 1998; Sun 1999), the merger also existed even in Qingdao, one of the most industrialized "open coastal cities" in China.[9] In the Nawon factory, the merger appeared as a by-product of global-local collaboration and a legacy of the socialist past: officials and the criminal underworld gained personal benefits through this insidious alliance, while sacrificing the interests of the Han-Chinese workers and later exerting detrimental effects on the foreign management.

THE FACTORY REGIME IN THE AGE OF GLOBAL CAPITALISM

The factory regime of the multinational corporation that I researched changed rapidly, and the changes demonstrate that the factory was closely connected to the global chain of garment production as well as to the political and economic environment of its host country. Here, the term "factory regime" indicates the political and economic methods and power structure to maintain stable labor-management relations, whose prime target is to minimize labor unrest and maximize production efficiency (Burawoy 1985: 87). While its functions are related to effectively governing the shop floor, the exact form of a factory regime is subject to changes that occur outside the shop floor, such as the ups and downs in the market for a factory's products, the degree of state intervention, the variable costs of labor reproduction, and the changing status of a regional industry in the global economy (Burawoy 1985: 261). Michael Burawoy's pioneering research on the rise and fall of different factory regimes demonstrates that the process of production is not simply confined to the labor process on the shop floor but also is linked to the broader context of local communities and government policies. According to Burawoy, the first "despotic" factory regime appeared in the late nineteenth century, when management enjoyed the autocratic control of workers on the shop floor. He traces despotic control back to the early development of historical capitalism in England. Under the prevailing idea of self-regulating, laissez-faire capitalism, workers were exposed to the "whip of the market" (12), suffering from periodic large-scale layoffs caused by cyclic market downturns. Over time, their situation got worse, this because there were neither strong labor unions nor an effective state welfare system that could protect the interests of labor during hard times. This situation allowed management to maintain highly authoritarian control over workers and coerce them into accepting rigid labor discipline (123–24). What brought an end to the regime were changes from outside the shop floor that occurred during the mid-twentieth century. These included the rise of the welfare state, the formation of strong labor unions, and the emergence of an "economy of scale" that could bear the high cost of providing employee welfare. Burawoy calls this new factory regime "hegemonic," because, under the new regime, workers came to work more by their consent than by economic or political coercion. Under the hegemonic regime, at the same time, management resorted less to autocratic methods of labor control (262–63).

The transformation of the factory regime at Nawon was unusually rapid, which reflects its high vulnerability to the pressure from the global chain of garment production and the Chinese government's intervention into corporate operations. According to Burawoy, in the West it took several decades for the initial form of factory regime to begin to shed its despotic characteristics. At Nawon, however, this change took place within the span of a few years. During the first several years of its operation in China, the management of Nawon controlled the shop floor with highly authoritarian methods of labor discipline and harsh punishments. Until the early 2000s, the vast reservoir of cheap Chinese labor in the countryside explained management's despotic control, since it greatly weakened local labor's negotiating power. During that time, the Chinese government's noninterventionist, pro-management attitudes also contributed to creating and maintaining a despotic factory regime.

The initial factory regime, however, only lasted several years and changed into another type as management constantly changed its shop-floor personnel organization. There was a close relation between the rapid transformation of the factory regime and Nawon's strong connection to the global chain of garment production, especially its subjection to the ever-increasing demand to cut prices. As products of the recent development in global capitalism, MNCs are under constant pressure to cut production costs and reduce lead time, thus forcing them to restructure their shop-floor organizations. The changes often result in the transformation of the existing factory regime, to the extent that they reduce managerial resources that have supported the regime. At Nawon, global capitalism's incessant demand for price cuts forced management to reshuffle its personnel organization of the shop floor, which resulted in a quick change of its factory regime. The highly labor-intensive production process of the factory rendered management vulnerable to the global demand for price cuts, making it hard for management to maintain its existing factory regime. This vulnerability induced management to make use of various political resources available on the shop floor at different moments of its business in China, which contributed to constant changes in the factory regime.

The Chinese government played a critical role in the creation of the factory regime and its rapid changes. Since the early 2000s, the government has gradually changed its role from a local collaborator with transnational capital to a supervisor of MNCs. Because its largely noninterventionist, pro-management polices during the 1990s greatly contributed to the formation of the despotic regime of the factory, any change in the government's policies and practices could lead to change in the factory regime. From the mid-2000s, for example, the Chinese government, alarmed by the growing gap between the rich and the poor and between the urban and the rural, began to emphasize labor welfare and economic equity (Lin 2003; Saich 2007; Wu and Perloff 2005). This reflects a broad change in the basic guidelines of government policies, which now emphasize both high-speed economic growth and the containment of social discontent, especially among the poor and underprivileged. The emphasis on worker welfare and economic equity, however, brought new burdens of growing labor costs and welfare expenditures to the management of Nawon. It is certain that the policy changes improved the workers' situation, since the government increased the minimum wage and enhanced its supervision of individual workshops. The changes also put certain limits on the degree and type of labor control management could exercise and gave more leverage to workers in their relations with management. However, for the management of Nawon, which had been suffering from rapidly rising labor costs and a subsequent fall in profit rates, the growing supervision by the Chinese government only indicated that its golden years in China would end soon.

Most of all, the policy changes caused Nawon's management to consider the opportunity cost of capital, the relative profitability of one production site vis-à-vis another. The headquarters of Nawon in particular quickly began a search for a better place for its future production, one that could promise higher profitability. The decision to relocate is additional evidence of the structural vulnerability of the factory regime at Nawon, which at this time did not take the form of "hegemonic despotism." In the factory regime that has developed relatively recently in countries such as the United States, Great Britain, and Japan, management has the power to force concessions from workers on many key issues, such as wages and benefits. In those countries, management has won concessions by threatening workers with the possibility of overseas relocation for higher profit rates. This factory regime is hegemonic, because management secures the concessions through "peaceful" processes such as collective negotiations. Yet, at the same time, it is despotic, because management attains its objectives by using the threat of factory closure (Burawoy 1985: 150). Contrary to the forms of management analyzed in Burawoy's comparative case studies, the management at Nawon did not regard the time-consuming and often painful process of collective bargaining with its Chinese employees as a necessary step before its final decision to relocate. Rather, the decision grew out of the ever-increasing market pressure to reduce production costs and the stiff competition among garment factories, which greatly decreased Nawon's profit margins. The decision also resulted from the Chinese government's tightening supervision over labor conditions and business practices of the factory, which worsened the business environment in China. The government's new emphasis on remedying the huge income gap within China spurred an unprecedentedly rapid increase in wages, which was a severe blow to management. As we will see, the policy changes of the Chinese government, together with the rapidly changing conditions of the global garment industry, induced Nawon's management to decide to relocate from China to Vietnam and to ignore the option of collective bargaining with its Chinese employees.

HAN-CHINESE WORKERS AND THE (IM)POSSIBILITY OF RESISTANCE

This book analyzes the conditions that explain both the resistance and the submission of the Han-Chinese workers at Nawon, which contributes to the key discussion about the resistance potential of socially marginalized people (for example, Ching Kwan Lee 2000a, 2000b; Ong 1987; Rofel 1999; Scott 1985). In the multinational factory of Nawon, Han-Chinese workers struggled to find ways to resist labor control but eventually succumbed to the factory regime. By referring to their subjection to management, I do not intend to deny the workers' potential to resist management's control. On the contrary, my ethnographic data indicate that the workers constantly sought to find loopholes in management's supervision and, to a certain degree, achieved small successes during the early period of the factory. At the very beginning of its local operation, the Korean management believed that it could easily discipline the untrained Han-Chinese workers by using its advanced knowledge and skills of labor surveillance and training. However, management soon realized that it could not easily incorporate the workers into the factory's operations. Especially during the early period of factory operations in China, the workers developed strategies of subtle resistance, and thus revealed the limited power of "universal" methods of labor control. Because of the resistance, management had to revise its initial training program and make changes in its methods of labor supervision.[10] The chapters that follow discuss how misrecognitions, tensions, and occasional conflicts on the shop floor hampered the programs of labor control, thus forcing management to constantly change them to better fit the local context.

The workers' resistance and its positive results did not last long. Management swiftly revised its methods of labor surveillance and discipline when it noticed their shortcomings. The workers, through the process of the repeated success and failure of their resistance, gradually set by themselves the limit of their resistance and accepted the ultimate authority of management. This was surprising because they did so even when they still felt management's labor control to be highly authoritarian and sometimes oppressive. The direct reasons of the submission were the constantly evolving methods of labor control and discipline, management's threat of penalties, and the local network of labor surveillance operated by village government officials and gangs.

Behind the direct reasons, however, there was the Han-Chinese workers' tacit approval of management based on its ability to guarantee them "decent" wages. At Nawon, the workers *consented to* management's orders because they believed that "decent" wages, a corporate reward for their submission, would at least give them a chance to change their fate as the daughters of poor farmers. To the workers, adequate wages were much more tangible than the seemingly elusive and dangerous cause of resistance. I will show the complex mechanism that led the workers to regard "decent" wages as the most important reason for working. The mechanism here involves the large seasonal fluctuations in garment orders, the positive functional relation between order amounts and wages, and the Korean management's exceptional ability to secure subcontract orders large enough to create "decent" wages. Management's ability to get a sizeable volume of orders and thus pay "decent" wages on time made Nawon distinguished from other garment factories nearby, which suffered from frequent workers' protests against late- and non-payment of wages. The Han-Chinese workers of the Nawon factory were prepared to endure strict labor control as long as they received what they consider to be adequate wages on time.

The Han-Chinese workers' unusual experiences and memories on the shop floor made their relationship with management complex and nuanced, which also contributed to both the possibilities and the impossibilities of labor resistance. The workers viewed their relationship with management not as entirely based on terminable contracts and economic calculations. They also viewed the relationship as embedded in feelings of trust and personal concern, which had accumulated through their long-term interactions with management on the shop floor. The factory regime at Nawon had the characteristic of "despotic paternalism" because the workers had basic trust in management that, they believed, made extra efforts to secure adequate wages *for* them. The labor-management relationship embedded in the exchanges of trust and paternalist concern explained the unprecedented workers' strike in 2002, which targeted a new plant manager from Guatemala. Unlike his predecessors, the plant manager pushed hard a new agenda of a "higher level of globalization," under which he greatly increased production speed and tightened labor control, while ignoring the trust and concern that underlay the preexisting labor-management relationship. The strike clearly shows how the Han-Chinese workers' trust in the management, which had effectively contained the potential for workers' resistance, triggered the workers' protest against the new plant manager, since he kept ignoring the subtleties of the preexisting relationship on the shop floor.

Han-Chinese workers' particular self-image contributes to the impossibility of workers' resistance. On the shop floor of Nawon, Han-Chinese workers often made self-disparaging comments that they are "daughters of small peasants." With these comments, they implied that they could neither openly express their grievances against management nor organize collective action such as strikes because they were poor and powerless, just like their parents in remote farming villages. Their habitual comments also served to perpetuate their subordinate status in the factory and the local community. Like the daily practice of "self-damnation" of British working class students (Willis 1981 [1977]: 174–75), the Han-Chinese workers' casual comments on their humble self-image reveal the subtle mechanism of ideology that made the workers themselves contribute to reproducing the negative values and practices of "small peasants" (Liu 2000: 16). The mechanism became more effective as the workers were subject to the paternalist control of management and the daily supervision of the pro-management local government officials. Later chapters will explore how the workers reproduced their own group identity as "little working girls," which was closely associated with the widespread social stigmatization of Chinese farmers as "dumb and gullible."

THE GLOBALIZING KOREAN GARMENT INDUSTRY AND ITS RELOCATION TO CHINA

A more complete understanding of the global-local collaboration and its effects within the Special Economic Zones of China requires some historical background on the collaboration among the parties involved, which includes the Chinese government's opening up of its economy, the rise in wages in South Korea, and the subsequent exodus of Korean corporations from South Korea.

After the rapid industrialization of South Korea during the 1960s and the 1970s, massive strikes broke out in the year 1987. To quell the nationwide protests, the military government of South Korea made an important political concession to the Korean people, who demanded greater political democracy and economic equity (Cumings 2005).[11] The overall democratization of Korean society, however, triggered a large number of labor protests in many corporations. Korean workers, who had suffered from low wages and poor working conditions under the military regime, believed that it was the right time for them to demand long-delayed compensation for their years of sacrifice in building the "national economy" (Amsden 1989; Hokyu Kim 2006a, 2006b). This led to more than seven thousand labor strikes during the short period of two months between July and August 1987, most of which involved demands for instant and large wage increases (CIFSJD 1987; Hart-Landsberg 1993; ICIME 1988).[12]

As a result of the unprecedented labor protests, wages almost doubled during the three following years, significantly decreasing the profits of Korean enterprises in labor-intensive light industries (Lee and Song 1994). Garment manufacturers were among the hardest hit because they were heavily dependent on human labor. Many garment manufacturers were vulnerable to the buyers' practice of price squeezing, because they made products under contract to big brand-name companies in the United States and Japan, such as NIKE, UMBRO, and Sean John (Gereffi 1994).[13] To overcome the difficulties, many corporations began to move their production facilities to countries that had cheaper labor, including Mexico, Guatemala, Honduras, Panama, and later, Indonesia, Bangladesh, Vietnam, and China (KOFOTI 1992, 2005; Lee and Song 1994; Park and Park 1989; Peterson 1992, 1994; Song 1989). Although it was relatively late in joining the list, China quickly attracted the largest overseas investment made by Korean garment corporations, and by 2002 it had received 31.7 percent of their overseas investment (EIBK 2003).

The huge wage difference between the two countries expedited the rapid relocation of Korean apparel manufacturers to China. As of the year 2000, the average hourly wage of Korean workers in the textile industry was US$5.32, while that of their Chinese counterparts was only US$0.69 (Werner International 2001). For the small- and medium-sized Korean corporations that felt the increasing pressure of high labor costs in Korea, the vast reservoir of cheap labor in China was the biggest attraction of overseas investment. In fact, by the end of the year 2005, more than 95 percent of Korean firms directly investing in China were small- and medium-sized enterprises (Juyeong Kim 2006).[14]

The recent relocation of Korean garment corporations to China is an obvious consequence of the global nature of capital, permanently looking for better business conditions that guarantee higher profits. In this context, the owners and managers of capital incessantly seek to decrease turnover time and production costs by overcoming or evading geographical and institutional barriers (Harvey 1982: 402–3; Marx and Engels 1992 [1848]: 21–22). Before the 1987 wage hike, South Korea was an ideal place for profit maximization of transnational capital because of its low labor costs in relation to business profits and the high education level of its workers. At that time, Korean workers had to work 54 hours a week on average while suffering from a low standard of living and poor working conditions. The South Korean government denied workers' rights to organize and take collective action, believing that active labor unions would dissuade many MNCs from investing in the country (Cumings 2005; Eckert et al. 1990; Janelli and Janelli 1993; Choongsoon Kim 1992).

Korean corporations in the light, labor-intensive industrial sectors hastened their relocation to other countries because the 1987 wage hike and double-digit wage increases thereafter removed most of their relative production advantages in South Korea. The overseas relocation of South Korean garment corporations reflects the "deterritorialization process" of capital as they overcame the deterioration of profits by relocating production facilities to other regions (Brenner 1999: 64; Harvey 2000: 58; Lefebvre 1976: 55–57).

Though transnational capital tends to expand the global chain of production through constant relocations, it still needs relatively fixed and immobile infrastructures once relocated to a new place. It thus requires the government of the host country to integrate and coordinate technological capacities, natural goods, public and private forms of fixed capital, infrastructural configurations, and "proper" social relations of production (Gottdiener 1985, 1987; Swyngedouw 1992). The Korean MNCs also required these upon their relocation to China and, the Chinese government, as the local partner of MNCs, promptly responded to the need by offering an "investment-friendly" environment. The Chinese government's quick response to the MNCs' demands attracted a considerable amount of foreign investment not solely from South Korea. At the end of the year 2002, China became the second-largest recipient country of foreign direct investment globally, surpassed only by the United States (Hong Kong Trade

Development Council 2003). The active and extensive operations of MNCs in China led to its reputation as the "world's factory" (Agence France Presse 2003; BBC News 2002; Escobar 2005; Kikuchi 2002). By providing favorable conditions for MNCs, China became an ideal destination for reterritorializing transnational capital.[15]

THE FIELDWORK

My fieldwork took place from June 2002 to May 2003. I first visited Qingdao in the summer of 2002. After two months of preliminary research, I went to Qingdao and stayed at Nawon for most of the fieldwork period. During that time, I also conducted short-term research in Pingshan County, Shandong Province, the hometown of most of the Han-Chinese employees of the factory. During my fieldwork, I conducted participant-observation on the shop floor to analyze everyday interactions between foreign management and Chinese workers. I also conducted personal in-depth interviews with employees of Nawon, including Han-Chinese workers, Korean-Chinese interpreters, and Korean managers, to uncover their memory of the changes that had occurred in the corporation over the past ten years. Most interviews, except for some with the Korean executives at Nawon Korea, were conducted as a series of long and informal dialogues.

My Korean nationality put me in an extraordinary research situation at Nawon, where a small number of Koreans supervised hundreds of Chinese workers. First of all, thanks to my Korean nationality and status as a graduate student from one of the best-known foreign universities in Korea (Harvard), both the Korean managers of the Nawon plant in Qingdao and the executives of Nawon Korea were quite willing to give me access, although not in full, to factory diaries, statistics, and business correspondence between the plant and Nawon Korea. In fact, their generous understanding of my long-term stay also originated from their slight misunderstanding of my fieldwork: when I introduced my study as a part of research on "corporate culture," they understood the term in the context of the study of business administration, which regards culture as a tool to enable foreign management to effectively control foreign workers who have a different "culture." Therefore, they quite frankly talked with me about their notions of cultural differences between Korea and China, and how the differences convinced them of the necessity of extraordinary methods of labor discipline and surveillance.

Among the Chinese employees, I first came to be familiar with the Korean-Chinese interpreters. What made this possible was their role in this multinational factory as "cultural brokers" between Koreans and Han-Chinese. The interpreters provided me with precious information about the history of Nawon and the intertwined power relations in and around the factory, which involved the Korean executives of Nawon Korea, the government officials of Fuyang village, and the village gang.

Building rapport with the Han-Chinese workers was very difficult and time-consuming. At first, they viewed my presence on the shop floor with deep suspicion; they believed I was another Korean manager disguised as an "innocent Ph.D. student." My relationship with the Korean-Chinese interpreters only deepened their suspicion, because many of them had ill-feelings against the Korean-Chinese as the agents of management—a result of management's preference for the small number of ethnic Koreans as their local business assistants. Especially during the first several weeks of my fieldwork, many Han-Chinese workers even avoided making eye contact with me just as they did with the Korean managers, because they regarded me as another Korean manager. After the first several weeks of my fieldwork, I realized that I should go beyond the role of simple observer in order to establish rapport with the workers. I thought the only possible and maybe the most efficient way to build rapport would be to work side by side with the workers. Only by working night and day on the shop floor would I be able to convince them that I was different from the Korean managers. After getting permission from the management, I began my shop-floor career as an "apprentice folder" in the finishing section, because folding finished clothes into plastic bags does not require the high-level of skills necessary for sewing and tailoring.[16] Fortunately, the relatively low labor intensity of the job gave me frequent opportunities to talk with the workers. Beginning with the folder position, I changed job positions two times during the fieldwork to make as many acquaintances as possible among the workers.

The strange presence of a Korean "worker" on the shop floor made Han-Chinese workers feel uncomfortable. Their initial uneasy feeling, however, gradually diminished as they realized that my everyday presence on the shop floor did not cause them any harm. They observed that, unlike the Korean managers, I did not pay attention to mistakes they made on the production line. In addition, again unlike the Korean managers, who always assumed an authoritarian attitude, I asked the workers to teach me almost everything about the tasks that I did, such as the proper way of folding and packing garments, the rules of garment inspection, and the technique of loading as many garment boxes as possible in freight containers. My attitude on the shop floor surprised many workers because they never expected such behavior from the Korean managers. Sometimes I tried to further reassure them by taking the role of an informant who collected some useful information from the management. For example, when they were extremely tired because of endless overtime, I got information about the work schedule from the management and let the workers know when overtime would eventually end. Occasional after-hours eating and drinking sessions with Han-Chinese workers also greatly helped me to develop rapport with them. In the multinational Nawon factory, national and ethnic divisions among employees were quite rigid, making commensality between Koreans and Han-Chinese workers virtually nonexistent.[17] Therefore, the occasional meetings for drinking and dining helped convince the Han-Chinese workers that I was not part of management.

Interviews with Han-Chinese workers were conducted in Chinese. Although I had good relationships with the Korean-Chinese interpreters, I did not ask their help in communicating with the Han-Chinese workers. The interpreters, as a group heavily favored by the Korean management, were in constant tension with the Han-Chinese workers, who were the most underprivileged in the factory and thus resented the privileged status of the Korean-Chinese. I did not tape-record dialogues with any of the groups in the workshop. While recording equipment is useful for analyzing interviews conducted in more or less artificial settings, it is not appropriate in the middle of the tense situation of a shop floor. Instead of using recorders, which might interrupt the natural flow of events, I took notes as best I could afterward.

STRUCTURE OF THE BOOK

Chapter Two analyzes how spatial divisions and different living conditions at Nawon served to maintain the factory hierarchy. In the factory there was an intimate correspondence between one's rank in the factory hierarchy and his/her living location and quality. The particular spatial divisions and the conditions of living in the factory operated as powerful instruments of social distinction. They inscribed national and ethnic differences into *both* the factory employees' bodies and their consciousness, thus contributing to the foreign management's control of local labor. The discriminating effect of spatial divisions and different living conditions became powerful when they operated through the most intimate human feelings of comfort and cleanliness. In the Nawon factory, for example, Korean residents affirmed their superior hierarchical status through the high-quality of their living arrangements. In contrast, the Han-Chinese workers' poorer working and living conditions created and maintained their self-image as "dirty country bumpkins," corresponding to their lowest place in the factory hierarchy. Especially, the Han-Chinese workers' pungent body odor, a result of their poor living conditions, generated a powerful racial prejudice against them.

Chapter Three examines the new meanings of class, ethnic, and social differences that are created and maintained by the local presence of a multinational factory. In post-socialist China, the socialist or Maoist term "class" is rarely used. It has been replaced by politically neutral expressions such as "stratum" or "social status." Using ethnographic data collected during my fieldwork, I analyze the complex meanings of the term "white-collar" as it is used to describe the prestigious social status of high-paid office workers in contemporary Chinese society. At Nawon, the division between white- and blue-collar employees was clearly marked by differentiated wage payments and corporate benefits. At the same time, however, the division overlapped with multiple cultural and political meanings that cannot be explained solely by the differences in income and corporate benefits. This chapter investigates the backgrounds of the Korean-Chinese, who held the preponderance of the prestigious white-collar jobs at Nawon, including the Korean-Chinese ethnic enmity toward Han-Chinese, Korean managers' belief in the superiority of Korean culture, and their deep-rooted historical doubt of Sino-centrism.[18] The historical marginality of Korean-Chinese made the white- and blue-collar division in the factory highly political. The new division between office and shop-floor jobs greatly enhanced management's control of labor by creating a deep inner schism among the local workers. The chapter also examines the social and political implications of the emergence of Korean-Chinese as a "rich ethnic minority," which runs counter to the common interethnic division of labor wherein the minorities occupy marginal and low-paid jobs.

Chapter Four looks into the transformation of rural Chinese women into industrial workers and the process through which management's particular mode of labor discipline gradually penetrates their minds and bodies. In addition to discussing the effectiveness of disciplinary measures, it also discusses the Han-Chinese workers' reaction to them. The workers had their own critical consciousness of a proper level of body discipline and work diligence. As Nawon's methods of labor discipline and punishment infringed on their ideas about proper discipline and work ethics, the workers developed their own tactics to evade management's control. My analysis demonstrates that the actual process of labor discipline is a dialectical one that ultimately leads to the mutual transformation of workers and management. The chapter therefore analyzes the effects of specific disciplining measures adopted in different stages of the worker-training program.

Nawon's foreign management gradually departed from its initial methods based on the "universal" concepts of labor supervision and rational principles of reward and punishment, since it had to change disciplinary methods according to the workers' reactions to them. At the end of its continuing transformation, the worker-training program of the factory came to embody distinctive elements of South Korean work culture, such as collective punishment, militaristic disciplinary methods, and the Confucian idea of body discipline. This is an example of locally embedded globalization, in that management increasingly relied on its own concepts of bodily discipline and punishment, while still maintaining its facade as an agent of universal, West-oriented industrialism.

Chapter Five examines the political implications of national and ethnic consciousness for the formation of the factory regimes at Nawon. It shows how the interethnic circumstances of China and the management's non-Western origins influenced the management's responses to the pressure and the formation of factory regimes. First, it examines management's unique ideas of the Korean nation and its national superiority over Han-Chinese. Management wielded these to rationalize its discriminatory treatment of the two ethnic groups of Korean-Chinese and Han-Chinese in the factory. The idea of Korean national superiority also contributed to creating a factory regime that depended on the close collaboration between Koreans and Korean-Chinese. Second, it analyzes how the industrial trainee program at the mother factory in Korea, open only to a limited number of Han-Chinese workers, drove the workers to compete with one another for access to the "Korean dream." The workers hoped that, using the program, they could change their fate as "daughters of poor farmers." The limited chances to join the program reduced the workers' expression of grievances against management by promoting competition for the limited opportunities. The program also created new, internal schisms among the workers between those who had been to Korea and those who had not, thus eventually consolidating management's control of the shop floor.

Chapter Six analyzes the increasing tension between the Korean management and grassroots Chinese government officials against the backdrop of the "merger of the black and the white," a case of post-socialist malaise (Yunxiang Yan 2003: 27). As previously mentioned, the benefits conferred by the Chinese government had been a key condition for the smooth operation of Nawon. The benefits offered by local government officials increasingly took on an unofficial nature, as management more and more relied on "special" support from village officials. Nawon's management increasingly had to deal with falling profits, a shrinking number of Korean and Korean-Chinese managerial staff, and deteriorating factory facilities. The village officials provided extra but indispensible support for the management, such as village-level surveillance of Han-Chinese workers and tip-offs about sudden government inspections of the shop floor. Management's growing reliance on this kind of special support from the local power holders, however, allowed the latter to intervene in the factory's operations. As the local power holders' intervention grew to an alarming level, management attempted to restore the principle of "independent management." The growing tension between the foreign management and the local officials culminated in the sudden death of a plant manager of the factory in a mysterious car accident. Management's ultimate inability to find the exact cause of his death, as well as rumors of a local conspiracy, only deepened its anxiety about the influence of the local power holders. The collision fundamentally transformed the existing mode of global-local collaboration in the factory, eroding the tripartite collusion among the foreign management, the village officials, and a local criminal organization.

Chapter Seven analyzes the limits of globalization by describing the new developments on the shop floor after the plant manager's death. After the fatal incident, management clearly realized that it could no longer rely on the unofficial support of the local power holders. In its effort to restore shop-floor control, management chose to push forward a "higher level of globalization."

By correcting its excessive reliance on the local, management hoped to resolve all the recent problems created by the local power holders' deep intervention to the factory. As part of its new managerial push, management decided to hire a new plant manager from a Guatemalan *maquila* factory, expecting he would introduce managerial principles and practices much more global than those of Nawon. No one in the factory exactly knew what "globalization" meant, but the "global standards" of the new managerial practices instantly reinforced management's labor supervision and increased the intensity of labor on the shop floor. These changes brought by the new global management triggered a Han-Chinese workers' strike, eventually leading to the new plant manager's disgraceful resignation. The unprecedented workers' strike also resulted from the "global" management's blatant ignorance of the local characteristics in the factory, such as the Han-Chinese workers' expectation of "decent" wages and the previous management's paternalist attitude toward the workers. Under the previous management, Korean managers often made a personal effort to get some subcontract orders. When the main contract orders from Nawon were insufficient to ensure wages well over a minimal level, such extra efforts of the managers were critical to maintaining workers' wages above a certain level. The workers had regarded the efforts as subtle expressions of the managers' personal concern about them. The new "global" management, however, could not understand the subtle connection between "decent" wages and the management's extra effort to get subcontract orders, thus creating friction on the shop floor. By violating the subtle moral code between management and labor, the management brought in from the Guatemalan *maquila* factory inadvertently caused the Han-Chinese workers to break their political silence and to go on strike.

Chapter Eight concludes the book by speculating on the future of Nawon and the groups of people involved in its local operations. Since the beginning of the year 2005, both the Chinese government and the Chinese Communist Party have repeatedly cautioned against the growing income gap between the rich and the poor as a potential cause of social instability (Jing 2006). To address this problem, for the first time since the implementation of the "reform and openness" policy, the Chinese government amended its regulations on minimum wages and raised the threshold of the monthly personal income tax (Tak 2006a; Xinhua News Agency 2005b). With these changes, the government intended to improve the quality of life of low-income people, specifically those who had been relatively underprivileged since the beginning of the economic reform. In accordance with the central government's new policies, Chinese local governments increased local minimum wages. They also vowed to tighten their supervision of transnational corporations, focusing on their corporate tax payments and working conditions.

For the MNCs that had already been suffering from rising labor costs in China, the changes in the government's polices meant that China would no longer be their promised land. We still have to wait to see whether the rapidly growing labor costs in China will trigger an exodus of MNCs to other countries. Until very recently, many corporations continued their operations in China because the country had other advantages aside from labor costs. These advantages, such as good infrastructure, efficient business services, and the potential for a large consumer market, offset the disadvantages of rapidly increasing labor costs. In this context, recent developments at Nawon and Nawon Korea, its headquarters in South Korea, give us a precious insight into how an MNC decides whether to relocate under rapidly changing local and international market situations. The management's reaction to the recent policy changes and the resulting wage hikes reveal the dynamics of global capitalism that lead investors to constantly move around the world, searching for relatively favorable conditions for profit maximization.

Finally, the concluding chapter highlights the increasingly troubled workers' situation at Nawon, which was created by the factory's deteriorating financial condition and a gloomy rumor about an impending factory closedown. The global movement of transnational capital is not only about the relatively free movement of capital and MNCs. It is also about the local workers who bear the grueling reality of sweatshop labor. Just like the dazzling scenes of consumption in Qingdao obscure the gray-colored factory buildings in its industrial zones, the flexible movement of transnational capital and foreign management have diverted our attention away from the sedentary and boring life of local workers. Coming from remote farming villages, many of the Nawon workers are bound to spend most of the prime time of their life in the dusty workshop, located half a world away from here. The impending relocation of this MNC *from* China gave rise to the local workers' worry, despair, and anger, as it dashed their tenuous hope for a better future.

The Politics of Spatial Divisions and the Living Environment

THE KOREAN MISSION: MODERNIZING CHINA

> Ten years ago, the very location of our factory
> buildings was in an abysmal swamp. It was so deep
> and muddy that we felt it was really difficult to walk
> around even wearing long rubber boots. Once stuck
> in the mud, we couldn't take even one step without
> someone else's help. The swamp was full of foul water
> polluted by sewage and kitchen garbage. The stinking
> water almost suffocated us. Ah, and the flies! Clouds
> of annoying flies always hovered over the foul swamp
> water. Around the building site, we couldn't find
> public phone booths, toilets, or even a single small
> retail shop to buy basic personal necessities.
>
> —recollections of a Korean manager

On a humid summer afternoon in 1993, guided by local government officials, a group of Koreans arrived at a plot of barren land near Fuyang village. The local government proposed that the land be used as the location for factories. What the Koreans found, however, was not neatly leveled ground ready for construction but an expanse of swamp filled with mud, foul water, and garbage. A member of the observation team dispatched by Nawon Korea, now retired manager Lee, remembered his first impression of China as "unattended, wild, and dirty." Although recommended by the local government, he said, "The site was a total wasteland that no one had ever touched." The virtual lack of public services such as pay phones and toilets further frustrated the foreign visitors. To buy basic personal necessities, they needed to take a slow bus for an hour to reach a small retail shop. The bathroom in the guest house arranged by the village government did not have hot water and even the cold tap water had a strong rusty smell. Several Koreans remembered that using the bathrooms in rural villages was particularly grim; there were no "modern" toilets, just a small pit surrounded by walls on three sides. "Sometimes the toilet space bordered on a pigsty of a farmer's house and I couldn't bear the nasty smell," Lee recalled.

In addition to the initial disappointment, the inefficiency of the "Communist" bureaucracy delayed the construction process. Korean management asked the local government to provide construction machinery and materials in order to transform the swamp into a factory site. Contrary to their initial promise to provide facilities, however, government officials failed to provide enough and timely machinery and materials. Because Nawon was one of the first FDI factories in the area, the local government did not have any prior experience in dealing with foreign investors. During the initial phase of the construction, therefore, it was common for the Korean managers at Nawon to encounter government officials who were reluctant to deal with foreigners. Although they advertised themselves as open to foreign investors and lured the Koreans into their district with the promise of "wholehearted service," the officials were still wary of the foreign presence in their region. For example, they tried to supervise every step of the Korean businessmen by following complicated administrative procedures. The procedures were so inefficient that the Korean managers often had to prepare identical sets of documents and visit several local bureaus (with different authorities) just to borrow a dump truck.

Recollecting their bitter times in China, the Korean managers superimposed the image of Korea during the 1960s on the image of China in the 1990s. In both casual conversations and formal interviews, the Korean managers, all in their late fifties, pointed out that the landscape of the Chinese countryside was similar to that of the Korean countryside that they remember from their childhood. Having grown up in a poverty-stricken society after the Korean War (1950–1953), the managers believed that the "backward" living conditions of the Chinese countryside were not completely foreign to them. Rather, they argued that their childhood experiences helped them to endure the miserable life in China. In their eyes, the bare wilderness of the Chinese countryside was an exact replica of the Korean countryside in the 1960s.

The fact that most of the Han-Chinese workers Nawon recruited were from Pingshan, one of the poorest regions (C. *pinkun diqu*) in Shandong province, reinforced the image of Chinese villages as backward and underdeveloped. The recruitment from Pingshan was the result of the provincial government's special request, as the government officials believed that the new jobs at Nawon could decrease the high unemployment rate in a poor, overpopulated farming region. Nawon Korea agreed to the request, because the officials at the same time guaranteed that the region would be a stable source of cheap labor—one of the key conditions that attracted many MNCs to China. Finally, in the early winter of 1993, a few weeks before the completion of factory construction, a Korean observation team explored farming villages in Pingshan looking for cheap labor, accompanied by the head of Fuyang village. According to the explanation of a former Korean manager who joined the expedition, the villagers of Pingshan seemed far more backward than those in Qingdao:

> I couldn't believe my eyes. Every adult I saw there wore a "Mao Zedong uniform." . . . They seemed to live in the Mao era. When we walked along the village streets, people we encountered always gave us a suspicious look as if we were aliens and whispered something to one another. All the village streets were narrow and unpaved and, therefore, thick yellow dust rose with each step we took. Everything was covered with dust. It didn't take an hour for the dust to completely cover the cleaned surface of the table in our room. At night, because it was early winter, we needed a heated room. The boarding house we lodged in, however, didn't have any proper heating system and we couldn't get enough sleep because the room temperature was really low. Our one-week stay in Pingshan, in every sense, was a quick replay of wartime life during the Korean War.

Several Korean managers in their late fifties still regarded China as the Communist party-state that had invaded Korea during the Korean War and had brought them suffering. "In the winter of 1952," one of the managers painfully recalled, "our family left behind everything in our hometown and fled from the invading Chinese army." He closed his eyes as if recalling some bad memory. "After the cease-fire agreement in the summer of 1953," he continued, "nothing remained in our home village except ashes. All of our family's property was burned." Although the postwar prosperity of South Korea made such traumatic wartime memories sink into oblivion, Chinese farmers in Pingshan wearing "Mao uniforms" suddenly reminded the managers of their nearly forgotten wartime memories. With their lingering memory of burning houses and abandoned corpses on the street, it may have been easy for the managers to view the Chinese farmers in "Mao uniforms" as the reincarnation of the Communist invaders during the war. After returning from their trip to Pingshan, the managers were convinced that China was still locked in a Communist era that had already disappeared from the stage of world history.

In this way, the South Korean managers, who came to China following the quest of multinational corporations for cheap labor, unexpectedly encountered their past in a remote corner of the Chinese countryside. During their first journey, they noted the obvious signs of China's "premodernity" in its abandoned swamplands, backward villages, and the low living standards of the farmers. The managers argued that China, if it really wanted to become a prosperous country, should go through the same modernization process that their motherland Korea had gone through thirty years before. They believed that modernization, understood as a synonym for industrialization, was a historically universal stage that every nation needed to pass through in order to be prosperous.

The Korean managers' understanding of China as fixed in the underdeveloped Communist past had significant implications for the design of factory architecture and the use of factory space. The managers believed that Nawon should be modeled on the design of their South Korean mother factory, because China was located well behind in the linear progressive process of modernization which South Korea had already gone through. The basic construction of factory buildings, in this context, reflected the Korean managers' feeling of national superiority over China and their will to discipline the people of a "backward" country. The building architecture and the resulting spatial divisions at Nawon, however, are not simple material expressions of the alleged South Korean superiority to China. In more subtle ways, the management utilized the spatial divisions as a method to maintain hierarchical order among its employees by making the divisions reflect national and ethnic divisions as well as different organizational statuses.

CREATING A FACTORY HIERARCHY: SPATIAL DIVISIONS AND DIFFERENT LIVING CONDITIONS

The management of corporations has widely used space as a key method to maintain its hierarchical superiority to labor. Ever since Frederick Taylor argued that a clear hierarchical difference between management and labor should be the precondition for "scientific management" (Taylor 1947 [1911]: 54), spatial divisions between management and labor have been a norm of industry. As early as the late nineteenth century, the hierarchical difference between management and labor became apparent not only in the factory but also in the everyday lives of workers and management outside the factory (Engels 2009 [1887]). The division was widespread even in the socialist countries such as the Soviet Union and China. The socialist governments officially promoted workers' rights over those of management and attempted to create an "equal and cooperative" management-labor relationship. However, when they adopted Taylorism to increase productivity, they also introduced its assumption of professional management, according to which managers, distinct from workers, "scientifically" administer the corporation. In the socialist countries, the adoption of Taylorist principles eventually contributed to reestablishing management's status as superior to rank-and-file workers (Berliner 1957; Priestley 1963; Walder 1986). The reestablished authority of management was well expressed in the spatial division between production sites and management's offices (Rofel 1999: 269).

The spatial division and architecture also reinforce the hierarchical differences among various parts of a corporation, as well as the basic and fundamental division between labor and management. As a powerful boundary-building mechanism operating at the level of everyday life, they reflect and maintain the power relations among the factions and individuals in a corporation (Ho 2009: 73–85). They act on the living experiences of employees and make them physically experience the subtle and pervasive distinguishing effects of managerial power, which in the end inscribe hierarchical differences deep in the bodies and consciousness of the employees.

The Korean managers at Nawon had clear ideas of how they should use the space and architecture of their factory to maintain the hierarchical difference between foreign management and local labor. They came to understand the power effect of particular spatial divisions and architecture through their experience of shop-floor management in South Korea. Nawon Korea, the parent of Nawon, began operations in South Korea as a contract factory that fulfilled foreign buyers' orders. As a factory located at the low end of the global chain of garment production, it was natural for Nawon Korea to adopt the basic factory architecture and shop-floor organization common to foreign garment factories. Here, the basic architecture and shop-floor organization reflected the hierarchical difference between management and labor, as commonly expressed in separate workplaces for managerial staff and rank-and-file workers.

Nawon Korea designed Nawon referring to the common pattern: it divided its space into two parts, one assigned to the exclusive use of management and the other to the workers. The thick soundproofed wall between the factory office and the shop floor clearly reflected and maintained the division between management and labor. The spatial division made it cumbersome for the workers on the shop floor to access the factory office. From the shop floor to the office, every worker had to go through two doors—the first to the hallway and the second to the main office. The thick rubber blind hanging over the first door kept the shop-floor workers from seeing the hallway even when the door was open. Factory regulations enhanced the division between the shop floor and the main office. According to the regulations, shop-floor workers had to use the small "workers' door" located on a different side of the building (Figure 2-1), while the office workers were allowed to use the main entrance.

At Nawon, however, the factory's architecture and spatial divisions did not simply mark the distinction between labor and management. They also reflected national and ethnic differences, as the management considered Korean-Chinese as more reliable local employees than Han-Chinese. In

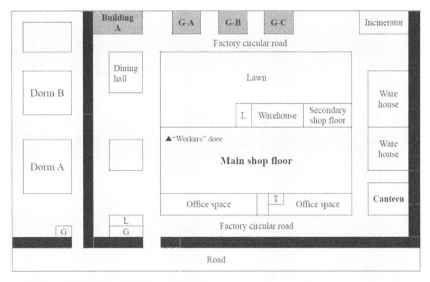

Figure 2-1. The Spatial Divisions at Nawon. Source: Author

the factory, the majority of Han-Chinese employees worked on the dusty shop floor as rank-and-file workers, while the small number of Korean-Chinese worked in the office as intermediary managerial staff. The division between office and shop floor overlapped with the ethnic division between Korean-Chinese and Han-Chinese, thus creating and enhancing an inner schism among local labor.

There is another special condition of Nawon that made its management very interested in the use of space. From the very beginning of Nawon, Nawon Korea ordered all employees—including Koreans, Korean-Chinese, and Han-Chinese—of its branch factory to live on the factory premises. By making labor and management live in the same factory compound, Nawon Korea intended to maximize labor efficiency, decrease labor costs, and facilitate management's control of labor. The policy made the spatial divisions extend well beyond the offices and the shop floor, into the everyday living spaces of the factory employees. Nawon Korea's decision to allow the high-ranking expatriate Korean managers to bring their families from

Korea and live together with them made the spatial divisions at Nawon more complicated: for the Korean families, management established Korean living quarters on the factory premises, thus adding another clear-cut division to the existing spatial divisions.

The fact that Nawon had both residential buildings and production facilities created additional dimensions within the spatial divisions, which led to subtle and intricate effects of social distinctions and discrimination. In the factory, management used not only spatial divisions but every dimension of daily life within the divisions to maintain hierarchical relations between Koreans, Korean-Chinese, and Han-Chinese. As Bourdieu observed in the North African Kabyle society, spatial organizations of everyday life serve to constitute and maintain a particular social order (Bourdieu 1970). They carry power effects by assigning people to distinctive places and governing their everyday routines. Everyday practices, seemingly politically benign, eventually create palpable power effects, as people gradually come to regard the practices as hardly alterable routines and accept their social and economic statuses in the divided spaces (Bourdieu 1977: 177–78).

In using spatial divisions and different working and living conditions within the divided spaces for its managerial purposes, the Nawon management divided the factory space, with Koreans occupying the innermost quarters, Korean-Chinese living in-between, and Han-Chinese residing on the margins of the factory premises. This three-tiered spatial division literally corresponded to their different statuses in the factory hierarchy. At Nawon, Koreans occupied the top portion of the factory hierarchy, monopolizing the top managerial positions such as factory president, plant manager, and financial manager. Korean-Chinese were at the middle of the hierarchical division working as interpreters, mediating between Koreans and Han-Chinese. Finally, the majority of Han-Chinese were at the bottom as rank-and-file workers. In the following sections, I show how the correlation between spatial division and factory hierarchy facilitated management's control. Two contrasting effects of spatial divisions contributed to management's labor control: first, the Korean-Chinese living quarters' closeness to the Korean residential area made the Korean-Chinese interpreters feel close to the management, and second, the spatial marginality of the Han-Chinese workers' dormitories created and enhanced their lowest and most marginal status in the factory hierarchy.

The spatial division within the factory premises brought about another effect of social distinction, as the management matched the three discrete living conditions to the three-tired spatial divisions in the factory. If the comfortable and superior living conditions of the Korean residents (the expatriate Korean managers and their families) confirmed their idea of national superiority on a daily basis, the Han-Chinese workers realized their marginal status in the factory whenever they thought of the shabbiness of their dorm rooms. At the same time, the Korean-Chinese interpreters felt satisfied with their living conditions close as they were to those of the Korean residents, thus reinforcing their sense of closeness to the Korean management. As we will see, the different conditions of daily life in the factory complex operated as powerful instruments of factory power, inscribing the overlapping differences in the factory hierarchy and ethnicity deep into the factory employees' bodies and consciousness. The most striking expression of this distinguishing effect was in the Han-Chinese workers' pungent body odor. The odor, as result of their poor working and living conditions, created a powerful stigma against the Han-Chinese workers and further marginalized them as the most underprivileged group in the factory.

The "German" Houses: A monument to Korean national pride

The living space of the Korean managerial staff and their families consisted of three houses with distinctive architectural and spatial characteristics. Factory employees called the three buildings "German" houses because they resembled the historic German buildings in Qingdao that had been built when the city was a German concession. The three houses' unusual architectural design set them apart from their surroundings (G-A, G-B, and G-C in Figure 2-1). In contrast to the simply rectangular gray factory buildings (scornfully called "matchboxes" by the Chinese workers), the houses had sloping red slate roofs, large picture windows in the living room, and outer walls decorated with small gravel bricks. The three houses, designed by a Korean architect who graduated from a famous design school in the United States, were testimony to the Korean management's effort to reproduce their "modern" Korean houses in "backward" China.

In 2002, two out of the three expatriate Korean managers lived in the German houses together with their families. The factory president and his family lived in house A, and the plant manager and his family lived in house C. House B was reserved for foreign buyers and the executives of Nawon Korea who occasionally visited Nawon on business. Nawon Korea provided the houses for the two Korean managers and allowed them to live with their families as corporate benefits of the two top managerial positions in the factory. The remaining Korean manager lived in an individual room (not a house) located on the upper level of Building A. He did not get the privilege of living with his family in a separate house because of his relatively low position (financial manager) in the firm, as a subordinate of the factory president and the plant manager.

As the living space of the highest-ranked managerial staff and their families, the German houses had clear spatial characteristics. First of all, they were secluded both from the world outside the factory wall and from the production area of Nawon. Although there was no physical boundary indicating the space was reserved just for Koreans, even the most casual visitor to the factory could easily recognize the Korean residential area, which was well apart from the main factory buildings (Figure 2-1). The German houses in the area were secluded from the outside world in another sense, as the main factory building located to the south of the houses effectively blocked any gaze from outside the factory wall. At the main factory gate, one could see only the gray factory buildings and warehouses, which hid the German houses behind them. Insulated from other factory buildings and the world outside the factory, the Korean residential area occupied the most interior part of the factory site and formed a distinct space open only to Koreans.

The architectural design of the German houses played a critical function in surveillance. The four-feet-high foundation of the houses gave the Korean residents of the houses a good view of the factory, while the high foundation allowed people outside to see only a limited part of the inner space of the houses. The Nawon president's comment on his morning routine showed well what the high foundation of the Korean houses meant to the residents of the houses:

> It's usually about six in the morning. After taking a quick shower, I sit deep in my armchair and drink tea. It's the most peaceful time of the whole day. My daily schedule is full of stress. Soothing choosy foreign buyers, urging managers to supervise workers more effectively, and pointing out workers idling in the production lines—everything requires lots of my energy and I usually feel completely exhausted by the evening. The

personal tea time early every morning reinvigorates my exhausted mind and body. Resting in the armchair and looking down at all factory buildings through the window, I regain confidence in my ability to tackle difficult business tasks. Sometimes, I meditate on the day's events while looking down at the factory buildings, and this makes me realize again that I'm the owner of this factory and have the authority to control the whole factory operation.

Korean residents of the houses knew well how the commanding view over the factory contributed to maintaining their high status in the factory hierarchy: they could have a near-complete view of the factory from the windows of their houses, while outsiders could not see the indoor space of their houses. This imbalance between Koreans and non-Koreans became more apparent by thin white curtains that the management installed on every window facing the main factory buildings. I realized that the Korean residents kept those curtains closed day and night. The factory president's wife once said that it was because they did not want the Chinese workers to see even the smallest part of their private space. According to her, the curtain was a two-birds-with-one-stone solution, eliminating the possible peeping of Chinese workers and, at the same time, securing the Korean residents' view of the whole factory. "Even the least educated Chinese worker wouldn't dare look through the curtain," she said, "because he couldn't figure out whether there were people inside behind the curtain."

Korean-Chinese living quarters: A marker of intermediaries

The Korean-Chinese residential area revealed how spatial divisions and living conditions served management, making the Korean-Chinese employees a group loyal to the management. Especially during the early period of Nawon, the Korean managers heavily relied on the Korean-Chinese for their business operations in China. Having limited local knowledge about China, the management urgently needed to create reliable local assistants. In order to make the Korean-Chinese employees function as intermediaries or "cultural brokers" between Koreans and Han-Chinese workers, the Korean managers believed that they should keep the Korean-Chinese close to management. The location of the Korean-Chinese living quarters clearly revealed the Korean management's intention to create a group of "loyal" Korean-Chinese. From the earliest stage of the architectural design of the factory, the management put the

Korean-Chinese living quarters close to the three German houses. In contrast, the management built the Han-Chinese workers' dormitories completely separated from the main factory site (Figure 2-1). Even though they were Chinese citizens, the Korean-Chinese interpreters were in the same factory space and even used the same building with some Korean managers, except those who lived in the German houses with their families.

The exceptional living conditions of the Korean-Chinese residential quarters greatly contributed to the management's effort to mold the Korean-Chinese employees into pro-management employees (Figure 2-2). The management offered the Korean-Chinese a list of benefits in their everyday living, not much different from those given to the expatriate Korean managers. A short description of their living quarters clearly shows the benefits they received from management, as a part of the preferential treatment for their intermediary place in the factory hierarchy. For example, in every room of the Korean-Chinese, management installed four bunk beds and allowed each interpreter to use the whole set of the beds as his personal space. Because the interpreters used the extra space of the upper level bed as personal storage, their shared rooms always seemed well organized and much less crowded than those of the Han-Chinese workers. Management also allowed them to keep electrical devices in their rooms, such as electric water pots and blankets, which were not allowed in the Han-Chinese workers' dormitories. Finally, their bathrooms were equipped with Western-style bathtubs, washstands, and gas water heaters imported from South Korea. In fact, except for the interpreters having to share a room with two or three Korean-Chinese roommates, the basic arrangement of their rooms was similar to that of the expatriate Korean managers living on the upper level (Figure 2-2).

Korean-Chinese commensality with Koreans created another space shared by the two groups, thus making the Korean-Chinese interpreters feel closer to the management. From the very first day of Nawon, the Korean-Chinese interpreters ate in the dining hall that was originally built for the exclusive use of the Korean managers. The quality of food and the menu were exactly the same as those offered to the Korean managers. Of course, a rigid difference between the Koreans and Korean-Chinese still existed. The Korean-Chinese interpreters, for example,

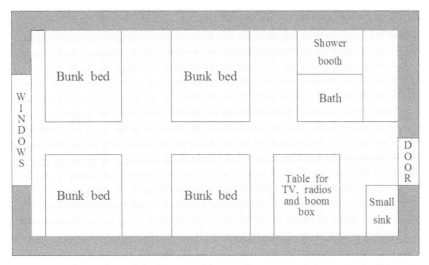

Figure 2-2. Floor Plan of the Korean-Chinese Interpreters' Room in Building A.
Source: Author

could not share a table with the Korean managerial staff. Among the six
tables in the dining hall, three were always reserved for Koreans, and not
a single interpreter was allowed to use them even if there was no other
seat available.[1]

The management's preferential treatment of Korean-Chinese employees
made those employees generally satisfied with the living and working
conditions of the factory. Their satisfaction primarily came from their
co-residence and commensality with the Korean managers. The Korean-
Chinese employees expressed an even stronger sense of satisfaction when
they compared their living conditions with those of the Han-Chinese
workers living in the factory dormitories. The huge difference in the living
conditions between the two ethnic groups made the Korean-Chinese
employees feel superior to the Han-Chinese. In view of common ethnic
relations in China, the Korean-Chinese feeling of ethnic superiority was
quite unusual. In China, Han-Chinese, the absolute ethnic majority,
maintain their superior statuses over ethnic minorities, including Korean-
Chinese, in economic, political, and cultural aspects. At Nawon, however,
the management put its Korean-Chinese employees in working and living
places much better than those of the Han-Chinese workers and thus

completely overturning the dominant pattern of ethnic relations in China. This, at the same time, made the Korean-Chinese interpreters feel closer to management, because it was that very management that put them on an intermediary plane in the factory hierarchy and provided the exceptional benefits that corresponded to their status.

Even though the management allowed the Korean-Chinese employees to share the living space and some key benefits with the Korean managers, it still differentiated between Koreans and Korean-Chinese. Korean managers at Nawon repeatedly made it clear that the shared living space in Building A should not create any confusion in the factory hierarchy. They argued that the Korean-Chinese must be the Korean management's subordinates under all circumstances. A close look at the space assignment and living patterns in Building A reveals how the Korean management maintained the hierarchical difference *in spite of* the shared living arrangements.

In the two-story building, Korean managers, one expatriate and one visiting, occupied the upper level, while the Korean-Chinese lived on the lower level. I learned about the subtle meaning of "living on the upper level" during a casual conversation with an expatriate Korean manager. In January, the outside temperature would fall to 20 degrees F and sometimes remain unchanged for days. Because the low temperature usually came with strong winds, it felt even colder. Unlike the German houses, built with quality construction materials, the ten-year-old Building A had thin walls with poor insulation. Because cold drafts blew in through the openings of the shabby window frames, it was hard for the residents to get a good sleep on cold winter nights. Despite their better insulation, in the house's upper level the temperature was lower than that of the lower level because the upper-level rooms were more directly exposed to the cold weather. This is why, especially during winter, the Korean managers living on the upper level used to complain of the low room temperature.

Interestingly, despite the low temperature in the upper level rooms, the Korean managers insisted that they *should* live on the upper level. They argued that people who gave orders should take a superior position in every respect, including their living space. Following the hierarchical order of the factory, managers should live in the upper-level rooms, while the Korean-Chinese interpreters were ordered to live on the lower level—the right place in view of their position in the factory hierarchy. For the managers, it would be simply an upside-down situation if the subordinates lived over the heads of their bosses. Any idea associating the interpreters with the upper-level rooms, they believed, violated the hierarchical order that began with the Korean factory president at its top and the interpreters somewhere between the Korean managerial staff and the Han-Chinese workers.

Most of all, the co-residence in Building A did not lead to any meaningful interactions between the two groups. During my fieldwork I observed no significant interaction between the managers and the interpreters except at several official banquets. The virtually nonexistent interaction between the two mainly resulted from their different use of time after work: while the Korean-Chinese interpreters went back to their rooms and usually spent their free time watching Korean TV programs broadcasted by a satellite relay, the Korean managers of Building A often went to Korean restaurants and bars to enjoy their social life. In fact, the different lifestyles of the two groups were an extension of their relationship on the shop floor, largely determined by their different places in the factory hierarchy. According to the role of an interpreter stipulated in the factory regulations, there was not a single functional overlap between the Koreans and the Korean-Chinese at Nawon. It was the Korean managers who held the power to begin and terminate orders in the workshop; the Korean-Chinese interpreters simply mediated between the Korean managers and the Han-Chinese workers. Such a wide social distance between the two groups both reflected and reinforced the factory hierarchy.

Factory dormitories and the spatial marginality of the Han-Chinese workers

While the Korean-Chinese employees lived close to the Koreans, the Han-Chinese workers lived in the factory dormitories, as noted earlier, completely separated from the living space of the Koreans and the Korean-Chinese. The Han-Chinese workers' dormitories were separated from the main factory area by six-foot-high concrete walls. The management further enhanced the spatial separation by installing two checkpoints that controlled the workers' movement between the dormitories and the main factory (Figure 2-1). With the checkpoints, the management made it very clear that not a single Han-Chinese worker could pass through the gates unchecked. This strict regulation made the Han-Chinese workers realize how they were separated from the main factory area not only by the high wall but by the extra surveillance methods. Every time the workers returned to the dormitories through the factory main gate, two female staff from the Personnel Affairs Division checked their bodies for any contraband owned by the factory, such as finished clothes and garment parts. Management restricted workers' access to the main factory area even during "free" weekends with no overtime. To get some hot water from the factory canteen, workers had to go through the vexing inspection by the security guards at the gate. Even after the security checks, they could not stay inside the factory site more than fifteen minutes per entry.

The factory dormitories' peripheral location reflected most Han-Chinese employees' statuses in the factory hierarchy. Except for two white-collar workers in the factory office and about twenty intermediary staff in the workshop, most Han-Chinese employees of the factory were rank-and-file workers who occupied the lowest place in the factory hierarchy. Their lowly hierarchical status also explains the big difference between their living quarters and those of the Korean-Chinese. The location of the Han-Chinese workers' dormitories reflected management's view of them as necessary resources for the factory operations but, unlike the Korean-Chinese interpreters, not as crucial staff. More specifically, it was the management's double need for easy labor mobilization and efficient labor control that determined the location of the Han-Chinese workers' dormitories. Since the late 1980s, the advancement in electronic point-of-sale technology using bar codes has greatly increased the command of retailers over garment factories. With this technology, retailers now make a real-time monitoring of consumer purchases and promptly reorder products just in time to restock their shelves. "Just-in-time" inventory procurement led to a new requirement that garment factories provide timely delivery. Under the "just-in-time" or "quick response" system, many garment factories, including Nawon, felt increasing pressure to deliver smaller orders in less time to meet tightly planned shipping schedules (Black and Chen 1995). Because of the volatile and unpredictable nature of orders, the management frequently required the Han-Chinese workers to work overtime, sometimes for stretches of three to four consecutive weeks. If the workers had lived in private rental houses scattered outside the factory, it would have been extremely difficult for the management to arrange for a large number of workers to show up on the shop floor on time. The management could put the workers within reach only by locating the dormitories right beside the factory main area. At the same time, however, the management well understood that the Han-Chinese workers' living in the dormitories could also be a threat to management, because the collective nature of the residence arrangements could possibly create and enhance solidarity among the workers. As preemptive measures to ward off possible labor unrest, the management established the concrete walls, the two checkpoints equipped with steel gates, and strict regulations that restricted workers' movement.

The Han-Chinese workers' daily life in the dormitories reveals how different living conditions contributed to creating and maintaining the hierarchical order in the factory. The Han-Chinese workers' living conditions in the factory were the poorest among the factory employees, as they had the lowest hierarchical status. In fact, their living conditions were much worse than what one might expect from the actual hierarchical difference between them and the Korean-Chinese employees. First, the basic spatial design of the dormitories was very different from the Korean-Chinese living quarters. In the dormitories, each floor had nine different-sized rooms and one shared lavatory.[2] According to room size, management installed four to six bunk beds and assigned seven to ten workers to each room. The high room occupancy created the most visible difference in the everyday life of the Han-Chinese workers and the Korean-Chinese interpreters: while a Han-Chinese worker had to live with six to nine people, a Korean-Chinese interpreter shared his or her room with only three. That made the Han-Chinese workers' rooms always look crowded, in contrast to the spacious rooms of the Korean-Chinese. The Han-Chinese workers always felt it difficult to keep their rooms clean and tidy because the management allowed them to use only one or two berths per room as shared storage space.[3] Because of the limited room space, the workers described their small rooms as "hopelessly dirty and totally disorganized" (Figure 2-3).

The Han-Chinese workers' poor living conditions functioned as a subtle mechanism to create and maintain the differences between them and the Korean-Chinese interpreters. The most striking condition was the absence of heating in their dormitories. As previously mentioned, management permitted the Korean-Chinese interpreters to use personal electric heaters in their rooms. They also enjoyed a warm shower in the rooms, thanks to the Western-style bathrooms equipped with gas heating. In contrast, the Han-Chinese workers' dormitories completely lacked heating, and the

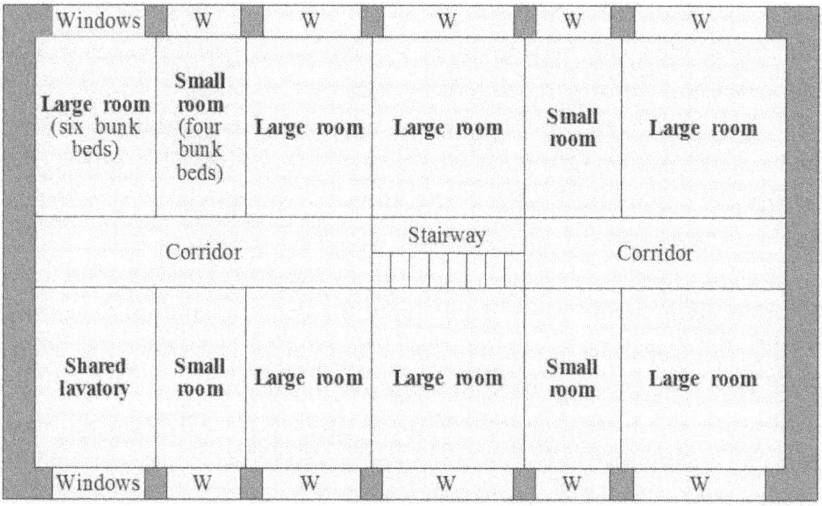

Windows	W	W	W	W	W
Large room (six bunk beds)	Small room (four bunk beds)	Large room	Large room	Small room	Large room
Corridor			Stairway	Corridor	
Shared lavatory	Small room	Large room	Large room	Small room	Large room
Windows	W	W	W	W	W

Figure 2-3. Floor Plan of the Han-Chinese Workers' Dormitories.
Source: Author

shared lavatories on each floor did not have any showers. The workers could not warm their rooms with electric heaters because the rooms had only one electric outlet, and that was installed on the ceiling for a light bulb. Factory regulations that strictly banned the use of heavy electric devices only made the already poor living conditions worse. In this situation, the indoor temperature of the dormitories sometimes fell below freezing during the winter. In chilly winter mornings, the Han-Chinese workers found the water inside their small plastic tea bottles thinly crusted with ice. They had to endure the low room temperature with only blankets for warmth and, as a result, many workers suffered from chilblains during the coldest time of the winter.

The Han-Chinese workers' poor living conditions even made their time-spending patterns different from those of the interpreters. The Han-Chinese workers spent an average of 35 percent of their free time washing clothes, while the interpreters spent only 5 percent of theirs in the same task. Their frequent overtime, which often lasted until 11 p.m., explains the long washing hours. Especially during the high-order season, the workers nearly ran out of clean clothes as overtime continued for three or four consecutive weeks. That was why, on the rare occasions of when the workers got their one day off, they rushed to the lavatory to wash their dirty clothes piled up in their rooms. "If a worker doesn't wash her clothes on that day," a Han-Chinese worker said, "she'd have to wear her dirty ones for an additional one or two weeks." The highly limited washing space in the dormitories took more free time from the workers because the shared lavatory on each level of the dormitories had only twelve water taps. For this reason, many workers simply gave up the chance to go outside, because they felt tired when they finished washing; even the remaining time after washing was not enough for them to take a nap. The Korean-Chinese interpreters, in contrast, spent their holidays quite leisurely, because they could use electric washing machines installed in their living quarters. While the workers spent much of their free time standing in the long line for their turn at washing clothes, the interpreters enjoyed watching TV, shopping, and exercising.

NATIONAL/ETHNIC "NATURE": RESULTS OF DIFFERENT LIVING CONDITIONS

The living conditions at Nawon that varied according to one's hierarchical status had the subtle but enduring effect of reinforcing social distinctions and discrimination. They created national and ethnic stereotypes of the residents, heavily stigmatizing the Han-Chinese workers living in the factory dormitories. The living conditions had such effects because they operated in the context of the everyday routines and affected the most intimate human feelings of (dis)comfort, (in)convenience, and (un)cleanliness. In the factory dormitories, the Han-Chinese workers had to endure various discomforts and inconveniences, created by the poor living conditions of the buildings. The everyday difficulty of keeping good individual hygiene made the workers compromise their standards of bodily cleanliness. The Korean residents (the Korean managers and their families) and the Korean-Chinese employees regarded the Han-Chinese workers' unclean dorm rooms and sweaty bodies as strong evidence of the ethnic inferiority of Han-Chinese. In the following sections, I show how the different living conditions in the factory changed the factory residents' view of national and ethnic differences and thus led them to believe the differences to be inherent and unchanging group characteristics. In short, the residents' perception of "others" contributed to creating national and ethnic stereotypes. The stereotypes eventually consolidated management's control of labor, because they widened the existing ethnic schism between the Han-Chinese and the Korean-Chinese.

The "Harmful influence" of Han-Chinese workers

Ignorance and evasion are the two terms that best describe the Korean residents' understanding of Han-Chinese workers. The families of the factory president and the plant manager could not remember meeting with the workers even once. Their complete lack of contact with the workers was surprising, because they had lived at Nawon for almost a decade. For example, three Korean children living in the Korean residential area, the children of the factory president and the plant manager, said that they had never talked with the Han-Chinese workers during their five-to-seven-year stay in the factory. They spent most of their time outside the factory and thus regarded their home in the factory as a place only for sleeping and doing their homework. Because the three young Koreans attended school in downtown Qingdao and joined after-school activities, they left their home around seven in the morning and returned at almost seven in the evening. There was not the slightest chance for them to see the Han-Chinese workers because they went to school well before the beginning of the factory routine and came back home in the middle of overtime operations. The unusual pattern of their daily routine completely severed their life from the daily activities of the factory. Their complete lack of contact with the Han-Chinese workers at Nawon was surprising because they kept close relationships with their Han-Chinese classmates at their school. When I asked about the reason for their non-contact with the workers, they at first looked puzzled, shrugging their shoulders. "They're workers," one of the Korean students replied. "There's virtually nothing for us to share with each other."

Behind the puzzled response, I found their parents' strong desire to prevent their children from having contact with the workers. The two mothers of the Korean students at Nawon said that they kept their children from contact with the Han-Chinese workers, not only because it was not necessary but also because it could be harmful to the children's development. "As parents," the mother of one of the students argued, "we should provide the best environment for our kids." The two Korean mothers' intense concern about their children's education was not special considering the feverish devotion of many South Korean parents to their children (Park and Abelmann 2004: 645–54; Abelmann 2007: 115–30). At Nawon, however, the parental fear of "lagging behind" of their counterparts in South Korea made their concern about their children much more intense. "Living among the *backward* Chinese workers from the countryside," the other Korean mother argued, "has already brought many disadvantages to our children." This shared, deep anxiety of "lagging behind" drove the parents to make every effort to protect their children from the possible negative influence of the factory environment, particularly from the "bad" influence of the Han-Chinese workers, the close human expression of the "backwardness" of a "Communist country." The fact that most Han-Chinese workers in the factory came from Pingshan, one of the poorest regions in Shandong province, confirmed the parents' belief in their "backwardness." One of the two mothers argued:

> We know that China, especially since early 2000, has rapidly developed. But the development has mostly affected the cities. It hasn't brought any significant change to the rural areas. The Han-Chinese workers in our factory are still uncultured and undereducated because they came from the backward countryside . . . This is why, we, as parents, should provide the best environment for our kids and keep them away from the workers.

The Korean residents' perception of China and the Han-Chinese workers was widely shared by the Korean parents living in other nearby Korean multinational corporations. Many of them did not hesitate to say that the workers were a real threat to their children's successful development: "Because the workers came from the most *backward* countryside and only got a middle school education," a Korean mother of a middle school student said, "they lack even the most basic etiquette of *cultured* people. If we left our children in open contact with the workers, it could do a real harm to our children's future." The Korean residents assumed that there was plenty of evidence that proved the uncultured and backward nature of the Han-Chinese workers. Even though they never actually saw the workers' rooms in the factory dormitories, many Korean mothers frequently referred to the "dark and overcrowded" rooms in the dormitories as evidence of the

Han-Chinese workers' lack of social etiquette and discipline. The mothers hoped that their children would grow up to be successful just like the students in the home country. They believed that they should use every means possible to realize that hope.

The Korean residents' stereotyped view of Han-Chinese workers reveals the subtle effect of social distinction and discrimination created by the spatial divisions and the different living conditions. The Korean residents were largely satisfied with their life in the factory, insofar as it proved the Korean national superiority to Han-Chinese and protected their everyday life from the "harmful" influence of the Han-Chinese workers. Meanwhile, the spatial divisions blocked a correct understanding of the workers. In fact, the deep division made the Korean residents ignore the actual situation in the factory dormitories and eventually deny the Han-Chinese workers' coevalness (Fabian 1983). In their eyes, the workers were not their contemporaries who merited their understanding.[4]

"The smell of Han-Chinese"

Smell is not simply a biological and psychological but also a cultural phenomenon (Classen et al. 1994: 8). The attractive or repulsive nature of an olfactory experience makes odor an effective device for categorizing different groups according to certain cultural values. Different odors have been ascribed to different social classes and ethnic groups. George Orwell once argued that the "real secret of class distinctions in the West" could be "summed up in four frightful words . . . the lower class smell" (Orwell 1937: 159). The upper- and middle-classes in nineteenth-century Europe often pointed to the "filthy" living conditions of the working class and the malodor reeking from them as markers of social class. This contrasted with the sanitary, thus, odorless life of the upper- and middle-classes. The pungent odor of the working class was not simply an actual foul smell caused by their poor working and living conditions. Instead, it reflected the collective judgment of upper- and middle-class people who considered them not only physically but morally repulsive.

Body odor also functions as a marker of ethnic or national identity, thanks to the commonsensical belief that food affects body odor. Sweet relishes and spices were believed to contribute to the distinctive body odor of Indians, and lean mutton was regarded as the cause of the "Arab odor" (Doty 1972: 149–50). However, a given ethnic odor is not simply regarded as a result of consuming a particular food item. Rather, it is considered intrinsic to the group, becoming a quasi-inherited trait that is as inalterable as skin color (Largey and Watson 1977; Synnott 1993: 194–202). In the pre-emancipation American South, for example, there was a prevailing stereotype of "repulsive-smelling" blacks. At that time, African Americans were not considered part of the same civilization as whites in part because they were believed to have a smell "extremely disagreeable to white people" (Classen et al. 1994: 20; Corbin 1986: 38, 209). Even today, people of the host country often regard immigrants and migrant workers as having a different body smell, thus making them the objects of mistrust as "foul foreigners" (Classen 1993: 92).

At Nawon, odor strengthened the existing divisions between different ethnic and national groups in the factory, thus reinforcing management's control of the shop floor. The Han-Chinese workers' pungent body smell was at the center of the powerful dividing effect based on odor. I realized this on the very first day of my research on the shop floor. After I spent several weeks in the main office, the Korean managers finally allowed me to do some "fieldwork" on the shop floor. Early one morning, I pushed open the door leading to the workshop and followed a Han-Chinese worker who would show me every corner of the production lines. At the very moment I stepped onto the shop floor, what struck me hard was neither the scene of a tightly organized shop floor nor the loud operating noise of sewing machines. When I took one step into the shop floor, I noticed a strong odor. "What's this strange odor?" I asked myself. Walking through the production lines, I realized that the whole shop floor was filled with the same odor, one that resembled something rancid.

Later, a Korean-Chinese interpreter informed me of the source: the Han-Chinese workers. During the summer, the temperature of the shop floor sometimes went up near 100 degrees and working uniforms became soaked in sweat after several hours of work. "Because the workers neither wash their hair nor take baths often," the interpreter said, "the whole shop floor is filled with such a strange odor—something fermenting or rotten." Several visiting Korean managers, who were not accustomed to the odor, expressed their acute embarrassment at the "obnoxious odor." Among them, a female manager complained that she could only stay in the workshop for a short time because the odor made her nearly sick. "They are girls in the prime time of their youth," she once complained. "Why don't they care for their own bodies? I can't believe that the horrible odor comes from such young girls who should be concerned about caring for their beauty." Although their responses toward the odor varied, all the Korean managers agreed on one point: the Han-Chinese workers' unsanitary lifestyle produced the odor.

The Korean-Chinese interpreters' reaction to the odor was even more negative than that of the Korean managers. At first, I expected that their attitude might be different from that of the Koreans, maybe more or less sympathetic to the Han-Chinese workers suffering from poor working and living conditions. Owing to their intermediary role as "cultural brokers" at Nawon, the interpreters spent much more time with the Han-Chinese workers on the shop floor than the Korean managers did. This, I supposed, may have given them more of an opportunity to understand what really created the odor, including the high shop-floor temperature, the poor living conditions of the dormitories, and the everyday difficulties of washing clothes. On the contrary, the Korean-Chinese interpreters' attitude toward the odor was more critical than that of the Korean managers. The interpreters often complained of the odor, calling it *Han-Chinese odor*. "Han-Chinese are always dirtier than we Korean-Chinese," a Korean-Chinese interpreter argued, "because they *originally* lack the idea of what the word 'clean' means." At the same time, the interpreters believed that the idea of cleanliness is inherent in the life of Korean-Chinese as an important part of their culture. Their awareness of the ethnic difference, expressed in the different level of bodily cleanliness, was very strong: several women interpreters even said that they were really reluctant to make physical contact with the Han-Chinese workers because they were "not clean."

Both the Korean residents and the Korean-Chinese interpreters acknowledged that the Han-Chinese workers' poor working and living conditions made their bodies smelly. Several of them, however, still argued that the odor was not a simple result of the poor conditions: "As you see," an interpreter said, "there are cheap public bathhouses near the factory. But many Han-Chinese workers still don't use them often. They simply don't like to wash—it's their nature." His argument reflects some actual facts, because there were only a few Han-Chinese workers who visited the bathhouse more than once a week. The real reason of the body smell, of course, was not in their ethnic "nature" but in their everyday difficulties keeping their bodies clean: "To use the bathhouses," a worker replied to my question about their rare visit to the bathhouses, "I have to walk down the dusty road for at least fifteen minutes." In fact, many workers regarded using the public bathhouses more than twice a month as a waste of time and money. Instead, they said that they went to the factory canteen, where they could use hot water from the faucets located at the corner of the building, to wash their hair. It was not an easy routine, however, because the workers had to pass through the two checkpoints to get to the canteen, accompanied by the security guards' rude questions and suspicious gaze.

To some extent, the idea of "clean Koreans" and "neat Korean-Chinese" was not completely imaginary: thanks to their good living conditions, both the Korean residents and the Korean-Chinese interpreters kept their bodies clean and odorless, in sharp contrast to the Han-Chinese workers' dirty bodies and pungent odor. In the same context, one may argue that the pungent body odor directly resulted from the Han-Chinese workers' poor living conditions, because those conditions made it very difficult for the workers to take showers or baths in the dormitories. However, the Korean-Chinese interpreters' comment about "Han-Chinese odor" indicates that the body odor carried political implications that could not be fully explained by the relation between the odor and the poor living environment. As the Korean-Chinese interpreters called the pungent odor in workshop "Han-Chinese odor," the odor came to indicate more than the Han-Chinese workers' dirty bodies, the physical source of the odor. Rather, the expression strongly suggested that the odor was somehow intrinsic to the workers as a part of their ethnicity. As the Korean-Chinese interpreters regarded the body odor as an expression of Han-Chinese ethnic characteristics and contrasted it with the clean bodies of the Korean-Chinese, the ethnic division between the two groups of employees deepened.

Han-Chinese workers: Social stigma and the fantasy of the foreign

The spatial divisions in the factory, with Han-Chinese as the most underprivileged, the Korean-Chinese employees in an intermediate position, and the Koreans residents on top, meant more than a simple distinction between us and the other. Instead, the distinction was heavily charged with negative ideas of backwardness, poverty, and uncleanness. This is in fact the very process of social stigmatization that made the Han-Chinese workers "the inferior other" (Parker and Aggleton 2003; Yang et al. 2008). In the stigmatizing process, those with power impose negative meanings on the powerless, which strengthens the existing social order and hierarchy. At Nawon, the Korean management designed the spatial divisions and put the Han-Chinese workers in a marginal area. The management also was the source of the poor living conditions of the workers that eventually imposed on them the negative meanings of backward, uncultured, and unclean. The stigmatization contributed to management's control of labor since it heightened the ethnic consciousness of the Korean-Chinese and deepened the schisms among the local employees.

The Han-Chinese workers were fully aware of how their poor working and living conditions created and maintained the humiliating symbols of stigma, such as pungent body odor, rough skin, and dirty hair. They pointed out that the symbols of stigma resulted from the lack of hot bathing water and the shortage of free time, not from any ethnic or group nature. Their clear understanding of the body odor and its causes seemed to negate the Korean-Chinese employees' essentializing statements that regarded the odor as an expression of an alleged Han-Chinese ethnic trait. However, the Han-Chinese workers' critical insight into the stigmatization did not lead to any open negation of the process, such as a protest against the poor living and working conditions in the factory. Many workers, instead, said that they did not care much about the living conditions because they were already "accustomed" to them (C. *xiguanle*).

It was a clear fact that their dorm rooms were very cold in the winter. Their rough faces afflicted with chilblains were the physical evidence of the poor conditions. At the same time, however, they said that they did not consider it an unusually serious problem because they had become accustomed to the low room temperature. They also knew that many nearby factory dormitories offered the same poor living conditions. Some workers even said, rather cynically, that they did not care much about the low room temperature because the indoor temperature of the farming houses back in the countryside of Pingshan was just the same as that of their dorm rooms. "We're country bumpkins," a worker said. "There is nothing particular that we can't endure . . . we have very simple expectations."

The Han-Chinese workers' attitudes toward their inferior living and working conditions are good examples of a typical attitude among many migrant workers in China (Jacka 2006). Coming from the poor and underdeveloped countryside, many of the workers had relatively low expectations for their living conditions in the factory dormitories. Their main concern, instead, was to receive wages on time and to save them for their future use such as for marriage expenses and a dowry. Undoubtedly, the workers felt uncomfortable because of their poor working and living conditions. At the same time, however, they believed they could manage to endure as long as management paid them their wages on time.

The local Chinese government's cooperative relationship with the Korean management of Nawon reinforced the disciplinary power of the spatial division. Shortly after the factory began operations, the officials of Fuyang village near the factory joined in supervising the labor at the factory. During the early years of operations, the managers, with their limited knowledge of the Chinese language and the local situation, struggled to discipline the newly hired Han-Chinese workers fresh from the countryside. The management realized that the village officials could control the workers much better than could the Korean managers because they themselves were Han-Chinese and had in-depth local knowledge.

The officials of Fuyang village welcomed management's request to participate in labor control. The officials knew very well how Nawon, one of nineteen multinational corporations in the region, could greatly contribute to the development of their village by generating tax revenue. Thanks to the revenue brought by multinational corporations, Chinese local governments have been able to launch ambitious public projects, such as new public apartments and daycare centers, updated school facilities, and new roads. The officials thought that they should support the smooth operation of the foreign corporations and attract even more foreign investment.[5]

Furthermore, the village officials viewed the large group of migrant workers at Nawon as a potential threat to public security. Migrant workers come from the countryside to work in the cities and thus are not registered as urban residents. To get urban residential status, they have to meet various official requirements such as having a record of long-term residence and income tax payments. Such strict and costly requirements often force them to keep their nonlocal, "migrant" status.[6] It is a common suspicion widely shared by the urban residents that migrant workers from remote rural areas tend to be less attentive to regulations and laws, because they are less educated and disciplined.[7] The village officials' view of the workers reflected the common prejudice against the migrant workers. "Migrant workers are poor and uneducated," a local public security officer argued. "They tend to do bad things and just run away." The large and even growing economic urban-rural gap only reinforced urban residents' negative view of the workers.[8]

In their joint control of the Han-Chinese workers, the village government regulated the workers' life outside the factory. Management transferred the administrative duties of the factory dormitories to the village government, including the control of the two gatehouses at the main dormitory entrance. The village officials recruited the administrative staff of the dormitories from among village residents. They enforced the nighttime curfew throughout the dormitories and checked for workers' misconduct in their dorm rooms. When security guards, all village residents, found a breach of dormitory regulations or a violation of the curfew, they promptly reported the case to the village officials and the management.

The village officials' administration of the dormitories made the spatial division between the dormitories and the main factory premises virtually inviolable. The Han-Chinese workers well understood that curfew violations would not only be punished by the management but would also incur the wrath of the village officials. The officials, according to the workers, could cancel the residential permits of the workers any time if they believed that the workers were "troublemakers." A Han-Chinese worker argued: "The [village] officials never care about our living conditions in the dormitories. They're only concerned about how to control us. Why don't they pay attention to us? It's so clear! Foreign corporations have brought them money." The discriminatory policy against migrants and the high cost of urban living dashed the Han-Chinese workers' hope for a decent future life in the cities. The systemic discrimination eventually contributed to the workers' acceptance of their marginality in the factory, which was obviously marked by the spatial division and different living conditions.

The spatial divisions in the living quarters at Nawon also contributed to the Han-Chinese workers' misrecognition of Korean women residents and their fantasy of the foreign women from a neighboring country. During my fieldwork, the workers often asked me about the age of the factory president's wife. When I estimated her age as around the early fifties, they seemed surprised. One of the workers said:

Are you kidding me? It was only about three months ago that I saw her in front of the Korean house [i.e., German house A]. At that time, she seemed to be waiting for her child to return from school. Although I couldn't get a clear view of her, I could recognize she wore a beautiful evening dress. Oh, and her pearly face shining with the rising full moon! She looked just like a young lady in her early forties. . . . And now you say that she's already over fifty? My mother in Pingshan is also in her early fifties, but her skin is rough and dark; her face is already full of countless wrinkles!

In the factory, stories about the beauty of Korean women widely circulated among the Han-Chinese workers. Another worker talked about how she unexpectedly encountered the factory president's daughter and came to realize her beauty. As an inspector of the finishing section, she saw the president's daughter on her way to German house B, where she was supposed to wash stained garments using a washing machine at the back of the house. Although the encounter was short, she argued that she remembered the details of the Korean girl's appearance. When the worker talked about her "fairy-like" appearance, she used expressions such as "curly, glossy hair," "soft and fair skin," "large black eyes," and "patrician nose." Other workers also used similar terms when they described the women living in the Korean houses.

The Han-Chinese workers' misrecognition of Korean women's beauty further reinforced their stigmatized image of themselves as "country bumpkins." The negative feedback ran through their comparison of Korean women's beauty with their image of themselves as dirty and unkempt, which was also expressed in contrasts between "white and fair" Korean hands and their "dark and rough" hands. At Nawon, the hands of most Han-Chinese workers were far from the feminine ideal that appeared in the women's beauty magazines they occasionally read. Their rough hands resulted from a specific rule of the management that did not allow them to wear gloves even during the winter. Gloves, according to the management, would certainly decrease work speed and increase the defect rate, since they prevented workers from having an "accurate feel" via their bare fingertips. As they were exposed to the cold temperature of the shop floor for an extended time, the Han-Chinese workers' hands gradually lost their original fairness and bore the marks of chilblains. This, again, had a profound effect on the Han-Chinese workers' self-image. When they described their hands as rough like "those of peasant women," the workers almost always pointed out how "tender and snow white" the Korean women's hands were. With their rough hands, the workers gradually came to believe that they lacked key female attractions symbolized by "delicate and fair" skin and accepted a disparaging self-image as "country bumpkins" as an unavoidable part of their everyday life.[9] This is another subtle but enduring effect of the different living conditions, one that enhanced and perpetuated the Han-Chinese workers' self-humiliating image and prompted them to accept the lowest place in the factory hierarchy.

CONCLUSION

As it relocated production facilities from South Korea to China, the Korean management at Nawon also imported the spatial designs and architecture of the mother factory. These embodied the prime principle of advanced industrialism, highlighting the clear division between management and labor. The spatial designs and architecture also embodied the management's effort to satisfy the demands of global garment production, especially the need for flexible labor suitable for the "just-in-time" production system. The management established a collective living place of Han Chinese workers outside the main factory premises. The peripheral but still close location of the Han-Chinese workers' dormitories functioned as an effective method of labor control and mobilization, helping the management to make timely delivery of orders.

In the factory, however, the spatial divisions and architecture carried multiple meanings that cannot be neatly explained either by the hierarchical difference between management and labor or by the incessant demand of the global just-in-time production system. They also reflected the foreign management's feeling of superiority over "backward" local labor, a feeling that often denies the coevalness of the local employees and treats them as underdeveloped, child-like subjects. Management's foreign origin made the meanings of the spatial divisions very complex. With the collective memory of the Korean War, the Korean managers questioned the Han-Chinese employees' reliability and their loyalty to the South Korean management. Instead, the management regarded the Korean-Chinese as trustworthy local assistants in its operations in China, because it understood Korean-Chinese as de facto Koreans. The management's suspicion of Han-Chinese and its preference for Korean-Chinese brought about a unique spatial division and hierarchy. The management intended to transform the Korean-Chinese employees into reliable local assistants or "cultural brokers" by putting their living place close to that of the Koreans and offering them superior living conditions.

The different living conditions had the most subtle and pervasive effects of social distinction and discrimination, because they created and enhanced stereotypes, stigmas, and misrecognitions among the factory residents. The Korean residents and the Korean-Chinese employees of the factory received the most positive effects brought about by the living arrangements: the best living conditions in the secluded space of the German houses made the Korean residents feel superior to the Korean-Chinese and the Han-Chinese workers. The Korean-Chinese employees also enjoyed the benefits of their exclusive living accommodations, characterized by their spatial closeness to Korean housing and commensality with the Korean managers. Their quality living caused a remarkable distinguishing effect because their accommodations, far superior to those of the Han-Chinese workers, enhanced their ethnic consciousness and created a wide social distance from the workers. The Nawon management carefully designed the Korean-Chinese living space and offered better living conditions to them as part of its effort to turn the Korean-Chinese into a group of pro-management local employees.

The everyday living of Han-Chinese workers revealed the most powerful influence of the different living conditions, because they affected the intimate human feelings of comfort, convenience, and cleanliness. The workers repeatedly felt their status in the factory as the most underprivileged when they realized how their rough and de-feminized appearance sharply contrasted with "Korean beauty." The Han-Chinese workers' pungent body odor became the prime example of the powerful stigma imposed on the workers when the Korean-Chinese employees referred to the odor as a Han-Chinese ethnic trait.

At Nawon, all the power effects created by the spatial divisions and different living conditions demonstrate the "porosity of the human body," the close relationship between the human body, self-image, and the surrounding world (Harvey 1996: 218–19). The effects demonstrated how the human body and self-consciousness are vulnerable to power, especially when it acts on the body and consciousness through the most mundane context of everyday life. In the Nawon factory, the spatial divisions and different living conditions served as powerful managerial tools to create and maintain a distinctive hierarchical order in the factory. Operating through the everyday practices of the factory employees and residents, the spatial divisions and the different living conditions created social closeness *and* distance. In particular, they divided the local labor along lines of two ethnic affiliations—the Korean-Chinese and the Han-Chinese—thus contributing to management's control of local labor.

The controlling mechanism of the spatial divisions and the different living conditions, however, only give us a limited understanding of the whole managerial strategy of labor control and its effects on the factory employees. They only revealed management's power that operated *outside* the workplaces, setting up the large framework of power relations between Koreans, Korean-Chinese, and Han-Chinese. We still need to look into the everyday interactions in the office and on the shop floor in order to understand the micro-operations and effects of managerial power. The next chapter explores how the multinational management secured its control of the factory office by manipulating ethnic and class differences among its local employees.

THREE

The Politics of Nationality, Ethnicity, and Status

The Factory Office

"NEW" WHITE-COLLAR WORKERS AND THE IMPLICATIONS FOR MANAGERIAL POLITICS

In China, the term "stratum" (C. *jieceng*) has become increasingly popular. In contrast, "class" (C. *jieji*), once a politically correct term, has become rare. Since the launch of the reform and openness policy in the 1980s, both intellectuals and the common people of China have become growingly reluctant to use the word "class" because it invokes the political chaos brought by radical Maoism (Zhang 2008: 23–26). During the radical Maoist period before the 1980s, the political slogan of "perpetual class struggle" dominated the entire Chinese society. Especially during the most tumultuous period of Cultural Revolution, many people with outstanding political, economic, or social backgrounds were condemned as the "enemies of the working class" and were purged (Bian 1994: 93–94). Since the 1980s, the Chinese government and the Chinese Communist Party (CCP) have officially denounced radical Maoism as an "historical error." Instead, they took a new path, "socialism with Chinese characteristics," with a new emphasis on economic development and practicalism. In the process of this huge political change, the new term "stratum"—considered politically more neutral than the notorious Maoist terminology—has gradually replaced "class."

The growing popularity of the terms such as blue- and white-collar (C. *lanling* and *bailing*) originated from the same political change. During the radical Maoist period, at least in theory, even a single internal difference in the working class was not tolerated. According to the dominant tenets of radical Maoism, the Chinese working class, as the leading class of the socialist revolution, should be internally homogeneous; every job should be treated and paid equally, insofar as it requires the same amount of quantifiable human labor measured by time spent in the production process. This logic has long disappeared since the Chinese government and the CCP took their capitalist turn with the economic reform. Now, a new logic of "quality labor" justifies the rapidly growing differences in the once highly homogeneous Chinese working class (Anagnost 2004). With the multiplying internal differentiations, the term "white-collar," originally imported from the United States, came to symbolize office jobs with high salaries held mostly by people with advanced degrees and new knowledge (Dai 2001; Wang 2004). In contrast, the term "blue-collar" came to mean jobs with low wages and long work hours that require less education and less sophisticated social backgrounds. In the new dichotomy of white- and blue-collar jobs, the former appear to be highly coveted and sought after, while the latter are less desirable.

A careful observation of the common use of the two terms reveals that they often imply more than functional differentiation. The term "white-collar" describes the new and growing body of managerial personnel. They develop company projects, set production targets, and issue orders that people who work on the shop floor are expected to fulfill. In contrast, the term "blue-collar" indicates traditional working-class people who spend most of their work hours on the shop floor and carry out management's orders. The diversification of the working class into the two "collars" implies a hierarchical relationship between the two, with white-collar workers usually assuming a commanding status superior to that of blue-collar workers. White-collar workers have become the new dominating group as they have gained more political and economic influence than that of blue-collar workers. However, the official political rhetoric of China does not acknowledge the implicit hierarchical difference between white- and blue-collar workers. In the official version of post-Mao politics, people with different individual skills are expected to work "harmoniously" with one another, since they are functionally dependent on one another (Xin 2004; Xing 2005). From this perspective, the internal diversification of the Chinese working class seems politically benign or neutral insofar as it indicates improving labor quality and diversifying social strata to the level of those in the developed countries.

The common and the official understandings of the division between white- and blue-collar workers, which are based on functionalism and political neutrality, have come under scholarly scrutiny. In fact, the division has been a key topic in the study of industrial organization and class politics (see, for example, Mills 1956; Bourdieu 1984; Weiss 1988). Especially scholars in the Marxist tradition argue that the rise of white-collar workers, as a new quasi-class, has created a deep division within the working class and, consequently, weaken class solidarity. It is a fact that white-collar workers receive better treatment from management and have incomes higher than blue-collar workers. This does not mean, however, that their status is fundamentally different from that of the traditional working class, insofar as they are still hired and paid by management (Dreyfuss 1977 [1938]; Snyder 1973: 22). Marxist scholars thus understand the creation of white-collar jobs as a part of a managerial effort to control labor. In that effort, management seeks to weaken the solidarity of the working class by creating internal schisms within it. Some scholars further insist that the very existence of white-collar workers, or a distinctive white-collar consciousness, is an illusion, because white-collar workers do not possess any means of production (Abercrombie and Urry 1983: 103; Aronowitz 1992: 291–322; Mills 1956: 211; Oppenheimer 1973).

At Nawon, the white- and the blue-collar division bears rich political implications. The division can neither be neatly explained by individual workers' different skills and functions nor be easily reduced to simple class politics narrowly defined in economic terms. Instead, the division was embedded in multiple ideologies such as nation, nationalism, and ethnicity, and thus created powerful political effects on the relations between management and labor. The particular division in the Nawon factory created and enhanced schisms among local labor and eventually contributed to management's control of labor. From the very beginning of its operations in China, the foreign management from South Korea filled most of the office job positions with Korean-Chinese. As a result, the white- and the blue-collar division came to overlap with the ethnic division between Korean-Chinese and Han-Chinese. The preferential recruitment of Korean-Chinese resulted from the management's memory of the Korean War, its unique understanding of nationality or ethnicity, and the collective Korean historical imagination of Sino-centrism. The strong preference for Korean-Chinese widened the existing schism between Han-Chinese and Korean-Chinese employees, allowing management to take full advantage of the white- and the blue-collar division.

The transformation of Korean-Chinese into a wealthy ethnic minority created remarkable political effects at Nawon, this because the transformation overturned the dominant ethnic power relationship of China. In national ethnic politics, Han-Chinese occupy the political, economic, and cultural high ground because they are the ethnic majority, composing about 92 percent of the Chinese population. In contrast, many Korean-Chinese suffer from social and economic disadvantages because of their status as a historically recent ethnic minority. Consequently, they have developed a collective feeling of being discriminated against by Han-Chinese. Taking white-collar jobs at Nawon led the Korean-Chinese to believe that they finally got a much-anticipated chance to change their fate as an underprivileged ethnic minority. As they realized the importance of their current jobs and tried to sustain the ethnic monopoly on the white-collar positions, the Korean-Chinese in the corporation became more vocal in expressing their "Korean-ness." Here, "Korean-ness" indicates the strong Korean cultural affiliation of Korean-Chinese, which is based on their sense of cultural authenticity as Koreans and belief in their embodiment of idealized traditional Korean culture. The concept of "Korean-ness" explains how the Korean-Chinese white-collar workers took advantage of their cultural affinity with South Korea to secure their place in mainstream Chinese society.

WHITE-COLLAR FORMATION AND THE POLITICS OF HISTORICAL IMAGINATION AND NATIONAL SUPERIORITY

Fear of Han-Chinese imperialism

At Nawon, the white- and blue-collar division was apparent even in the spatial arrangement of the main factory building. Sound-proofed thick

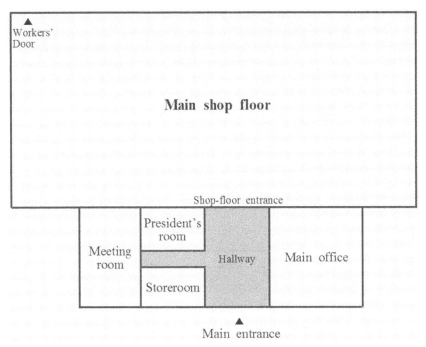

Figure 3-1. Spatial Divisions of the Factory Main Building. Source: Author

walls divided the indoor space into two areas, one assigned to the office and the other to the production area (Figure 3-1). In addition to the apparent spatial division, the high-quality work environment of the main office created a more subtle but highly pervasive distinction between the white- and the blue-collar workers in the factory. In the workshop, with no air-conditioning, shop-floor workers suffered from the extremely high (in the summer) and low (in the winter) indoor temperatures. In contrast, office workers enjoyed the air-conditioned office environment where some of them even complained about the "freezing cold" (in the summer) and the "unnecessarily warm" room temperatures (in the winter). As mentioned in Chapter Two, the differences in the workplace temperature created an enduring difference between the white-collar and the blue-collar workers by engraving the difference deep into the their bodies. Thanks to the comfortable, air-conditioned work environment, the office workers could keep their bodies clean and odorless. The office workers' odorless bodies stood in stark contrast to the shop-floor workers' dirty bodies and pungent odor, which elicited expressions of repugnance among the office workers.[1]

The office workers' clean and fair skin provided another outstanding symbol of white-collar jobs, because it also contrasted with the shop-floor workers' dark and rough skin that suffered from chilblains. Finally, the office workers were exempt from overtime, which was deeply envied by the workers on the shop floor. The office workers could leave the factory at five each day, except for the ones on overtime duty.[2]

The division of the office space according to different functions and hierarchical statuses of the employees also contributed to management's control of labor. In the office, the desks of the two expatriate Korean managers were located at a prime spot where they could easily observe all the office workers. Under the watchful eyes of the Korean managers, eight office workers kept records on material stocks, calculated salaries, dealt with external affairs with government officials and buyers, and provided interpretation between Korean and Chinese. Because of the deep involvement of the Korean-Chinese workers in the key factory operations, the managers would say that without their services the factory simply could not operate. Their significance in the factory's operations, however, did not mean that the office workers held much authority over the factory's affairs. If any situation arose that even slightly extended beyond the authority granted to them, the office workers had to consult the Korean managers. "You shouldn't be too creative," an office worker said. "If you are, you'll soon realize you're in big trouble with the managers." Her statement testified to management's determination to maintain the clear hierarchical difference between foreign management and local labor.

Despite their subordination to the management's powerful authority, the small number of office workers formed the most privileged group among the Chinese employees. This was obvious in, among other things, the long list of benefits offered to the office workers. First of all, a marked wage difference between the two groups distinguished the office workers from the blue-collar workers on the shop floor. In China, this sort of wage disparity is the most common but key benefit that management offers the growing number of white-collar workers (Guthrie 1999: 79–82; Zhang 2000: 87). At the Nawon plant, the distinguishing mechanism not only appeared in the difference in wages. In the everyday workplace of the factory, management set up minute but highly effective methods of distinctions that caused the office workers to feel superior to their shop-floor counterparts. For example, the company's dress code created visible differences. The office workers were allowed to wear ordinary, colorful clothes, insofar as they did not violate the factory dress codes that required "decent" clothing. Their colorful clothing contrasted with the shop-floor workers' dull and gray work uniforms, distinguishing the office workers from those on the shop floor.

A close look at the organization of the office personnel, however, reveals an unusual feature of the white-collar workers in the Nawon factory that does not match the general definition of white-collar (see Table 3-1).

As Table 3-1 shows, the most outstanding feature of the main office employees is their ethnic composition. While Han-Chinese constituted an overwhelming 94 percent of the factory's total workforce, they held only 25 percent of office jobs (two out of eight). The dominance of Korean-Chinese among the managerial staff shows a significant difference from the general pattern of interethnic division of labor. According to the common pattern, minority groups are usually overrepresented in marginal or low-paid jobs, owing to economic, social, and cultural discrimination (DeAnda 1996). It is also said that immigrants tend to take relatively menial and marginal jobs because they are not familiar with the culture of the host country (Lamphere 1992). Taken together, the two statements suggest that the social status of a minority group tends to be worse if they are recent immigrants.

The social and economic status of Korean-Chinese in China seems to perfectly fit these statements. Most Korean-Chinese are descendants of poor farmers who migrated from Korea in the early twentieth century. Since the first Korean flow to northeast China in the 1860s, many Korean farmers migrated to China. Some fled from abject poverty and severe droughts. Later, many were forced out of their homeland by the policy of the Japanese colonial government that intended to open farmland in northeast China using Korean labor. Particularly during the first half of the twentieth century, the migration policy of the Japanese colonial government rapidly increased the Korean population of the region, from less than a half million in 1920 to about 1.3 million in 1941.[3] This policy made Korean-Chinese a historically recent ethnic minority of China. Their two hundred years of settlement history is far shorter than that of other ethnic groups in the country (Seongjun Choe 1999; Mackerras 2003). Furthermore, the largest group of Korean-Chinese have lived as self-employed farmers in a remote region of northeast China, infamous for its slow economic and social development compared with rapidly developing southeast China (for

TABLE 3-1. Organization of Main Office Personnel, June 2002

Ethnicity / Nationality	Name (age)	Place of birth	Education level	Duties
Korean	Bak (51)	Yongan (South Korea)	B. A.	General plant manager
	Moon (43)	Yongan (South Korea)	B. A.	General financial manager
Korean-Chinese	Yoo Joonja (34)	Yanji, Jilin Province	High school	Triple interpretation and paperwork related to customs
	Kim Hyesook (29)	Huadian, Jilin Province	College graduate	Everyday statistics, including actual number of workers in the factory
	Choi Minjung (28)	Yanji, Jilin Province	Vocational high school	Financial affairs such as calculating workers' salaries and tax payments
	Kim Jihwan (25)	Yanji, Jilin Province	Vocational high school	Managing main materials, such as textiles
	Roh Youngra (19)	Yanji, Jilin Province	High school	Managing "auxiliary" materials, including buttons, zippers, OEM labels, and packing boxes
	Yoon Soonae (21)	Yanji (city proper), Jilin Province	High school	Secretary of Dyeing Department
Han-Chinese	Li Meihua (33)	Qingdao, Shandong	Vocational high school	Managing affairs related to customs office, tax office, maritime and port authority. It was said that she had many acquaintances in government bureaus
	Zhang Zhenmei (27)	Qingdao, Shandong	College	Managing deposits and withdrawals of factory money including money for immediate use

Source: Author

example, Ching Kwan Lee 1999, 2000a, 2000b). That the Korean-Chinese were concentrated in "backward" farming villages in northeast China maintained and reinforced their minority image and status.

However, at Nawon, as we have pointed out, the Korean-Chinese held job positions higher than those of their Han-Chinese counterparts and enjoyed exceptional corporate benefits. Thus the dominant status of Han-Chinese in Chinese society was completely overturned in the factory. The reversed ethnic relationship at Nawon cannot simply be explained away as a by-product of the functional division between white- and blue-collar jobs. According to a functionalist approach, the white- and the blue-collar division comes from individuals' different abilities to meet the specific needs of a firm. On the face of it, this functionalist approach seems to explain the reversed ethnic relationship at the Nawon plant since at Nawon the Korean-Chinese had an official job title of "interpreter," in addition to holding other, more usual job titles. This implies that they got their current jobs because they were bilingual in Chinese and Korean. Born into Korean-speaking families, the Korean-Chinese workers acquired their Korean as they grew up. Many of them also achieved an advanced proficiency in Korean while they attended Korean-medium schools. Their bilingualism distinguished them from the Han-Chinese workers, who only spoke Chinese, and assured them the privileged white-collar jobs in the factory.

Interestingly, the Korean managers at Nawon argued that, when they first arrived in Qingdao, Korean-Chinese were not their first choices for the interpreter positions. According to them, management originally preferred Han-Chinese interpreters, because it believed that, in addition to Korean language competence, they were likely to have a "local knowledge" of China that might be deeper than that of Korean-Chinese. However, the supply of Han-Chinese interpreters could not meet the fast-growing demand by the increasing number of South Korean corporations in China. The managers said that the local Chinese government failed to provide qualified Han-Chinese interpreters for their factory, and therefore, they had to find alternatives by themselves. It was quite a relief for them to find Korean-Chinese, as they quickly met the urgent need for interpreters. According to the managers' explanations, there was nothing unusual about the predominantly Korean-Chinese managerial staff: it resulted from the management's choice based on supply and demand in the labor market.

However, the following comments of a Korean manager revealed an interesting fact behind the dominantly Korean-Chinese managerial staff:

> Even when, by good fortune, we interviewed Han-Chinese interpreters with a good command of Korean, we were quite reluctant to hire them. . . . In the end, we decided not to recruit Han-Chinese to take the office jobs, because we worried that they had an antagonistic feeling against us from South Korea. . . . Who knows? They may have been brainwashed by Korean language teachers from North Korea and contaminated by the anti-South propaganda fabricated by North Korea.

His comment about North Korea and the "untrustworthy" Han-Chinese indicated that the reversed ethnic power relations in the factory can be fully explained neither by different individual abilities nor by the supply and demand of the labor market. Management's memory of the recent history between China and North Korea largely contributed to its suspicion of Han-Chinese. While South Korea had no diplomatic relations with China before 1993, North Korea has kept a close relationship with China since its establishment in 1948. This relationship is reflected in diplomatic rhetoric such as "brotherly" (C. *xiongdi*) and "blood-tied" (C. *xuemeng*) allies that has appeared on official occasions since the Korean War (1950–1953).[4] Especially at the beginning of their operations in China, the Korean managers believed that such a close relationship between the two countries may have affected what Han-Chinese thought about the management from South Korea. "South Korea," another manager said, "is still in a hostile relationship with North Korea, the blood-tied ally of China. I worried that Chinese people's familiarity with North Korea made them less loyal or somewhat hostile to us." They suspected that the Han-Chinese interpreters may have been deeply influenced by North Korea, as they learned the Korean language and culture through channels connected to that country.

The management's notion of untrustworthy Han-Chinese was not extraordinary. It reflected South Korean mistrust of China. Common expressions such as "China suspicion" or "the China threat" demonstrate the common South Korean view of China as potentially an imperialist country. The image depicts China as a country that incessantly seeks military, economic, and cultural hegemony in neighboring regions. Many South Koreans think that China is basically an imperialist country that clings to its grand vision of its status as the "Central Kingdom,"[5] imposing Sino-centric international relations on neighboring countries. Many South

Koreans remember China as a country that invaded Korea many times and forced Korea to take the status of a tributary nation.[6] South Korean mass media, history books, and Internet discussion boards spread and maintain this watchful view of China. It is not difficult to find newspaper or journal articles arguing that China has increased its influence over East Asia. They commonly warn Koreans about the impending resurgence of China as the local hegemonic country (Goo 2009; Il-Kweon Kim 1985; Kwon 2008).

Nawon management's doubts about Han-Chinese loyalty to its corporation were rooted in the popular discourse about China. The management suspected that, sooner or later, China would attempt to regain its hegemonic status in East Asia once it successfully emerges as a regional economic powerhouse. Currently, the Chinese government welcomes Korean corporations as a source of foreign investment. The seemingly friendly attitude of the Chinese officials, the managers thought, would turn hostile if South Korea no longer remained a profitable business partner. "Although now we supervise Han-Chinese on the shop floor," a Korean manager once said, "I imagine someday China will rise again and try to resume her status as an imperialist country." According to the managers, the Han-Chinese employees might only reluctantly acknowledge the Korean management's authority just as their government was only superficially friendly to them. "Who knows?" another Korean manager argued. "The Han-Chinese on the shop floor may feel it particularly hard to endure our control because we're people from a small country, South Korea."

Managerial politics of nation, nationality, and ethnicity

To the management, with its lingering suspicion of Han-Chinese, Korean-Chinese appeared as ideal alternatives to Han-Chinese interpreters. During the early period of their operations in China, the managers believed that Korean-Chinese were much more reliable than Han-Chinese, because they are de facto Korean. In fact, the management's belief in Korean-Chinese trustworthiness, which contrasted with the idea of "unreliable" Han-Chinese, was another key factor that led management to create a managerial office staff that was predominantly Korean-Chinese. However, the logic that justified management's suspicion of Han-Chinese contradicts management's trust in Korean-Chinese. It was management's main argument that the close relationship between China and North Korea had affected Han-Chinese and created an alleged pro-North Korean (or anti-South Korean) attitude. Ironically, the same logic strongly implies that Korean-Chinese were not free of the North Korean influence. In fact, most Korean-Chinese had more chances to be influenced by North Korea because they were born and grew up in a region in northeast China that borders North Korea. In addition to the question of geographical proximity, many Korean-Chinese have relatives in North Korea. Using their blood ties, many Korean-Chinese have been to the country renowned for its reclusiveness (Kang 2008). Their close ties to North Korea suggest that Korean-Chinese were no less exposed to North Korean influence than Han-Chinese.

The Korean managers acknowledged that Korean-Chinese might not be free from North Korean influence, but they still insisted that Korean-Chinese were different from Han-Chinese because they are members of the Korean nation. The managers' casual comments about the standards of ideal office workers in their factory revealed the meaning of "being a Korean." According to the managers, what made the Korean-Chinese "Korean" was not just their language skills, but their knowledge of the "culture" of their factory. The managers thought that Korean-Chinese retained a "Korean identity" and commanded "an intuitive sense" of Korean culture. That made Korean-Chinese ideal office workers, while making their Han-Chinese counterparts unqualified for the job.

The managers' comments about Korean-Chinese and their Korean nature, however, made it more difficult for me to figure out the meaning of "being a Korean." The meaning was elusive because the managers used key concepts such as "Korean identity" and "Korean culture" with no explanation. They seemed to believe that the meanings were simply self-evident. The unclear concepts only became clear when the managers contrasted alleged Korean-Chinese characteristics with those of the Han-Chinese. In a casual after-hours drinking session, a Korean manager visiting from Nawon Korea complained about the slow bodily movement of Han-Chinese employees and contrasted it with the fast movements of Korean-Chinese. "Whenever I ask a Korean-Chinese to bring something," he contended, "she brings it immediately. Korean-Chinese are different from the slow Han-Chinese." Another manager, who sat beside him, added:

> Han-Chinese employees' slow movement is not a simple matter. They always respond slowly to our instructions even when we deal with rush

orders. . . . That's why we often shout "Quickly, quickly" at them. I think their slow bodily movement reflects the deep-rooted Han-Chinese defiance of us. They just don't dare openly resist our authority because we pay them. In contrast, Korean-Chinese office workers seldom show such a defiant attitude. *As Koreans*, they know how to take a proper attitude toward their superiors. In general, they're obedient because they know the virtue of order and deference. Han-Chinese workers don't have that virtue. . . . They don't even know how to bow to us [emphasis by the interviewee].

Conjuring up certain group characteristics and contrasting them with those of the other is a common method for drawing and maintaining boundaries between "us" and "them" (Crang 1998: 60). Distinctive group characteristics also justify existing hierarchical relations. In the process, the group with superior or desirable characteristics establishes its prevailing status over those without such characteristics, thus marking clear hierarchical boundaries (Barth 1969; Cohen 1985; de Certeau 1988 [1975]; Yang et al. 2008). The Korean managers' contrast between Korean-Chinese and Han-Chinese shows how they used contrasting ethnic characteristics to distinguish Korean-Chinese from Han-Chinese and justify the superior status of the Korean-Chinese. The comments of the Korean managers show two contrasting sets of national or ethnic characteristics: first, Korean-Chinese agility versus Han-Chinese slowness, and second, Korean-Chinese obedience versus Han-Chinese defiance. According to the managers, the desirable characteristics of Korean-Chinese made them more suitable for the office jobs than Han-Chinese.

However, the management's following explanation for the origins of the contrasting characteristics reveals that it constructed them in a highly arbitrary way. Korean managers thought that Han-Chinese workers moved slowly because they were born and grew up in the backward Chinese countryside: "In the farming villages of China," a Korean manager said, "people live according to the rhythm of nature, getting up with the rising sun and falling asleep with the setting sun." Korean managers asserted that the Han-Chinese workers' slowness was almost second nature, deeply engrained in their bodies and minds from their earliest childhood. Interestingly, when the managers tried to explain the agility of Korean-Chinese, they did not refer to the Korean-Chinese social background as the origin of this supposedly ethnic merit. As Table 3-1 shows, the Korean-Chinese office workers had an urban or suburban background that contrasted with the Han-Chinese workers' rural social roots. The managers could have used the Korean-Chinese employees' urban background to explain their agility, just as they found the origin of the Han-Chinese slowness in their rural background. Instead, the Korean managers thought that the urban background of the Korean-Chinese did not distinguish them from the Han-Chinese workers, because the small cities of northeast China were not much different in their "backwardness" from the Han-Chinese workers' rural villages. Instead, the management regarded the common characteristics of the Korean nation as the main reason of the agility of the Korean-Chinese. A senior Korean manager said:

> Koreans are famous for their indomitable spirit. Although born and raised in China, Korean-Chinese still retain that Korean national trait *deep inside their bones*. Thanks to their innate virtues of diligence and unyielding endurance, many Korean-Chinese won in the fierce competition with Han-Chinese farmers. Some of them even escaped the wretched life of farmers and moved to cities and got respectable jobs [emphasis by the interviewee].

The Korean managers' explanation about the origins of Korean-Chinese agility reveals how they arbitrarily constructed the contrasting ethnic characteristics. Adopting a version of environmental determinism, they placed the origin of Han-Chinese slowness in their social background of backward villages. They believed that Han-Chinese workers were slow by nature because they had been deeply influenced by the slow rhythm of life in the farming villages. When they explained the origin of the Korean-Chinese agility, however, they did not adopt the same logic of environmental determinism. Instead, the managers argued that Korean-Chinese had desirable ethnic traits because they are members of the Korean nation, which by nature is characterized by unyielding endurance and diligence.

Management's contrast between Korean-Chinese obedience and Han-Chinese defiance further shows how it arbitrarily constructed the contrasting ethnic characteristics. At this time, management used the concept of Confucianism and identified the origin of Korean-Chinese obedience in the Confucian tradition. Korean managers at Nawon used Confucianism in a fairly narrow way, emphasizing two Confucian virtues: submission to hierarchical superiors (K. *chung*) and unlimited filial piety (K. *hyo*). They argued that these two Confucian virtues greatly contributed to the corporate culture of their factory, such as deference to management and the unilateral, top-down flow of orders. It is in this very context that management placed the origin of the Korean-Chinese obedience. Korean managers argued that the Confucian virtues of diligence and obedience are deeply ingrained in the Korean-Chinese consciousness because they are part of the Korean nation, which inherited this ethic. They believed that the Confucian virtues contributed to the successful migration of Korean-Chinese to China and helped them establish their own autonomous area in northeast China.[7] In the same context, the management considered that the reversed ethnic power relationship in the factory was a consequence of Koreans' superior morality. The Korean managers contended that there was nothing strange about the dominance of the Korean-Chinese managerial staff because it simply reflected the Korean-Chinese moral superiority to Han-Chinese. Korean-Chinese could not but outdo Han-Chinese simply because ingrained in them were the Korean cultural tradition and the Confucian ideas of diligence and obedience.

Surprisingly, though the Nawon management frequently referred to Confucianism as the source of Korean-Chinese obedience, it did not have any formal knowledge about Confucian philosophy. Instead, the management's belief in the connection between the Korean Confucian tradition and the obedience of the Korean-Chinese was based on the Korean managers' personal thoughts and understandings of the ideology. A Korean manager claimed: "The Confucian tradition has been a part of our everyday life and is deeply ingrained in our spirit. This is why we can keep its principles such as diligence and obedience even without any comprehensive knowledge of the Confucian scriptures." This brief comment implies that the Confucianism emphasized by Korean managers is close to "routinized" or "everyday" Confucianism. The specific terminology indicates plebeian ideas and beliefs that are casually related to Confucianism, which originated not from any formal study but from common people's personal and often arbitrary understandings about it. Many Koreans do not hesitate to call some practices and principles "Confucian" even though they are not sure whether the practices and principles are rooted in the tradition. They do not question the exact origin because they believe that the ideology is truly widespread and deeply ingrained in the everyday life of Koreans and their consciousness (Janelli and Yim 1999; Choongsoon Kim 1992).

Management's idea of Han-Chinese defiance, however, contradicts the obvious and well-known historical fact that Confucianism originated in China and its key intellectual figures are mostly Chinese. Though Confucianism may have had a similar positive influence on Han-Chinese as it did on Koreans, management outright denied this possibility, referring to the harmful influence of radical Communism in China. Korean managers said that the Confucian tradition in China could not be sustained because of the devastating effects of Communist ideology, which peaked during the Cultural Revolution (1966–1976). In fact, Nawon management's belief in the deep and persisting influence of the radical Communism was so strong that some managers even denounced the Han-Chinese workers' excuses for their mistakes as "Communist verbosity." To the managers, the term indicated an allegedly deep-rooted tendency of Han-Chinese to claim their innocence by resorting to the rhetoric devised by the cadres of the CCP.

Thus management selectively used the concept of Confucianism to justify its strong preference for Korean-Chinese. On the one hand, it used the concept of Korean culture and its "everyday" Confucianism to explain the obedience of the Korean-Chinese. The Korean managers argued that the Korean-Chinese retained the same Confucian virtues because they are part of the Korean nation. The blood-related, quasi-inherited membership in the Korean nation protected the Korean-Chinese from the harmful influence of China's radical Communism. On the other hand, management did not apply the same logic of everyday Confucianism to Han-Chinese. While it emphasized the enduring influence of Confucianism on Koreans and Korean-Chinese, the management believed that the Confucian tradition did not have any comparable positive influence on Han-Chinese. Instead, the managers insisted that the radical Communism during the Maoist period eradicated most Confucian virtues and inculcated in Han-Chinese an attitude of defiance against authority.

The Korean managers' belief in the reliability of the Korean-Chinese and their assertion about the "Korean-ness" of the Korean-Chinese, however, hid another of management's views on Korean-Chinese, its unofficial suspicion of their integrity. The suspicion was unofficial, because, on official occasions, management always expressed its trust in the Korean-Chinese employees. The Korean managers expressed the suspicion only on private occasions such as after-hours drinking sessions. A Korean manager at Nawon Korea said: "Korean-Chinese employees have been an indispensable part of our business in China. However, too much reliance on them could be detrimental to our management. . . . At any moment, they could pursue their own interests at the expense of the interests of our company."

During my fieldwork in 2003, I heard several times stories about "bad" Korean-Chinese who had worked in other, nearby Korean corporations. According to the stories, they embezzled corporate funds and disappeared, taking advantage of the Korean management's limited knowledge of China and its reliance on them. Such stories about runaway Korean-Chinese reinforced the Korean management's suspicions about them. Several Korean managers of neighboring Korean corporations that had suffered from such embezzlement even argued that Korean-Chinese are less reliable than Han-Chinese because they betrayed their "brethren."

The Korean management at Nawon did not have such strong doubts about Korean-Chinese. First of all, Nawon had not experienced any embezzlement committed by a Korean-Chinese during the past ten years of its operation in China. In the factory, four senior Korean-Chinese employees (two in the office and the other two on the shop floor) had shown exceptional work performance since the very first day of the corporation. The long-term presence of the Korean-Chinese employees led management to have an unusually strong trust in them. In this context, the plant manager of Nawon even insisted that the four senior Korean-Chinese employees were more trustworthy than his own blood relatives.

However, several Korean managers who joined Nawon and Nawon Korea in the late 1990s did not share the positive view of Korean-Chinese. The relatively young Korean managers in their forties argued that they had a more "realistic" or practical view of Korean-Chinese, which was different from that of the "old" Korean managers who had worked in the corporation since the early 1990s. The younger managers said that the managerial view of Korean-Chinese during the time "somewhat" exaggerated and "over" idealized the Korean-ness of Korean-Chinese, while disregarding the actual situation of Korean-Chinese. In fact, the so-called idealized managerial view of Korean-Chinese reflected the romanticized images of Korean-Chinese, which were widely shared among many South Koreans during the early 1990s. Right after the normalization of diplomatic relations between South Korea and China in 1993, South Koreans came to watch and read many media reports about their "lost and found" brethren in China. Media images of Korean-Chinese who lived in the farming villages in northeast

China reminded many Koreans of their recent past, because the villages seemed to preserve the idyllic and pristine traditional culture of Korea that had disappeared in the rapid industrialization of South Korea (Gwak 2008). The Korean managers at that time shared the romanticized view of Korean-Chinese, and it contributed to their belief in the "Korean-ness" of Korean-Chinese.

After its decade-long operations in China, the management at Nawon argued that it should take a more "practical" view of Korean-Chinese. By that word, the Korean managers meant that they should officially maintain a close relationship with the Korean-Chinese employees, while unofficially keeping wary of their potential for "doing bad things." The management's nuanced view of Korean-Chinese was well expressed in the main office of the factory. Although the Korean-Chinese dominance was apparent inasmuch as they took most of the privileged white-collar jobs, the detailed job descriptions revealed the current management's nuanced approach to Korean-Chinese (Table 3-1). The two Han-Chinese office workers were in charge of the such crucial tasks as managing corporate funds and dealing with government officials, both of which involved the flow of "real" money. In contrast, the Korean-Chinese office workers had no access to the "real" money, even though they were in charge of other important tasks. Officially, the Korean management explained that jobs were assigned according to individual workers' different qualifications: management hired the Han-Chinese employees because they had the right qualifications for dealing with financial matters. In a private conversation, however, a Korean manager expressed the unofficial reason of these job assignments:

> It doesn't mean that we don't trust the Korean-Chinese employees. But who knows? Bad things happen. We know that it's very difficult to catch runaway Korean-Chinese, because they came from remote places in north-east China. . . . In contrast, it would be very unlikely for local Han-Chinese workers to do bad things. They know that it would be much easier for us to catch them.

Management's changing view of Korean-Chinese reveals its instrumental view of Korean-Chinese ethnicity and Korean nationality. To the managers, with their lingering suspicion of Han-Chinese, Korean-Chinese initially appeared as ideal alternatives to Han-Chinese interpreters. Especially during the early period of Nawon's operations in China, the managers believed that Korean-Chinese were much more reliable than

Han-Chinese, because they were considered de facto Koreans who shared blood ties with the Koreans in their ancestral land. Through the decade-long interactions with Korean-Chinese, however, the Korean management gradually became disillusioned with its initial view of Korean-Chinese as "lost and found" Korean brethren. Nawon management's nuanced view of Korean-Chinese, together with other Korean corporations' strong negative view of the ethnic group, clearly shows the fundamental arbitrariness in the managerial politics of ethnicity and nationality. Just as it arbitrarily constructed images of Han-Chinese, the Korean management constructed and destructed images of Korean-Chinese according to the corporation's changing business situation.

KOREAN-CHINESE OFFICE WORKERS:
ETHNIC YEARNING FOR SOCIAL SUCCESS

A reversal of fortune

The unique division between the blue- and the white-collar Nawon workers had its most visible distinguishing effects on the Korean-Chinese employees in the office, as it dramatically improved their economic and social status. The Korean-Chinese office workers believed that they had been victims of ethnic discrimination and were condemned to the status of the underprivileged in Chinese society. They argued that the Chinese government's repeated promise to treat ethnic minorities equally proved the reality of ethnic discrimination in China. "The promise of ethnic equality," a Korean-Chinese office worker said, "is only false government propaganda. If there were real ethnic equality, there would be no reason to have such slogans and campaigns."[8] The Korean-Chinese workers remembered that they had experienced various forms of daily discrimination since their earliest childhood. Hyesook, a Korean-Chinese office worker who had worked in the factory since 1996 (see Table 3-1), once talked about her traumatic childhood memories of ethnic discrimination. When she was still a baby, her entire family had to leave their hometown in the Korean-Chinese Yanbian autonomous region and move to a remote Han-Chinese village, following the order of the local revolutionary committee. Amid the social tumult of the Cultural Revolution, the party committee of her hometown ordered her parents, both junior middle school teachers at that time, to go to the village and live with the "poor and illiterate" farmers there. In the dominantly Han-Chinese village, Hyesook had to attend a nearby primary school where Han-Chinese constituted the majority of the students. It did not take a long time for her to encounter the reality of ethnic discrimination:

> When I attended the primary school, I participated in an annual school sports competition. Because I ran fastest in my class, I was sure I would win the first prize. So, in the short-distance race, I ran as fast as I could and came in first. But the referee said I came in second! He announced that a Han-Chinese boy won the race. Do you know what? He actually reached the finish line right behind me. Why? On my way home, I cried and cried. Later I asked my parents why the referee didn't give me the first prize. After a long silence, my father reluctantly said that it was only because we are not Han-Chinese.

With their own memories of ethnic discrimination, the Korean-Chinese office workers unanimously agreed that their minority status made it difficult for them to acquire high social status in China. At Nawon, however, they saw how the same status as an ethnic minority helped them acquire prestigious white-collar jobs. Furthermore, the Korean-Chinese office workers certainly expected that their current white-collar jobs would empower them to climb up the social ladder and finally secure a respectable social and economic status. This change would be guaranteed by their high income—more than double the average wage of the Han-Chinese workers on the shop floor.

The success stories of the Korean-Chinese coworkers confirmed their expectations that they would realize their dream in the foreseeable future. The story of Joonja, a Korean-Chinese in charge of customs-related affairs, is an exemplary case. Born in Yanji, the capital city of the Korean-Chinese Autonomous Prefecture, she had attended Korean-Chinese schools until she entered a vocational high school. Contrary to the common belief that it is nearly impossible for a Korean-Chinese woman to get a decent job, she had the good fortune to become an assistant accountant of a state-owned factory near Shenyang.[9] Despite her initial excitement, the job soon proved to be unsatisfactory. The factory paid her a small wage and barely guaranteed a meager annual pay increase. What disappointed her most was the unlikeliness of an opportunity of being promoted beyond her low-level office worker position. This she attributed to a glass ceiling against ethnic minorities: "If I had continued working in the factory," she recalled, "I might have ended my career as a petty female accountant."

Joonja was fortunate to see an advertisement on the bulletin board of a nearby Korean-Chinese employment agency. It was about an opening for Japanese-speaking Korean-Chinese in a South Korean multinational factory. At that time, the Korean management of Nawon needed an interpreter who could speak Korean, Chinese, and Japanese and help managers in their meetings with Japanese buyers. As usual, the management preferred a Korean-Chinese as the triple interpreter and her previous career at the Chinese factory made her stand out from the other candidates. After being hired, Joonja quickly won management's trust as she had successfully assisted Korean managers in their business meetings. "Finally," she said, "I got the right job after wasting time in the Chinese factory."

In the fall of 2001, Joonja and her husband, also a Korean-Chinese, who worked in a nearby Korean multinational factory, purchased a new condo in Qingdao. It was a memorable event for the young Korean-Chinese couple with a six-year-old daughter, because it was not common for people with nonlocal residence status to purchase houses outside the town in which they were registered:[10] "We were able to buy the condo with the money that we had made from our jobs in Korean companies." She did not forget to add that they could buy their new home thanks to a bank loan. They believed that the work certificate issued by Nawon helped them to obtain the loan. It was commonly believed that banks are generous to those who have jobs in foreign-invested companies. To Joonja, her office job at Nawon was a hard-earned bit of good fortune that brought her many benefits formerly unimaginable, such as a stable and considerable income, a lovely family, and a brand-new condo in Qingdao, a big city located in the prosperous coastal area of China. She regarded what she had achieved as key symbols of stable middle-class life. The achievement also convinced her that her family was now on the right track toward the mainstream of Chinese society. "There is *no official* discrimination against ethnic minorities in China," she said, "but it's a plain fact that I couldn't have achieved what I have if I had kept my previous job in the Han-Chinese-owned company" (her emphasis).

The Korean-Chinese office workers at Nawon regarded their achievement of white-collar-worker status not as merely a small personal event. Rather, with their shared memory of ethnic discrimination, they believed that their new status as white-collar workers in the factory was compensation for their underprivileged status in the predominantly Han-Chinese society.

They thought that their current jobs would contribute to improving their social and economic status, especially making them superior to the Han-Chinese workers. The growing popularity of white-collar jobs in China only increased their satisfaction with their current jobs: "White-collar jobs in foreign-invested companies," a Korean-Chinese office worker proudly declared, "are among the most envied in China nowadays. They're quite in vogue [C. *shimao*]." The Korean-Chinese office workers' high satisfaction with their current jobs clearly shows how those white-collar jobs empowered a once underprivileged ethnic minority, bringing it close to mainstream Chinese society.

A new Korean-Chinese consciousness

The Korean-Chinese office workers knew very well why management preferred them to Han-Chinese in its first recruitment of office workers. They got the high-paid white-collar jobs in the factory not simply because they spoke the two languages of Korean and Chinese. Rather, it was because they were members of the Korean nation and had the "desirable" cultural traits of Koreans. This understanding had a significant influence on the Korean-Chinese self-consciousness as an ethnic group, making them highly active in expressing their ethnic consciousness. Most Korean-Chinese office workers showed no reluctance to distinguish themselves from Han-Chinese. In the office and on the shop floor, they often compare themselves with Han-Chinese employees, emphasizing how the Korean-Chinese as a group were superior to Han-Chinese in everyday work performance. Their intermediary status between the Koreans and the Han-Chinese reinforced their sensitivity to ethnic differences. As cultural brokers who spoke for the Korean management's interests, sometimes they had to argue with local Chinese government officials and even exchanged fiery words with the Han-Chinese staff on the shop floor. This kind of stressful situation prompted the Korean-Chinese employees to more openly express their feelings of difference from the Han-Chinese and raised their ethnic consciousness to a new level.

This does not mean, however, that the Korean-Chinese consciousness observed at Nawon was entirely a recent creation of the particular situation in that factory. Rather, the arrival of South Korean multinational corporations in China galvanized the existing consciousness of Korean-Chinese, making them evaluate their status as an ethnic minority in a more positive way. The Korean-Chinese autonomous prefecture was established in northeast China well before the opening of the first South Korean factory in the late 1980s. Thus the Korean-Chinese may have developed an ethnic consciousness long before their first encounter with Korean multinational corporations in China. Korean-Chinese interpreters' comments about the history of their ancestors' migrations reflected the Korean-Chinese view of their own ethnicity. Korean-Chinese office workers often referred to their ancestors' successful migration to China as strong evidence of their ethnic "excellence," specifically the indomitable spirit of diligence and independence. A Korean-Chinese office worker proudly said:

> During the first cold winter of their early period of settlement, many of our ancestors lost at least one of their family members. Never discouraged by the initial loss, our ancestors became quickly adapted to the bitter-cold winter of the Northeast. They reclaimed a significant amount of wasteland and finally exceeded the Han-Chinese farmers in every respect.

The Nawon Korean-Chinese employees almost always expressed their belief in the excellence of the Korean-Chinese ethnicity by comparing themselves with Han-Chinese. They believed the virtues of Korean-Chinese as an ethnic group, most of all their spirit of diligence, made them prevail over the majority of the Han-Chinese workers in the factory. This positive self-evaluation gradually replaced their view of themselves as victims of ethnic discrimination. This implies that the new white-collar jobs in Korean multinational companies might transform Korean-Chinese from an underprivileged minority into a successful ethnic group, thus allowing them to enter mainstream Chinese society.

The discourse of Korean-Chinese ethnic excellence was not exclusive to the Korean-Chinese employees at Nawon. It was so widespread among Korean-Chinese that some Korean-Chinese intellectuals even published academic renditions of the popular discourse. For example, Yanbian University, the preeminent educational institution in the Yanbian Korean-Chinese Autonomous Prefecture, published a series of research papers on Korean-Chinese ethnic characteristics. In the papers, a group of Korean-Chinese scholars pointed out the "indomitable tenacity and diligence" of Korean-Chinese as the key reasons behind the successful settlement of Korean-Chinese in northeast China (Heo 1994: 101-2; Seongcheol Kim 1992: 161; Yeonglim Kim 1994: 178; Lim 1992: 124). In addition to the ethnic virtue of diligence, other scholars mentioned virtues such as high

adaptability and a strong entrepreneurial spirit. They argued that such
ethnic traits made Korean-Chinese an ethnic group suitable for the new
era of reform and openness (Choe 1994: 59; Hongwoo Lee 1994: 35). Some
Korean-Chinese scholars even contrasted "clean" Korean-Chinese with
"dirty" Han-Chinese and regarded cleanliness as a key Korean-Chinese
ethnic trait (Jeon 1994: 189; Park 1994: 225). This contrast reminds us
of the Korean-Chinese office workers' strong reaction to the pungent
body odor on the shop floor. As mentioned in Chapter Two, they called
the pungent smell "Han-Chinese odor," contrasting "neat and clean"
Korean-Chinese with "dirty and disorganized" Han-Chinese.[11] The
academic stereotyping was striking because it shows that even highly
educated Korean-Chinese intellectuals subscribed to the controversial
idea of ethnic hygiene. The surprising examples from the Korean-
Chinese research articles clearly show how the ethnic characterizations
and a belief in Korean-Chinese superiority (and Han-Chinese inferiority)
are widespread in Korean-Chinese society.

The Korean-Chinese belief in their ethnic excellence predates the arrival
of South Korean multinational corporations in China. Much of its current
expression, however, reflects the recent improvement in the social and
economic status of Korean-Chinese. It was the new job opportunities in
many South Korean multinational corporations in China that made the
improvement possible. As previously mentioned, Korean-Chinese had a
strong group consciousness as an ethnic minority that had been victimized
in the predominantly Han-Chinese society. The negative self-image has
gradually changed as the recent improvement in their social and economic
status made Korean-Chinese feel prouder of being ethnic Korean. This
does not mean there is no relationship between the preexisting Korean-
Chinese belief in their ethnic excellence and the current expression of
Korean-Chinese ethnic pride. However, without the new white-collar jobs
in the South Korean multinational corporations, many Korean-Chinese
could never have had the chance to express their belief in Korean-Chinese
excellence in such an open and positive way.

The current expression of Korean-Chinese ethnic superiority shows how
the multinational corporations from South Korea have affected the power
relationship between ethnic groups and transformed ethnic consciousness.
As we have pointed out, the management of Nawon gave its Korean-
Chinese workers the privileged white-collar jobs because it considered them

more reliable as local business assistants than the Han-Chinese. The new job opportunities greatly improved the economic and social status of the Korean-Chinese workers and eventually transformed their negative self-image as a victimized, disadvantaged ethnic minority into an image as a positive and successful ethnic group. This illustrates that, when multiple groups of people divided by ethnicity compete with one another for limited resources, ethnicity can be understood as a vehicle to advance the interests of one ethnic group over others (Glazer and Moynihan 1963: 17). At Nawon, the Korean-Chinese employees became more vocal in expressing their belief in the ethnic superiority of Korean-Chinese and paid much attention to distinguishing themselves from Han-Chinese. They thought that such distinctions helped them to maintain their higher status than that of the Han-Chinese employees and justified the exclusive corporate benefits they received from management. Ethnicity, in this context, might even be defined as strife between ethnic groups, in the course of which their members emphasize their identity and exclusiveness (Cohen 1969: 4). The growing ethnic consciousness and tension between the Korean-Chinese interpreters and the Han-Chinese workers reveals the political potential of ethnicity.

POLITICAL IMPLICATION OF THE WHITE-COLLAR-WORKER FORMATION

The Korean-Chinese office workers at Nawon believed that they *should* be different from their Han-Chinese counterparts to maintain their privileged white-collar status. Several Korean-Chinese workers even argued that to behave more like a Korean would further secure their white-collar jobs, because their Korean ethnicity was the key reason that management hired them. This shows that the white-collar consciousness in the multinational factory developed to a higher level since it overlapped with the Korean-Chinese ethnic desire to distinguish themselves from Han-Chinese.

This strong and unusual white-collar-worker consciousness created a deep division between the white- and the blue-collar workers in the factory. The division was clearly reflected in the virtual absence of social relations between the Korean-Chinese office workers and the Han-Chinese shop-floor workers. At Nawon, few Korean-Chinese office workers remembered the names of more than ten Han-Chinese workers on the shop floor. Even the senior Korean-Chinese office workers who had worked in the factory for almost a decade had trouble remembering their names. Moreover, the office workers had only very limited relationships with the few shop-floor workers whom they knew. Most of the time, they only had brief talks with the Han-Chinese workers related to factory affairs. A Korean-Chinese office worker explained why she had such weak relationships with the shop-floor workers:

> I can't find any common topics that I can talk with them about. They can never understand my life grappling with statistics and reports because they only received a junior middle school education. When I feel overwhelmed by tons of reports, they're only concerned with the lunch menu at the factory canteen. They eat differently, think differently, and sleep differently. They are *just Han-Chinese country bumpkins* [emphasis by the interviewee].

What, then, did the Han-Chinese workers on the shop floor think about the Korean-Chinese white-collar workers? The Han-Chinese workers looked upon the white-collar workers mostly from their everyday experience of the different working conditions between the shop floor and the office: "Our workplace is steaming hot and my work uniform is dull-colored," a Han-Chinese worker said, "but the Korean-Chinese work in the air-conditioned office. . . . They can wear fashionable clothes during work hours." This kind of observation on the differences between the office and the shop floor often led to comments that reflected their ill feeling toward the office workers: "While we bear the endless drudgery of stitching on this dusty shop floor," another Han-Chinese worker said, "the Korean-Chinese giggle with Korean managers in the office."

The Han-Chinese workers' idea of white-collar jobs was mixed with their ethnic enmity toward Korean-Chinese, a mirror image of the Korean-Chinese feeling of ethnic superiority to the Han-Chinese workers: "You know how the Korean-Chinese got the privileged [white-collar] jobs," a Han-Chinese line leader said. "It was only because they're ethnic Koreans." Many Han-Chinese workers believed that the management's ethnic preference for Korean-Chinese made them dominant in the white-collar work positions at Nawon. They thought that the Korean-Chinese predominance in the office was fundamentally unfair, because it was not individual abilities but inherited Korean ethnicity that brought most of the prestigious work positions to Korean-Chinese. For this reason, they did not fully accept the Korean-Chinese superior status in the factory hierarchy. A Han-Chinese worker argued:

> It's natural for Korean-Chinese to speak Korean and understand Korean culture. They happened to be born in a Korean-Chinese household and thus can speak Korean and know its culture. They got the white-collar jobs with no effort! To the extent that management preferred Korean-Chinese because of their ethnicity, then we, Han-Chinese, can't get the same desirable positions in the factory.

The common image of the Korean-Chinese as a group that was favored simply because it was an ethnic minority greatly contributed to the Han-Chinese workers' ill feeling against the Korean-Chinese office workers. Since in China it is generally believed that Korean-Chinese have an inferior social and economic status, mostly living in poor farming regions of backward northeast China, many Han-Chinese workers felt extremely jealous of the Korean-Chinese office workers. They believed that, at Nawon, the Korean-Chinese could occupy such prestigious positions only at the expense of the Han-Chinese. Han-Chinese workers argued that the Korean-Chinese in the office were arrogant and took advantage of their white-collar jobs to ignore them. In fact, many Han-Chinese workers tried to depreciate the Korean-Chinese predominance in the factory, arguing that the authority the Korean-Chinese exercised in the factory was effective only within the factory walls:

> The Korean-Chinese can behave as our superiors only thanks to the Korean management's support for them. They're just like the foxes that borrow the tigers' fierceness [C. *hujia huwei*]. If they lose the special support from the Korean management, they would be nothing! Their high status is only valid in a factory owned by Koreans.

As we have noted, the formation of white-collar workers at Nawon consolidated management's control of labor by creating a deep inner schism among the Chinese employees. This effect reminds us of the old colonial political structure based on "divide and rule." In the former British colonies, for instance, the British colonial officials tended to favor certain groups of people in the colonies as their local assistants. Such preferential or discriminatory policies were based on the colonial officials' preconceptions about the diverse ethnic or tribal groups of the colonies, especially about which ethnic groups had characteristics suitable for colonial intermediaries (Furnivall 1948: 305). This discriminatory colonial practice eventually promoted suspicions and antagonisms between groups of local people and made them compete against each other for favorable treatment by the rulers. At Nawon, the reversed ethnic division of labor, a result of the management's (mis)understandings of the Korean-Chinese and Han-Chinese ethnicity, had a similar effect. The overturned structure of the division of labor stirred up and increased antagonism between Korean-Chinese and Han-Chinese employees, which eventually weakened the potential for workers' solidarity. In particular, the gradual transformation of the Korean-Chinese into a wealthy ethnic minority made them apparently pro-management, while greatly increasing the Han-Chinese workers' antagonism toward the small number of the Korean-Chinese ethnic group.

In the Nawon factory, the formation of white-collar workers produced another strong pro-management effect, by creating a large social distance between the two Han-Chinese white-collar workers in the office and the Han-Chinese blue-collar workers on the shop floor. The relationship between the two groups might have been different from that between the Korean-Chinese office workers and the Han-Chinese shop-floor workers because there was no divisive effect from a difference in ethnicities. One might expect that being of the same ethnicity, the two groups would be more friendly, or, at least, less hostile. Contrary to expectations, however, the two Han-Chinese office workers viewed the shop-floor workers in a way not much different from that of the Korean-Chinese office workers. For example, just like the Korean-Chinese office workers, they had trouble remembering the names of the Han-Chinese workers on the shop floor, even though they had worked at Nawon for more than four years. The following statement of Zhenmei, one of the two Han-Chinese office workers, revealed that their view of the shop-floor workers was not much different from that of the Korean-Chinese office workers. She argued that there was nothing unusual in their virtually nonexistent social relationship with the shop-floor workers:

> Why do you expect that I'd have acquaintances on the shop floor? Most of them are from *backward and poor* farming villages that I've never been to. They didn't even finish junior middle school. . . . As you know, I'm really busy preparing documents that are submitted to management and to the corporate headquarters in Seoul. I have no time to pay attention to their

work and life in the factory. . . . They're just simple workers who are only concerned with their monthly wages. They have no interest in developing their career and individual qualities [emphasis by the interviewee].

As far as Zhenmei was concerned, that she shared the same Han-Chinese ethnicity with the shop-floor workers did not make any difference in her view of them. She believed there were fundamental differences between her and the shop-floor workers such as social background, level of education, and even personal interests. Zhenmei considered the workers on the shop floor uncultured and dirty and far outside of the range of suitable acquaintances. She even alluded to the pungent odor of the shop floor, calling it a "peasant odor." This shows how the divisive effect of the white- and the blue-collar division was very much buttressed by the urban prejudice against workers from the countryside, which itself reflected the wide social gap between the rural and the urban. Although they did not use the term "ethnicity" in distinguishing themselves from the shop-floor workers, the Han-Chinese office workers were always conscious of the sharp distinction between the white- and the blue-collar workers and intended to maintain the distinction.

The increasingly close relationship between the Han-Chinese and the Korean-Chinese office workers shows another result stemming from the formation of white-collar workers at Nawon, which, at this time, increased the strength of the internal ties among the privileged group of employees of different ethnicities. The office workers, both the Korean-Chinese and the Han-Chinese, called one another either elder or younger sister to express their feeling of closeness. The two Han-Chinese office workers said they felt much closer to their Korean-Chinese "officemates" than to the Han-Chinese shop-floor workers. This was because they believed that they shared "many things" together. Meihua, the other Han-Chinese office worker, once argued that they felt close to one another because they did the same office jobs and felt a similar kind of job stress, and, therefore, could better understand one another. Sometimes the office workers, both the Korean-Chinese and the Han-Chinese, went downtown together for shopping and other leisure activities. The close interethnic relationship indicated another power effect of the white-collar job formation, which, at this time, created social ties among the employees with different ethnicities. It revealed the multiple social consequences of the white- and the blue-collar division, which were articulated and rearticulated through the formation of "new" white-collar workers, the reversed ethnic division of labor, and the growing rural-urban division of post-socialist China.

CONCLUSION

Any thorough understanding of the white- and the blue-collar division in a local context must go beyond a functionalist framework that explains the division in terms of functional differentiation among individuals with different abilities. It also should depart from Marxist approaches, which assume a binary opposition between capitalists and workers. Although the binary framework offers an effective critique of the functionalist approach, it is not sophisticated enough to explain the actual divisions embedded in multiple concepts such as nation, nationalism, and ethnicity. The formation of white-collar workers at Nawon was very different from what the functional and the Marxist understandings would lead us to believe. In the multinational Nawon factory, inherited ethnicity as well as acquired personal qualifications determined an individual's eligibility for the prestigious white-collar work positions. At the same time, the white- and blue-collar division had complex dimensions that go beyond any binary framework. The division in the factory was embedded in distinctive concepts and ideas, such as the management's view of Korean nationalism and culture, the Korean suspicion of Sino-centrism, Korean-Chinese ethnic pride, and Han-Chinese ethnic animosity toward Korean-Chinese. Of particular importance was management's preference for Korean-Chinese, which had overturned ethnic power relations in the factory, thus bringing about the two escalating feelings of Korean-Chinese ethnic superiority and Han-Chinese ethnic animosity against the group of minority employees.

The uncommon white-collar job formation at Nawon fundamentally changed the social and economic status and ethnic consciousness of the Korean-Chinese. As members of an historically recent ethnic minority in China, the Korean-Chinese office workers shared a strong feeling that they were victims of ethnic discrimination. To the extent that they considered themselves underprivileged, the Korean-Chinese office workers regarded their high-paid white-collar jobs as long-delayed compensation for the discrimination. With their prestigious jobs, they thought they could improve their economic and social status and finally escape their once doomed fate as an ethnic minority. The white-collar jobs at Korean multinationals like Nawon have changed the Korean-Chinese self-image from being victims of ethnic discrimination to members of the rising middle class in China.

The formation of white-collar workers at Nawon has another important implication for the politics of ethnicity and ethnic consciousness, since it created a wide social distance between the Korean-Chinese office workers and the Han-Chinese shop-floor workers. The divisive effect was reinforced when the Korean-Chinese employees projected their collective yearning for social and economic success onto the white-collar jobs, while the Han-Chinese developed a feeling of ethnic animosity against Korean-Chinese. The newly emerging interethnic antagonism leads us to a broader discussion about the changing meanings of ethnicity in contemporary Chinese society. In the current social landscape of China, individuals of an ethnic group are constantly asked to reevaluate their own ethnicity as their class or status identifications change. What would determine the self-consciousness of Korean-Chinese if they successfully secure their space within the rising middle class of China? Would Korean ethnicity still be the key to their group identity? What would Han-Chinese, the overwhelming ethnic majority, think about the new middle-class membership of Korean-Chinese? Answers to these questions are still open: future changes in the Korean-Chinese ethnic consciousness largely depend on whether Korean-Chinese can successfully maintain their white-collar jobs and continue to climb the social ladder to middle-class status.

The Making of Chinese
Industrial Workers

THE SHOP FLOOR

The shop floor of Nawon was divided into three parts, respectively assigned to the cutting, the sewing, and the finishing sections. The Korean managers proudly said that all the details of the shop-floor design were identical to those of the Korean mother factory. "This is," a Korean manager argued, "the best possible arrangement for maximum productivity." The shop-floor design, as an exact replica of its South Korean counterpart, reflected the management's ambition to create in China another golden era of garment production. The managers made the shop floor a space where they could generate profits by combining cheap Chinese labor with their advanced knowledge of production and labor management.

The management's belief in efficient design of the shop floor was not an empty boast. In fact, the shop-floor organization at Nawon was the end result of the incessant demand of the garment manufacturing industry for maximum output with minimum cost. Garment manufacturing at Nawon was based on two different production systems, the hand-off and the flexible-work-group systems. While the sewing section was organized into twelve assembly lines under the hand-off system, the cutting and the finishing sections were organized into work units based on the flexible-work-group system (Figure

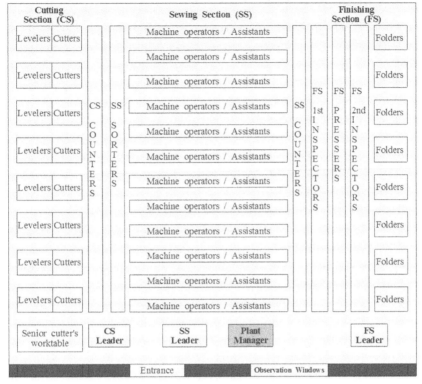

Figure 4-1. The Shop Floor of Nawon. Source: Author

4-1). The internal operations of each section reflected the difference in the two production systems. In the first system, as a sewing-section worker on the production line completed a garment, the worker promptly passed it to the next worker, just like a runner in a relay race. In the second system, workers in the cutting and the finishing sections moved from one worktable to another, according to changes in the workload. The application of the two different systems resulted from trial and error as the management searched for higher productivity. From repeated experiments on the shop floor, the managers at Nawon argued, they realized that the combination of the two systems created the optimum conditions for the highest productivity.[1] The hand-off system was the best for the sewing jobs, because it best fit a labor process tied to the high speed of sewing machines. The work-group system was particularly efficient for the jobs in the cutting and the finishing sections, because under the system workers could move from one part to another according to changes in the volume of products that went to (for the cutting section) or came from (for the finishing section) the sewing section.

The entire production sequence on the shop floor began with the senior tailor of the cutting section, who made pattern templates according to product specifications. After determining that templates had no errors, the materials department brought the required fabrics and accessories from the warehouse to the workshop. Sorters arranged the delivered fabric according to the production sequence. The levelers leveled off the bolts of fabric that were passed from the sorters and stacked them evenly. Depending on order amounts, sometimes the levelers stacked up over one hundred layers of fabric on the worktable. Piled fabrics were sent to the cutters. The cutters drew lines on thin paper patterns according to the templates. They put the paper on top of the piled fabrics and cut them along the lines drawn on the paper. The cutting-section counters grouped the cut fabric into bundles to be sewn together in the sewing section. Before passing the fabric bundles to the sewing section, they tagged small labels on every fabric part to track the individual parts through the whole production process.

The tasks of the sewing section began when the sewing-section sorters delivered the garment parts from the cutting section to the sewing machine operators. In 2003, there were twelve production lines in the sewing section and each line had twenty operators. More than two hundred operators performed different functions with their sewing machines, such as single-needle stitching or hemming. While the operators were at work, the sewing assistants, standing beside the worktables, helped the operators. The assistants trimmed and then delivered fabric parts from one operator to another. Each production line had a line leader, responsible for supervising individual operators and keeping lead time at a "reasonably good" level. At the end of each production line, the sewing-section counters counted up the number of sewn garments and handed them over to the finishing section.

Just like the other two sections, all operations of the finishing section began with the counters, who checked and recorded the number of garments delivered by the sewing-section counters. The received garments that needed special processes, such as buttoning, went to the appropriate workers—in this case, buttoners, who made buttonholes and attached buttons to the garments. Garments without buttons, together with those buttoned, went to the first quality checkers. Management divided the quality checkers into two groups. It placed the first group of checkers before the ironing workers and had them check for major defects such as derailed stitches and color mismatches. The ironing workers always had a heavy workload because each worker had to deal with garments that came from one production line of the sewing section. They often felt overwhelmed by the garments because the work of the sewing was faster than that of the ironing. The second quality checkers, who worked right after the ironing, measured the dimensions of the ironed garments and determined whether they were within the permitted range of product specification. Once they had passed the second quality check, the garments were sent to the folders, who folded and put them in plastic bags. The garment product in plastic bags went through a metal detector that checked for broken needles hidden in the garments. Finally, the male packers loaded labeled boxes with the finished product into export containers.

LOCAL LABOR, "GLOBAL" MANAGEMENT

In the summer of 2001, the personnel composition of the shop floor at Nawon had special characteristics. First of all, there was only one Korean manager on the shop floor supervising the entire manufacturing process. The minimal number of Korean managerial staff on the shop floor was highly unusual compared with other, nearby foreign garment factories. For example, a Korean garment factory that was only three blocks away from Nawon placed seven Korean managers on the shop floor to manage three hundred Chinese workers. The Nawon managerial staff on the shop floor also had a distinctive characteristic. On the shop floor of Nawon, Han-Chinese, not Korean-Chinese, held about 80 percent of the staff positions. The predominantly Han-Chinese staff sharply contrasted with that of the other South Korean garment factories, where about half of the managerial staff on the shop floor were Korean-Chinese. The personnel composition on the shop floor seemed to contradict a key assumption of the management, with its deep distrust of Han-Chinese obedience to the management. As analyzed in Chapter Three, the Korean managers considered the Han-Chinese workers unreliable because they viewed them as members of an ethnic group that had been tainted by Sino-centrism and Communist ideology. How could management allow Han-Chinese to hold most of the shop-floor staff positions if it was really afraid they might be defiant?

Management explained the predominantly Han-Chinese managerial staff on the shop floor as a result of Nawon's successful localization. Localization, a term commonly used in Korean business administration literature, is often measured by the ratio of the number of Koreans and that of "indigenous" people among managerial staff, where a higher ratio of indigenous people indicates a higher level of localization (Shanghai Asset Inc. 2005; Shin 1993). Successful localization, thus, means that management controls local labor with a small number of foreign managers. The single Korean manager on the shop floor indicates that the Nawon management had achieved the goal of controlling the shop floor with a minimal number of foreign managerial staff. In fact, the Korean managers of the factory boasted that their shop floor experienced virtually no labor disputes during the corporation's decade-long operation in China, while many nearby garment factories, both foreign-invested and Chinese-owned, suffered from frequent labor disputes.

How could the management keep its shop floor relatively peaceful, while giving most of the shop-floor staff positions to Han-Chinese, whom it considered unreliable? The annual company statistics on the composition of the shop-floor personnel from 1997 to 2001 give us a clue to the answer (Table 4-1).

As Table 4-1 shows, the number of Korean managers and Korean-Chinese interpreters on the shop floor gradually decreased during the five-year period from 1997 to 2001. During the same period, the number of Han-Chinese employees increased by almost 30 percent. In general, an increasing number of workers leads to a higher potential for labor disorder and thus creates a demand for additional managerial staff. It is a managerial truism that factories with a large number of workers have more managerial staff than smaller ones, unless they are equipped with extra supervising tools such as surveillance cameras. At Nawon, however, the management decreased the number of Korean managers and Korean-Chinese interpreters and recruited more and more Han-Chinese workers, while not installing any extra surveillance methods on the shop floor. The extraordinary situation at Nawon indicates that the management successfully supervised the workshop despite the steadily growing number of Han-Chinese workers and the shrinking number of the non-Han-Chinese managerial staff.

However, it would be a mistake to assume that the management established tight control over the workers with no difficulty. The gradual decrease in the number of Korean managers and Korean-Chinese employees implies that management may have experienced difficulties in establishing and maintaining efficient labor control. If management had

TABLE 4-1. Organization of Workshop Personnel, 1997–2001

	1997	1998	1999	2000	2001
Korean managers	8	6	4	3	2
Korean-Chinese interpreters	22	20	18	16	5
Han-Chinese workers	462	492	514	592	657

Source: Author

been so confident in its control of Han-Chinese workers, why did it take such a long time to decrease the non-Han-Chinese managerial staff? Later I learned that, during the first several years of the factory's operation from 1993 until 1996, management had placed a much larger number of Korean managers and Korean-Chinese interpreters on the shop floor. According to a senior Korean-Chinese worker in the office, there were about fifty Korean managers and Korean-Chinese interpreters in the workshop during that time. She also added it was only in 2000 that management began to give Han-Chinese some minor staff positions on the shop floor.

An executive of Nawon Korea argued that such a large number of managerial staff on the shop floor was necessary for the management to discipline untrained Han-Chinese workers. "We had to teach the young peasant girls," he said, "the factory's jobs from A to Z." The Korean managers at Nawon, who came to China dreaming of another golden age of garment manufacturing, faced the daunting task of disciplining young Han-Chinese women from the "backward" countryside. The task was more demanding because it was the very first time for the managers to supervise workers in a foreign country that had been completely unknown to them.[2] Coming from an allegedly much more modernized country, South Korea, the managers thought they had the right skills and know-how to quickly transform the untrained rural women into model industrial workers. Their view of the Chinese workers reflected the common attitude of multinational management toward local labor, regarding them as backward and, therefore, as the objects of disciplining and education (Fuller 2009: 39). The Korean managers believed they could fill the "backward" minds of the rural Chinese women with the key virtues of industrial labor, such as punctuality, accuracy, and orderliness. With a belief in the effectiveness of its managerial methods, management adopted "universal" surveillance methods such as observation windows. For management, "universal" methods meant the production techniques and managerial know-how that had originally been developed in the West and later proved their applicability in non-Western countries including South Korea.

The creation of industrial workers at Nawon, however, could never be completed by adopting "universal" methods of surveillance. Contrary to what management assumed, the young Han-Chinese women from remote farming villages were never empty containers waiting to be filled with the right contents, namely labor discipline. Instead, they reacted to the disciplinary measures with their own critical understandings of them, such as "voluntary" subordination, passive adjustment, and, occasionally, resistance. The workers' constant attempt to find loopholes in the disciplinary and surveillance methods repeatedly thwarted management's original plans for achieving labor discipline. Their reactions eventually caused management resort to other forms of training methods that were not "universal." The new methods of labor discipline originated from South Korean workplaces.

The fact that the Korean management had its own local, not "universal," characteristics made the detailed process of creating industrial workers more complex. Coming from one of the Asian NIEs that had achieved fast modernization,[3] Korean managers assumed that they were the messengers of advanced and "universal" scientific management. They believed it would be one of their first duties to "shower" the undisciplined Chinese workers with modern, "universal" disciplinary methods. However, unexpected resistance from the Han-Chinese workers caused management to resort to disciplining measures that had originated in the South Korean work culture. Management's version of South Korean work culture was a mixture of the historical legacies of the "militarized modernization" of South Korea (Moon 2005) and the Confucian idea of self-discipline (Choongsoon Kim 1992; Kyeong-Dong Kim 1994). At Nawon, this work culture inspired management to introduce new disciplinary methods that would correct the defects of the "universal" ones. With the new methods, management finally gained crucial momentum in transforming untrained "country bumpkins" into disciplined factory workers. My discussion of the creation of Han-Chinese industrial workers in the factory begins with management's observation windows, a symbol of "universal" methods of labor control.

CREATING INDUSTRIAL WORKERS

Observation windows and panoptic surveillance

It was the third day of my fieldwork at Nawon that I first felt the power of management's control of labor. The workshop was noisy and bustling as the Han-Chinese workers were returning to their positions from lunch break. Many of them were still chatting with others in low voices, waiting for the first inputs of their afternoon work quota. At the moment, the plant manager, Bak, was still in the factory main office, drinking coffee with visiting Japanese buyers. When he saw the hands of a wall clock pointing exactly at 1 p.m., he quickly stood up from his chair and went to the observation windows that were installed between the main office and the workshop (Figure 4-1). Because the afternoon work hours had just begun, I still could hear workers' low chatting voices mixed with the sound of the sewing machines. To my surprise, shortly after the plant manager stood in front of the windows and began to look into the workshop, the workers' chatting voices magically faded away. In less than a minute, only the noise of sewing machines filled the shop floor. To silence the hundreds of shop floor workers and induce them to concentrate on their work, the plant manager neither set out on a round of inspection nor yelled at idle workers. How could his simple watching have such a powerful effect over the entire workshop?

In a private interview, the plant manager proudly said that by just watching the workers through the windows he could instantly know how everything was going on the shop floor:

> I've worked in this company since the summer of 1996. . . . Don't you think my six-year career is long enough to know every possible situation on the shop floor? I fully understand the technical details of garment production. I also know the workers in key positions very well. I can figure out what's happening in the workshop from a worker's slightest body movement or facial expression. . . . Not a single worker can idle away time on the production lines. They can't escape my eyes.

This comment, together with the shop-floor workers' reaction to his gaze, reveals that the observation windows functioned as a powerful supervising device. What was intriguing was the Han-Chinese workers' response to the gaze: whenever they saw or felt someone watch them through the windows, they instantly increased their work speed and concentrated even harder on their work.

The observation windows, however, did not have any features that might contribute to such a powerful surveillance effect. They were just simple windows with plain glass; the only particular element was the opaque tape applied to the lower half. How could simple windows have a powerful labor-controlling effect? Almost a week later, a senior Korean-Chinese interpreter who had worked at Nawon since its establishment told me that the observation windows had only plain clear glass during the first several months of the factory's operation. It was only after the earliest period that the management applied opaque tape to the lower half of the windows. "The Korean managers made the change to the glass," the interpreter said, "to keep the Han-Chinese workers from looking into our office." As a newcomer to the factory, I could not understand how the half-blind windows could block the workers' sight into the office. The workers, I thought, still could easily look into the office because the top half of each large window was completely clear.

The Han-Chinese workers' body movements on the shop floor had the key to the answer. On the shop floor, the workers moved according to the technical requirements of each production process. For example, the movements of machine operators, the majority of the sewing-section workers, were confined to their worktables, because the stitching job required them to sit in front of their sewing machines and fixed their view on the worktables (Figure 4-2). The sitting work posture blocked their view of the main office because the lower part of the windows was taped over. A senior Han-Chinese worker recalled how they felt about the change to the windows:

> Before the management attached the opaque tape, we could glance into the office through the windows when Korean managers weren't watching the shop floor. We felt more or less relieved because we could see what the managers were doing in the office. . . . It was especially nice to guess when they would come to the workshop to check our work.

After the management applied the tape to the windows, the operators of the sewing section acutely felt the change. They worked closest to the observation windows, and thus were fully exposed to management's gaze (Figure 4-1). "After the managers applied the tape," a line leader of the sewing section said, "I could no longer relax my attention even when I

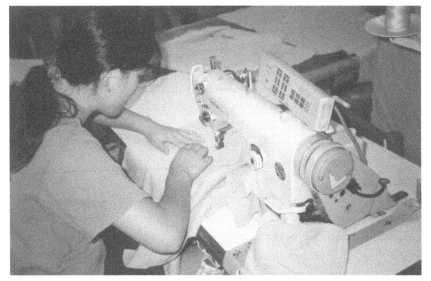

Figure 4-2. Typical Stitching Posture of a Sewing Machine Operator.
Source: Author

didn't have jobs on my worktable." The operators could no longer figure out the situation in the office because their sitting work posture kept them from seeing into the office. They had to rise by a couple of inches from their chairs to get even a quick glimpse of the office and not a single one of them would dare to do so. They could not know when the Korean managers would rise from the opposite side of the windows to look into the workshop.

For a while, the observation windows with the half-blind glass functioned as a highly effective labor-controlling device by giving management a panoptic view of the shop floor. Here, the term "panoptic" indicates a situation where those who are the targets of surveillance have a constant feeling of being watched although they do not know whether they are actually being watched. The controlling effect of a panoptic view can be powerful because those being watched are under the constant stress created by the unpredictable operation of the watchful power (Foucault 1995: 201). At a glance, the situation at Nawon may seem somewhat different from typical panoptic conditions because the half-blind windows equally blocked the view from the main office and from the shop floor. This was not the case, however, because the managers in the office could watch the entire shop floor whenever they wanted, while the machine operators had to risk the management's ire to get a glimpse of the office. In fear of being caught by the managers' watchful eyes, the workers dared not peer into the office.

The episode of the observation windows reflects how management tried to establish effective labor control. From the very beginning, management had clear ideas about how to design the shop floor, applying the managerial and technical know-how it had gained from the long-term managing experience in South Korea. Based on that know-how, management located the observation windows near the production lines of the sewing section, expecting that would maximize labor control. Why the sewing section? In garment manufacturing, sewing machine operators were at the core of the entire garment production process because their work speed determined overall lead time and product quality. Gaining firm control of the operators was the first and the most important objective of every manager. Only after establishing tight control over the operators could management extend its control over the entire production process.

Management expected that the new observation windows would also enhance the supervision of the workers in the cutting and the finishing sections. In management's view, the workers in the two sections always looked more or less disorganized because they worked under the flexible-work-group system. The folders in the finishing section, for example, moved from one worktable to another according to changes in the hourly output coming from the sewing section. Changes in hourly output were inevitable since each production line of the sewing section often had to deal with garments with different styles: simple-style garments needed little production time, but garments with extra accessories or with complex designs usually increased the lead time. Hence the workload coming to the workers in the finishing section varied, and this required them to move from one worktable to another. Management decided to apply the work-group system to the finishing section because it believed this system could better deal with the variability of the workload. The Korean managers, however, often said that they were always concerned about the frequent moves of workers on the shop floor. The workers in the cutting and finishing sections could move only with the permission of their work group leaders. The workers, however, still could get a little relief from the incessant flow of garments when they changed their work positions. The managers thought the workers took advantage of the work-group system by intentionally moving slowly when they changed their work positions.

The Korean managers believed that increasing the work speed of the sewing section, a direct result of management's enhanced control of the machine operators, would surely increase the work speed of the other two sections. The functional dependence of the two sections on the sewing section was the key. At one end of the work flow, cutting-section workers provided cut fabric for the sewing section as fast as they could to maintain the fast work speed of the sewing section. At the other end, the finishing section workers had to work until the machine operators finished the last piece of garment and sent it to them. In management's words, the two sections existed to guarantee the smooth operation of the sewing section. Management thought that it could prevent the workers' foot-dragging in the two sections by increasing the production speed. Speeding up the production rate of the machine operators would eventually increase the work rate of the entire workshop and, as a result, stop workers from slowing down operations.

"Red" Han-Chinese workers

Management, however, soon realized that the observation windows were of limited use in controlling workers in other work positions. The assistants in the sewing section were among the workers who were still relatively free from the panoptic control of management. The assistants' work posture created a blind spot in management's panoptic surveillance. During work hours, they stood in the small space on the left side of machine operators, trimming extra thread from garments and passing them to the next operators. Thanks to the standing work posture and frequent moving between worktables, the assistants could get a chance to see the office through the upper part of the observation windows.

When they installed the observation windows, the Korean managers did not expect that the assistants would cause such a problem. Based on their past experience of managing South Korean workers, they thought that the observation windows would be enough to control both the machine operators and the assistants. According to the managers, however, the Han-Chinese assistants behaved very differently from their South Korean counterparts. When they did paperwork or read newspapers in the office, the managers felt the assistants' eyes on the back of their necks. "It was an odd feeling," a Korean manager recalled, "similar to the feeling that I have when a person hostile to me stares at me." When he had such a feeling, he promptly turned his eyes in their direction: "Almost every time, my eyes met with an assistant's eyes."

At first, the management thought it would be easy to stop the Han-Chinese workers' peeping. Through careful observations, the Korean managers made a shortlist of "frequent peepers." Referring to the list, they decided to punish a Han-Chinese worker identified as "the most frequent peeper." They planned to use the punishment as a warning to other workers who often glanced over at the observation windows. With this in mind, the Korean managers called the worker, an assistant in the sewing section, to the office. When the unlucky worker came to the office, the Korean managers scolded her for the frequent peeping and for being distracted from her job. They also told her that her salary would be docked by 20 percent as a punishment for her negligence in carrying out her job. "We believed that such a punishment was reasonable," a Korean manager recalled, "because it's a fact that frequent peeping distracts workers from their jobs and thus increases the production defect rate."

To their surprise, however, the Han-Chinese assistant did not admit the accusation. Instead, she insisted she did not make any defective garments. She even asked the managers to provide her with detailed information about her alleged defects, such as the exact time and manner she caused problems in the production procedures. In the end, the Korean managers let the worker go back to the workshop. They decided not to punish her because they could not present any "concrete evidence" that could prove a relationship between her frequent peeping and a high defect rate. When the worker strongly denied the accusation, the managers realized that it was not that easy to punish workers only because they occasionally had glanced into the office. How could one prove that the peeping really caused any defects in the garments? Would peeping five times be enough to punish a worker? Why not four? The Han-Chinese worker's unexpected defiance made the managers realize the fundamental uncertainties in their standards of punishment.

The small, one-time dispute with a rank-and-file worker deeply frustrated the entire Korean management. Senior Korean managers from Nawon Korea who had observed the dispute in the office recalled that they had been literally shocked by the worker's defiant attitude. Their feeling of frustration ran particularly deep because in many South Korean workplaces such an outright challenge from a rank-and-file worker was nearly unimaginable. In South Korea, during the 1970s and most of the 1980s, a highly authoritarian, top-down relationship between management and labor was dominant in many workplaces. During that period, labor protests, if any, were quickly suppressed by the pro-management government. Thanks to the government's support, management could safely assume a highly authoritarian attitude toward labor and demand workers' "proper" respect (Janelli and Janelli 1993; Choongsoon Kim 1992; Won Kim 2005; Koo 1993, 2001). Accustomed to such a highly authoritarian work culture, the Korean managers at Nawon took the Han-Chinese worker's defiant attitude very seriously: What caused her to deny the accusation in such a bold way? What made the Han-Chinese worker different from her South Korean counterparts? To management, deeply offended by this unexpected event, it did not matter whether the defiant attitude of the assistant really represented the attitude of the majority of the Han-Chinese workers in the factory.

Management found an easy answer in the recent history of China: the reign of radical Communism. A senior Korean manager at Nawon Korea who had interrogated the assistant argued that such defiant behavior reflected the Han-Chinese workers' "deep-rooted redness." For the manager, red was the color of defiance and insubordination that originated from Communist propaganda about the conflicting interest between management and labor. Ironically, Korean managers conjured up the image of "red" Chinese workers at the very moment when the generation of the radical workers created by the Maoist movement was retiring (Ching Kwan Lee 2000a). Unlike the workers of the Maoist period, the Han-Chinese workers at Nawon did not experience any of the Maoist radical political campaigns. Instead, the young workers were more interested in the dazzling scene of consumer culture and its promise of pleasurable individual consumption (Rofel 1999: 188–90; Yunxiang Yan 2000: 223–25).

The Korean managers' idea of "red" Chinese workers came from a collective misrecognition, one of the local consequences of globalization. Globalization, understood as ever-intensifying transnational flows of capital, people, ideas, and cultural objects, is believed to improve people's understanding of different "cultures" and promote tolerance of cultural others (Lane 2006: 89–90). However, especially during its early period, intensifying transnational flows create misrecognitions among the people engaging in the process, leading them to understand objects, ideas, and people that they encounter in erroneous ways. In the multinational Nawon factory, the managers believed that radical Communism had heavily affected the young Han-Chinese workers, while the workers, then in their teens, actually had not been exposed to any radical political tenet. The misrecognition had important implications for shop-floor politics. Most of all, it justified the introduction of new labor-controlling methods that the management thought would be powerful enough to transform the allegedly "red" Han-Chinese workers into docile factory workers. The following sections explore how the management's misrecognition of local labor played a critical role in introducing new forms of labor discipline to the shop floor.

LOCAL TRANSFORMATION OF GLOBAL LABOR MANAGEMENT

The plant manager on the shop floor

The Korean managers realized that the brief confrontation in the office brought an unexpected positive result. On the day after the event, peeping from the shop floor virtually disappeared. "The Han-Chinese workers tried really hard not to meet my eyes," a senior manager said. "Even when I spoke to them, they didn't look at my face." Such a voluntary change among the workers, however, could not keep management from adopting more drastic methods of labor supervision. Although the managers acknowledged that the frequency of peeping had significantly decreased, they still thought that the change was only superficial. The Han-Chinese workers, they argued, only changed their way of peeping into a sneakier method, "just like Communists." A senior manager recalled that, even after the event, the sewing-section assistants still kept watching the main office when they delivered garments between worktables. The Han-Chinese workers' "cunning" behavior only strengthened management's belief in the necessity of additional labor-controlling measures, specially designed to fit the situation of "Communist" China.

In early November 1994, the Korean management decided to set up the plant manager's desk on the shop floor, in the middle of the sewing section

(Figure 4-1). With the change, the plant manager was expected to stay in the workshop from the beginning to the end of each work day. The location of the plant manager also reflected management's intention to maximize its control over the workers, taking advantage of the sewing section's significance in production procedures. The decision signaled management's departure from the previous managerial practices it considered "universal." According to "universal" principles regarding the hierarchical difference between management and labor, high-ranking managers such as a plant manager are to be in a place separated from the dusty and noisy workshop (Rofel 1999; Taylor 1947 [1911]). The management at Nawon initially maintained this difference between labor and management as a key "universal" principle, and hence created the spatial division between the shop floor and the main office.

The Nawon management considered the decision to put the plant manager's work desk on the shop floor a truly unprecedented move. Management compromised the principle of spatial hierarchy between management and labor to create a shock effect on the Han-Chinese workers. With the change in labor management, the plant manager began to conduct close, on-site labor supervision in the middle of the workshop. The power effect of the new labor supervision was obvious: it virtually trapped the Han-Chinese workers in an overpowering mode of surveillance. Among the workers on the shop floor, the sewing-section assistants most acutely felt the management's new presence on the shop floor. Senior Han-Chinese workers who worked as assistants at the time of the change remembered that they were badly shaken by the on-site presence of the manager. Because they worked standing facing him, their every movement was exposed to the plant manager's watchful eyes. The sewing-section workers felt the pressure of the close supervision so intensely that many of them even held their breath when they felt the manager's eyes on them.

Politics of a "peasant nature"

The change in Nawon's labor management immediately brought some positive results for management. In a managerial meeting memo written in December 1995, the Korean managers concluded that, under the plant manager's close supervision, the Han-Chinese workers came to concentrate much more on their jobs. The factory statistics for labor productivity at that time also show that workers produced more garments and the defect rate was low. The management's feeling of accomplishment, however, did not last long. About three months after the plant manager had begun his work inside the workshop, workers' distraction increased again when the manager was not on the shop floor. According to the work diary kept by the Korean-Chinese interpreters, the Han-Chinese workers on the shop floor increasingly showed signs of slackened labor discipline, such as reduced work speed, small talk, and negligence in their jobs during the manager's absence.[4] The rebounding product defect rate further confirmed the limited effects of the plant manager's shop-floor presence.

At this time, the Korean managers did not mention the Han-Chinese workers' "redness" as the reason for the limited effectiveness. Instead, they pointed to the "peasant nature" of the workers as the main culprit. The Korean managers argued that that nature had a much worse influence on the workers than did radical Communism because it was deeply ingrained in them from their earliest childhood. "The Han-Chinese workers were born and raised in the countryside," a senior Korean manager said. "This can explain why our initial attempt to discipline and control them was not that successful." As the preceding chapter has noted, the Han-Chinese workers' rural background was one of the reasons management commonly gave to justify the low status of the Han-Chinese in the factory. Management believed that the Han-Chinese workers' rural background, now expressed as their "peasant nature," also explained why they did not give up the practices of peeping and foot-dragging. Management considered that their persistent resistance to its orders originated from the stubbornness of farmers living in the backward countryside.[5] The Korean managers' new interest in the so-called peasant nature of the workers did not mean that they abandoned their concern about the harmful influence of Communism. "The [peasant] stubbornness only got worse," another senior manager asserted, "as it was combined with Communist propaganda of class struggle."

Management's statements about the workers' "peasant nature," however, were not based on actual knowledge of China's villages. Most Korean managers had never visited any village even for a short time; only a few managers stayed in rural villages when they visited Pingshan as members of the expedition team. With such limited knowledge and experience of the Chinese countryside, the Korean managers found evidence for the Han-Chinese workers' "peasant nature" from what they casually observed at Nawon. For example, a Korean manager, who neither had been to Pingshan nor had visited any nearby farming villages, insisted that the everyday commotion caused by the workers at the shop-floor entrance reflected their "peasant nature." In fact, the small size of the plant entrance was the main cause of the commotion. The entrance, nicknamed the "workers' door," was too narrow for such a large number of workers to go through within a short time (Figure 4-1). The manager, however, considered the commotion that sometimes developed into brief exchanges of fiery words among workers as clearly demonstrating their unruly nature. Other Korean managers also believed that they understood the peasant nature of the Han-Chinese workers, pointing out the loud chatting from the factory canteen during meal time: "They speak really loud just like shouting," another Korean manager argued. "Only peasants in the countryside speak in that way."

How can we understand the apparent discrepancy between the Korean managers' limited knowledge of the Chinese countryside and their strong belief in the rural origins of the Han-Chinese workers' indiscipline and disorder? Again, the discrepancy was caused by collective misrecognition, the shared misunderstanding about ideas, people, or goods in transnational settings. The Korean managers' belief in the Han-Chinese workers' "nature" was misrecognition because they conjectured that the Han-Chinese workers at Nawon were very similar to the Korean workers they had supervised in the past. In their statements about "peasant nature," the Korean managers often insisted that there were some shared characteristics between the Han-Chinese and Korean workers: they are young and uneducated women who came from poor rural villages. Convinced of the similarities, the Korean managers often said that the Han-Chinese workers on the shop floor reminded them of the Korean young women they had met in the garment factories of South Korea. A Korean manager explained how he instantly discovered the similarities between the two on the first day of his encounter with the Han-Chinese women:

It was the early winter of 1993. I visited Pingshan for the first time as a member of the expedition team. In a village there, I interviewed several young girls who wanted to work in our factory. When I asked them some basic questions about their families and education level, most of them felt it difficult to answer my questions. They were extremely cautious and sus-picious about strangers. . . . Those girls in their braids instantly reminded me of the young girls I had met in Korean factories twenty, even thirty years ago. Although not exactly in the same way, the Korean women workers also had bobbed their hair and were very cautious—they also felt it difficult to say even a single word to me in a straightforward way.

During the 1970s and the 1980s, many young Korean women left their rural hometowns and moved to urban industrial areas (Koo 1993, 2001; Oh 1983; Song 1989;). Many of them found jobs in garment factories and gradually became the major workforce of the Korean garment industry (Deyo 1989). Just like the Han-Chinese workers at Nawon, however, they did not have any experience of factory work and thus lacked key qualities needed by garment manufacturing, such as quick body movements and notions of labor discipline. "Except for the unusual perseverance acquired from the harsh life of poor peasants," a Korean executive of Nawon Korea recalled, "the young [Korean] peasant girls didn't know the importance of punctuality and perfection in factory work." To the managers with their lingering memory of Korean "factory girls," the Han-Chinese workers' unruly behavior only proved the fundamental similarities between them and their Korean counterparts in the past.

The rural background of many of the Korean managers also contributed to the collective misrecognition. Following the large flow of people out of the countryside, the managers left their rural hometowns and began their careers in the cities. Their relocation, however, did not rid them of their memory of idyllic rural village life and village people. It is this memory that led the managers to perceive the current Chinese villages as a near-exact replica of the Korean villages of the past and thus to believe in the backwardness of China. In the same manner, the Korean managers assumed that young Chinese workers from the villages did not have any idea of what factory jobs were like, because the workers had characteristics similar to those of the Korean farmers of the past. A senior manager at Nawon Korea, born and raised in a poor South Korean tenant farming family, argued that he instantly recognized that the young Han-Chinese women on the shop floor lacked discipline. He firmly believed that the Han-Chinese workers had grown up in a situation that was not much different from that of the Korean farmers in his memory. "Even though I have never visited Pingshan," he argued, "I instantly recognized that the Han-Chinese young girls lacked discipline. . . . They were mere country bumpkins."

The marching drill

The Korean management's misrecognition of the Han-Chinese workers justified its introduction of new forms of labor control and discipline. In a managerial meeting held after the peeping episode, the Korean managers concluded that their former labor-control measures, including the plant manager's on-site supervision, failed to fully accomplish their original objective. They needed extraordinary methods of labor control that would be "fundamental in their effects" and thus "could remove every aspect of peasant nature from the Han-Chinese workers' minds." The meeting memo clearly noted that removing the deep-rooted "peasant nature" as well as the "Communist" influence from the workers should be the foremost managerial task.[6]

To achieve this, management turned to disciplinary techniques and strategies that had been developed in many South Korean corporations in the past, especially during the 1970s and the early 1980s. At that time, many Korean corporations adopted strict labor regulations and strong disciplinary measures that were influenced by the direct and indirect intervention of the military government (Chun 2003; Hokyu Kim 2006a, 2006b; Lee and Song 1994; Moon 2005). These measures, inspired by military organization and tactics, included such things as a top-down flow of orders, a blind deference to superiors, and boot-camp-style training programs. Once adopted as new-worker disciplining methods, highly authoritarian practices of this sort had remained in effect in many Korean factories and functioned as the key support of authoritarian managerial practices (Choe et al. 1994; Choongsoon Kim 1992; Ko 1988; Koo 2001; Ok-jie Lee 1990).

A marching drill, the first disciplinary method introduced after the meeting, was inspired by the training programs of South Korean corporations. A managerial memo written in mid-summer 1995 explains how management structured the drill. Management demanded that all Han-Chinese workers gather in front of the main factory building at 7:30 a.m. every workday. The section leaders, who were all Korean-Chinese at that time, took a roll call. After the roll call, the managers ordered the workers to form columns according to their section affiliations. Under the lead of the Korean-Chinese interpreters in charge of each unit, the workers marched in file along the road that loops around the factory (Figure 2-1). After the drill, they entered the workshop column by column through the "workers' door" (Figure 4-1). From its procedures, it was clear the drill was modeled after a standard military troop review.

The Korean managers had clear reasoning for introducing the marching drill as the first method of the new labor management. A senior Korean manager insisted that drilling should be the first step in changing a person's basic mindset:

> The close-order drill in the military is one of the most effective training methods to change the human mind. To act in concert with other people will bring the spirit of self-sacrifice, concentration, and a high level of bodily discipline. As you may know, there is a popular saying in Korea, "To be a real man, one has to join the military." The hardships in the military can transform even the most disorganized person into a highly disciplined man. . . . The drill will bring a fundamental change to the peasant girls and eventually transform them into true industrial workers.

The manager, who had served in the South Korean Marine Corps, believed that through military training he had been born again as a diligent and self-disciplined man.[7] Thanks to his changed personality, he thought, he successfully climbed his way up the corporate ladder and finally got the position of plant manager at Nawon. It was an extraordinary achievement because of his humble social background as a son of a poor farming family. "Whenever I look back on the old days," he said, "I always feel a sense of gratitude to the military. If the military hadn't changed me, I would have remained a country hick." Based on his own self-transforming experience, he was confident that the military-style drill would erase the "bad" nature of the Han-Chinese workers. Although they did not have exactly the same experience as the plant manager's, other Korean managers agreed that the hardest time in their military career was when they were in the training camp. "Every morning in the camp," a Korean manager said, "began with the bugle call and an endless repetition of close-order drilling." Because there was always at least one trainee who could not keep step with others, they had to repeat the same drill until all of them moved in perfect order. Through the repeated drills and collective punishments, the managers thought they had gradually learned to comply with military order emphasizing "deference to the [combat] order" and "self-sacrifice for the interest of the whole" (Ministry of National Defense of Korea 1996). With their vivid memory of military training, the Korean managers at Nawon believed that the marching drill was certain to change unruly Han-Chinese rural women into model industrial workers. As the beneficiaries of military discipline, the managers thought that they well understood the most subtle mechanism of the drill. First, it would bring physical pain to the workers. Second, the pain would eliminate their "bad" nature, and eventually transform the rural women into model industrial workers.

The Han-Chinese workers' first response to the marching drill, however, was far short of what management had desired. A group leader of the finishing section recalled that most of the workers regarded the drill as another annoying daily routine that only wasted their time and energy. "We thought," the group leader said, "that it only makes our toilsome day more miserable." Dissatisfied, many workers failed to attend the drill on time. The management confronted this kind of resistance with heavy penalties, imposing a twenty-yuan fine on each worker who did not arrive on time.[8] More importantly, management applied a military-style collective punishment. When workers marched along the loop factory road, the plant manager, installed on a raised platform, observed the procession and pointed out workers who were out of step with their unit. Whenever a worker fell out of step, he ordered the unit leader to march the whole unit until the unlucky worker fell into step.

Although the heavy penalty instantly decreased the number of workers who were late, they showed no enthusiasm for the drill. A Han-Chinese line leader remembered that their procession was almost chaotic, especially during the first two weeks: "Many workers frequently yawned when they marched," she recalled. "Some of them even openly muttered words of discontent in the drill." Because of such strong reluctance, the first two weeks' drills lasted almost an hour, far exceeding management's original expectation of twenty minutes. The workers' disappointing performance only made the Korean managers more determined to continue the drill. In their eyes, the Han-Chinese workers' near-chaotic marching was the most apparent sign of their deep-rooted "peasant nature." "They should learn, through their own experience the beauty of joint movement and cooperation," a senior Korean manager at Nawon Korea insisted. "We believed that the drill would force them to work more in concert, more diligently."

Two weeks after the first day of the drill, the plant manager at Nawon decided to make a special announcement. To the workers gathered in front of his platform, he declared that he would continue the drill until they showed a significant improvement in marching. Sumin, the Korean-Chinese senior tailor of the cutting section, still had a clear memory of what the plant manager said in the announcement because he spoke through Sumin's interpretation. In his impromptu speech, the plant manager blamed the workers' noncooperation for the increased training time:

> Though originally expected to be a twenty-minute training, the drill has now lasted more than one hour. I know that such long training drains your energy that should be used in workshop. But the drill is our policy and we will never withdraw it simply because you don't cooperate. . . . Aren't you tired now? If you stop muttering and voluntarily participate in the drill, this drill would not last long. . . . Whether you can finish the drill within twenty minutes or not solely depends on your performance!

Since the very beginning of the drill, most of the Han-Chinese workers had thought that it was excessive and humiliating. They believed that it was only suitable for schoolchildren. A senior worker recalled that, at that time, several workers even suggested ways to resist management such as a boycott of the drill. However, many of them began to think differently as their initial anger at the drill subsided. After the plant manager's announcement, they worried that the management would never stop practicing the drill regardless of how they reacted to it. Another senior worker said:

> We finally decided to follow the plant manager's demand. We thought that we had no power to ask him to stop the drill. . . . How could we, *the daughters of petty peasants*, stand against management? While we are small migrant workers from the countryside, Koreans have lots of money and can do everything with it. Any form of protest would only jeopardize our jobs in the factory. We thought that there was no other way but to follow management's orders [emphasis by the interviewee].

Studies on the political agency of Chinese migrant workers point out that their social background of poor rural villages and unstable social status have contributed to their political passivity. The "collective inaction" of Chinese migrant workers has been most apparent in many multinational corporations that have hired a large number of workers from the countryside (Chan 1998a; Ching Kwan Lee 1998b; Pun 2005; Solinger 1999). At Nawon, the Han-Chinese worker's comment of "country bumpkins" revealed that they perceived themselves as powerless and politically weak. This negative self-image discouraged them from organizing resistance against management. Especially during the early period of Nawon, the workers—thinking of themselves as "poor peasant girls," ignorant of almost everything in and around the factory—never thought that they could resist the power of management. For workers who had just arrived at the factory from their remote farming villages in Pingshan, everything seemed strange and sometimes even hostile.

The foreignness of the management and the village government's involvement in labor control further weakened the Han-Chinese workers' potential for resistance. During the first year of their employment at Nawon, many workers from Pingshan thought that the factory came from a remote country that might be located somewhere in the West. According to a worker who had worked at Nawon since 1993, many workers, at least during the first year of their employment, vaguely assumed that the Korean managers they saw on the shop floor were not the part of the "real" management of the factory:

> We knew that this factory came from Korea. But we never imagined that Korea could be a neighboring country that is not in the West. Before we came to the factory, we believed that Koreans would have blue eyes, pale skin, and a long nose. Now it sounds totally silly, but some workers even thought that *real* managers from the West would come and take control of us if we didn't sincerely follow management's orders. They believed that the *real* foreign managers must be much stricter than the managers on the shop floor [emphasis by the interviewee].

The particular methods of labor discipline and the training program only further convinced the workers of the foreignness of the management. "They [managers] are not Chinese," another senior worker said, "and for that reason, we were afraid of how they'd respond if we continued to show how discontented we were with them."

The village government's involvement in labor control also discouraged the workers from organizing resistance to management. After they took over the administration of the factory dormitories from Nawon, village officials frequently visited the dormitories. It did not take much time for the workers to realize that the officials were interested not in the living conditions of the dormitories but in tighter control of them. The staff of the dormitories, all recruited from village residents, strictly supervised the workers. The local staff often threatened that they would inform management and the village officials if the workers did not follow their orders. These were not empty threats. The Han-Chinese workers clearly remembered that several times the village officials revoked the temporary residence permits of some workers whom the staff pointed out as "troublemakers." When workers were hired, the village officials collected their original residence card and issued a temporary card. Revocation of a temporary residence card meant that the worker's status in Qingdao became unstable. As they watched how the local staff's notice urged the village officials to revoke the temporary residence permit of a worker, the Han-Chinese workers at Nawon came to believe that the village officials took sides with the foreign management. This revelation further convinced the workers that any resistance to management's methods of labor discipline would not only be fruitless but also dangerous.

After the plant manager's announcement, management observed that the Han-Chinese workers gradually changing their attitude toward the drill. Sumin, the Korean-Chinese interpreter who had led the cutting section in the marching drill, recalled that he was quite surprised to see several Han-Chinese workers insulting a fellow worker who was out of step: "When the plant manager said that their practicing time had been increased because of her mistake," he said, "all workers in the unit looked sharply at the worker who'd made the mistake. I heard several of them muttering against her and calling her a moron." From the first day of the drilling, the Han-Chinese workers had been angry at management because it forced them to do a "childish march." Their strong dislike of the drill, however, gradually lost its potency as they faced management's determination to continue the drill. In this situation, more and more workers believed that the only possible way to reduce the practicing time was to follow management's orders. This change made the workers consider those who did not act in concert with others more irritating than the drill itself.

The image of workers cursing their colleagues who made mistakes in the drill indicates that they had begun to check on one another so as not to be punished by management. The Han-Chinese workers, through the repetitive drill, became subjected to their internal and mutual surveillance and criticism. Around late fall of 1995, the marching drill finally seemed to achieve its original objective. At that time, a Korean manager wrote down in a memo: "Workers' attitude in drill: very good. [I] could not find even a single worker who did not act in concert with others. They march in strict order, as if they were soldiers in a recruit training center. I can see their bodies are really tense."

The writing exercise and toilet cleaning: Engraving discipline in workers' bodies

The slow but clear success of the "marching drill" made the managers feel confident that they had finally gained momentum in disciplining the Han-Chinese workers. In the annual evaluation of labor management in 1995, the Korean managers concluded that the drill by and large raised the level of labor discipline among the workers by changing their view of the work order and factory hierarchy. They thought that the workers' improved performance in the drill reflected changes at a deeper level of their consciousness. "The marching drill changed workers from deep in their consciousness," a Korean manager said in a managerial meeting memo. "Now they march in concert *even without* our close supervision" (emphasis by the manager). The managers believed that the change in the workers' consciousness was critical in labor management because it would facilitate their labor supervision. "We can't watch every worker 24 hours a day," another Korean manager said in the same meeting; "we have to train the workers to do their jobs even without our on-site surveillance." The Korean managers believed that the deeper-level change in the workers' consciousness would make them react to management's requirements more voluntarily and thus reduce the need for costly on-site labor supervision.[9]

Revamping the training program of the newly hired Han-Chinese workers was management's next method for changing the workers' consciousness. Management set up the original training program in the spring of 1994, modeled after the program of the Korean mother factory. In the two-week training program, new workers had to attend a four-hour class in the morning and do some menial jobs in the afternoon. In the morning class, Korean-Chinese instructors taught the workers the factory regulations and the general work procedures. In the afternoon, the instructors had new workers clean the workshop and do simple, menial labor such as dumping trash or sorting out materials in the warehouse. Printed on rough paper, a twenty-five page manual entitled *Workshop Manual for New Workers* summarized what management believed the

TABLE 4-2. Outline of the *Workshop Manual for New Workers*

Part	Title	Content
I-1	General Principles	Honesty in work, Completion of work, Observation of order
I-2	Work Principles	Nine Essential Principles (Obey orders, Keep silence, Work honestly, Keep work position, Keep workshop clean, Protect tools, Report correctly, Move quickly, Make no errors) Nine Activities Not-allowed (Defiance, Chatting, Laziness, Absence, Dirtiness, Stealing, Wrong reports, Distraction, Nonobservance of formalities)
I-3	Thought Principles	Information on the labor contract, Contract period, Work days, Wage system, Incentive wage system, Absence restrictions, Working holidays, Leaves of absence, Conditions of warning and layoffs [Punishment process], Indemnity responsibility, etc.
I-4	Shop-Floor Principles during Work Hours	Maintaining machine and tools, Proper behavior during workshop entrance, Working and leaving times, Caring for work uniforms, Proper hand and hair care, etc.
I-5	Dormitory Principles	Duties of room forewomen, Rules for cleaning floor and maintenance, Rules for using lavatories, Proper behavior in corridors and rooms, Penalties for violating rules, Confiscation of personal electric devices, etc.
I-6	Factory Canteen Regulations	Rules for queuing, Proper dining behavior, Rules for returning leftover food, Rules for canteen supervisors, etc.
I-7	Factory Lavatory Regulations	Rules for maintenance, Responsibility for reporting problems, Time limit for each use
I-8	Reward and Punishment Principles	Reward classes and selection principles, Punishment procedures and layoff conditions
II	Section Rules and Principles of Individual Sections	Regulations and work principles for individual work positions

Source: Author

newly hired workers should learn (Table 4-2). The first half of the manual enumerated general regulations such as work hours, labor contracts, work evaluations, and punishment rules. The latter half included detailed instructions for individual work positions, required techniques, standards of product inspection, and so on.

At first, management expected that the two-week training program would be enough for the new workers to understand the overall organization of the factory and learn the workshop regulations. However, it soon realized that the original program could not instill factory discipline deep into the workers' consciousness. The Korean managers thought that they found the reason in the program's overreliance on simple classroom lectures. A Korean executive at Nawon Korea said:

> We asked the Korean-Chinese interpreters to repeat the same lecture about factory regulations during the two-week training program. We also distributed regulation booklets to the newly hired workers to help them memorize the regulations. But, despite all this, the workers acted as if they had never heard of the regulations and tended to search for loopholes in our supervision. . . . Even though they heard the same lectures more than five times, it made no noticeable difference in their actual behavior on the shop floor.

After several meetings, management decided to incorporate a new element into the training program: a "writing exercise." In the revised training courses, management no longer distributed a printed manual to the new workers. Instead, it gave the workers blank notebooks and required them to write down every line of the factory's regulations in the notebooks. In the new training courses, the newly hired workers hurried to write down the regulations when their Korean-Chinese instructor finished his explanation about each heading of the regulations, which were written on large boards. In addition, management set up a qualifying exam about the factory regulations at the end of the training program and asked all new workers to take it. It announced that their exam score would determine who among the newly hired workers—now called "temporary trainees"—would remain in the factory as regular workers. With the changes in the program, management began to recruit more new workers than the actual number of vacant positions on the shop floor. That meant that about 20 percent of the newly recruited workers had to go back to their hometown if they got a poor exam score. The temporary trainees

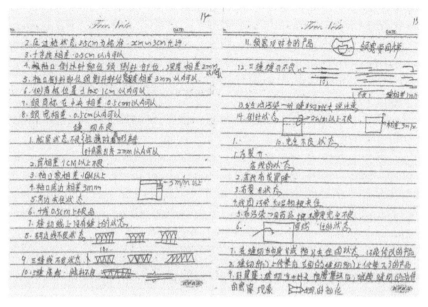

Figure 4-3. Notebook of a New Han-Chinese Worker.

realized that if they wanted to qualify as regular workers, they had to do their best in writing down the regulations, "like a copy machine," and memorize them as best as they could. Figure 4-3 presents an example of a notebook of a new worker who passed the qualifying exam and got a position on the shop floor.

The first group of Han-Chinese workers who went through the revised training program remembered that it greatly increased competition among them. A worker said that she had been really shocked to see several of her friends refuse to show their notebooks to other workers, even though they were close friends from the same village in Pingshan. "They were seriously worried," she said, "that their friends would get better exam scores and get jobs instead of them." Her testimony showed that the new training program spread the idea of competition among the workers, which was precisely what management intended. Management believed that the revamped program would change the workers' "peasant nature" that was tied to the rhythm of nature and thus lacked the idea of competition.

What management valued most, however, was not the increased competition among the workers. Instead, management praised the classroom scene of the trainees concentrating on writing down the factory regulations in their notebooks. The Korean managers found this fascinating because they believed that repeatedly writing down the regulations would have a certain disciplinary effect. A senior manager at Nawon Korea argued that the act of writing, when it was combined with a good writing posture, could ingrain discipline into new workers' bodies. His emphasis on good handwriting and its disciplinary effect reflected management's belief in the close relationship between repetitive body movement and changes in consciousness, as first expressed in the "marching drill." However, the Korean managers found the origin of the writing exercise not in their military experience but in the teachings of Confucius. The managers did not know its exact source but insisted that Confucius had mentioned a correlation between good handwriting with a high level of self-discipline and upright behavior:

> Every Korean knows that Confucius once taught his disciples that one's handwriting reflects his personality and degree of self-discipline. One can know what a person is by checking how he writes—both his handwriting and his writing posture. For this reason, new workers with good handwriting have a higher level of discipline than those who do not. This can explain why workers with good handwriting get higher scores in the qualifying exam. In contrast, many with bad handwriting probably will become troublemakers on the shop floor because they have a low level of self-discipline.

The Korean manager's belief in the disciplining effects of handwriting reflected a widespread idea in South Korea, an idea about handwriting and its relation with one's level of self-discipline. In South Korea it is widely believed that there is an essential relationship between one's proper behavior, correct speech, and good handwriting. This rather complex belief is summarized in the Korean phrase called *Shin-On-Seo-Pan*. *Shin* means one's appearance. A person with a fine presence is regarded as having a good personality. *On* means oratorical talent. A person whose words have clear logic receives high credit. *Seo* refers to handwriting. If one's handwriting is excellent, one is considered as having a high level of self-discipline and a noble personality. Finally, *Pan* means judgment. Without good judgment, one cannot be considered a fully developed individual. The management at Nawon referred to *Seo* to justify the new training program and its evaluation standards.[10]

The Korean managers' individual experience with the disciplinary effect of handwriting increased their confidence in the effectiveness of the "writing exercise." As school students, they participated in their schools' annual writing competitions. Many schools in South Korea organize such competitions because they believe in the disciplinary effects of the repeated practice of writing (for example, Daegu Metropolitan Office of Education, 2004). The managers agreed that the practice had such an effect. They remembered that the students who had won the grand prize at the competitions usually had been renowned for their good conduct and high exam scores. They also argued that, after practicing handwriting for quite a long time, they often had felt some degree of change in their mind and behavior. Thus management had every expectation that the writing exercise at Nawon would increase the Han-Chinese trainees' level of self-discipline and expedite their transformation into disciplined industrial workers.

Toilet cleaning was another new element of the revamped training program. In introducing the practice, management ordered every trainee to clean the workers' lavatories, the "most unwanted place" in the factory. In fact, assigning drudgery to newly hired workers has been a widespread practice in many workplaces. In the Western tradition of apprenticeship training, artisans impose simple and demanding tasks on apprentices (Herzfeld 2003). This is a form of a passage rite, and through it apprentices gradually come to accept their status at the bottom of the hierarchy (Bateson 1958 [1936]; van Gennep 1961). The practice of toilet cleaning at Nawon had a similar disciplining effect in that it confirmed the power of a management that could impose the demeaning practice on the workers.

The practice of toilet cleaning, however, had a more recent origin. First, the practice originated from worker training programs in Japan. Popular in large Japanese corporations until the 1980s, the training program assumed a mutual transformation of body and mind. According to this assumption, people can feel a sense of cleaning their own mind by doing arduous tasks such as long-distance running, taking cold showers, and, sometimes, cleaning toilets (Kondo 1990). By imposing unusual conditions on new workers, such programs can be expected to transform their minds and adjust them to accept particular company orientations (Rohlen 1974). Many South Korean corporations incorporated this Japanese idea into their initiation programs because they were influenced by the Japanese colonial domination of Korea (1910–1945) and, later, by the Japanese multinational corporations in South Korea (Chun 2003; Moon 2005). The old disciplinary method of Japanese origin unexpectedly appeared at Nawon where Korean managers struggled to transform rural Han-Chinese women into industrial workers.

The Korean managers said that toilet cleaning had an "ultimate" effect of transforming the minds of those who did this menial job because it cleaned and made empty their mind just like a well-cleaned toilet. The repetitive job of toilet cleaning, they thought, would contribute to management's labor discipline because it was easier to train those who had a clean and empty mind. The managers firmly believed in the disciplinary effect of toilet cleaning also because they had experienced the effect as newly hired workers long ago. Based on their personal experience, the managers insisted that the Han-Chinese trainees should undertake the arduous job of toilet cleaning as the first step in being changed into model industrial workers.

CONCLUSION: A LOCAL VERSION OF GLOBALIZATION

At the beginning of Nawon's operations in China, the Korean management declared that its factory operations should be based on "modern" and "universal" production technologies and managerial techniques (Management of Nawon 1994). The Korean managers thought they could apply "universal" managerial techniques to the workshop in China because they believed in the wide applicability of those techniques. The Han-Chinese workers' persistent resistance, however, proved that management's belief in their applicability was a mere illusion. Acknowledging the limits of universal labor-controlling methods, management found alternatives in its own knowledge of labor discipline in South Korea. This knowledge was a complex combination of the highly authoritarian South Korean work culture, a unique interpretation of Confucianism, and the historical Japanese influence on South Korean corporations.

Management's collective misrecognition of the Han-Chinese workers also played a key role in its decision to introduce the new, Korean methods of labor discipline. The Korean managers who supervised Chinese workers for the first time faced the unavoidable but daunting task of discovering the specific characteristics of the workers. The managers, however, found this extremely difficult. As expatriate managers of a medium-sized garment factory, they had neither the time nor the resources that would allow them to get a good understanding of the workers. Most of all, the incessant demand of the global garment market to set up a shop floor and quickly get it ready for production fundamentally impeded their understanding. Under the stressful situation of a multinational shop floor, they chose to understand the workers by referring to the frameworks that they were familiar with. When the Korean managers were unexpectedly challenged by a worker, they found the source of the challenge in China's radical Communism. This was a complete misrecognition, however, because the young Chinese workers on the shop floor had not experienced any of the radicalism during the Maoist period. The managers also assumed that the Han-Chinese workers at Nawon had the characteristics of "country bumpkins," referring to their memory of Korean women workers and South Korean villages of the past. This misrecognition had crucial implications for labor control at Nawon because it justified the application of the disciplining methods that management considered suitable for the Chinese shop floor.

In short, the non-Western origin of the Nawon's management created a unique situation on the shop floor in China. Just like Western management, the Korean management assumed its superior status as the agent of advanced industrialism and the bearer of the modern managerial techniques. When management encountered resistance from Han-Chinese labor, however, it gradually applied its own managerial methods with South Korean origins. Management decreased its emphasis on "universal" principles and increasingly turned to its own "local" methods in its desperate search for effective methods of labor control. The creation of industrial workers at Nawon demonstrated that the seemingly "universal" design of its shop floor was deeply embedded in "local" memories and disciplining methods, which contributed to its distinctive methods of labor discipline.

FIVE

Korean Management in a Chinese Workshop

Economic Globalization and the Changing Factory Regime

THE CHANGING FACTORY REGIME AT NAWON

The ultimate task of management is to reduce uncertainty in production and ensure profitability (Burawoy 1985: 27). On the everyday shop floor, this entails keeping employees working efficiently with no disruption in the production process. What is important here is the political dimension of production, including management's strategic control of its relationship with labor and the workers' reaction to management's control. Disciplining labor, the main topic of the preceding chapter, is one of the key elements of a factory regime, that is, the political-economic methods of controlling labor-management relations, mitigating possibilities of labor unrest and maximizing production efficiency (Burawoy 1985: 87).

The concept of factory regime illuminates another key aspect of shop-floor management: its connectedness with forces outside the factory. The exact mode of a factory regime is not solely determined by the power relationship between labor and management on the shop floor. The circumstances of the labor and product market, government policies on labor and industry, and relations between the factory and local communities also affect the formation of a factory regime. The exact modes of a factory regime can be diverse because the determinants of a factory regime differ from one locale to another. For example, a despotic factory regime could prevail where workers do not have the protection of resources such as unemployment insurance and labor unions, and thus solely depend on their jobs for survival. The workers' heavy dependence on their jobs greatly enhances management's authority, allowing it to control workers through despotic means such as threats of dismissal and imposing heavy penalties on workers who protest (for example, Chan 2001; Pun 2004). A hegemonic regime could emerge when management tries to secure its employees' "voluntary" consent to work, while resorting less to coercive measures of labor mobilization such as hefty fines and threats of dismissals. Such a regime is common when the government intervenes in factory management by implementing policies such as social welfare legislation to protect workers' interests (Burawoy 1985: 126). Management may also adopt less coercive measures of labor control and increase corporate benefits for its employees when a brisk market creates a demand for labor that is greater than the actual supply (for example, Jang 2009; Kessler 2007).

On the Nawon shop floor, the initial factory regime was highly authoritarian. During Nawon's first three years of operation (1994–1996), the factory regime, characterized by the South Koreans' monopoly of shop-floor authority, had clear and distinct features. During that time, management required that every employee, both Korean-Chinese and Han-Chinese, report to and get consent from the Korean managers about every issue on the shop floor. This highly authoritarian characteristic originated from the South Korean work culture, featuring top-down and military-like elements such as collective punishment and workers' deference to management (Chun 2003; Janelli and Janelli 1993: Moon 2005). The Nawon management's view of the Han-Chinese workers also contributed to creating the authoritarian factory regime. The Korean managers at Nawon defined their role as all-powerful instructors who discipline "backward" Han-Chinese workers.

The authoritarian factory regime was not immune to changes outside the factory, especially to the unpredictability of the garment industry. The unpredictability is caused by weather and seasonal changes, the just-in-time system, whimsical consumer tastes, and buyers' "price squeezing."[1] Many employees at Nawon marked their calendar with two alternating seasons that they called the high-order and low-order seasons. During the high-order season, workers on the shop floor were required to put in a lot of overtime to fulfill the high volume of orders. During the low-order season, however, overtime work became unusual because the factory received fewer orders. The buyers' way of placing orders caused the large difference between the two seasons. Because garments are a highly seasonal product, buyers tend to place their orders before a season begins. For the same reason, they require the contract factories to finish the order within a short time. This practice concentrates orders in seven or eight months of a year, creating the two alternating seasons (Green 1997: 139–42). The growing popularity of the just-in-time system has only widened the seasonal fluctuation in orders. At Nawon, management was always burdened with the fluctuation. During the high-order season, management often found it difficult to fulfill orders in time even with a lot of overtime. In contrast, during the low-order season, management struggled to find orders to run the production line and pay the worker's wages. The sharp contrast between the two seasons threatened the stability of the Nawon factory regime because both the excessive overtime (during the high-order season) and the reduction of wages (during the low-order season) tended to increase workers' grievances against management.

Since Nawon was located low on the global commodity chain of garment production, its factory regime was vulnerable to changing market demand (Appelbaum and Gereffi 1994: Cheng and Gereffi 1994). The management of the factory particularly suffered from the bad economic situation in Japan. Since the early 1990s, the Japanese retail garment market had been heavily affected by the long-term Japanese economic recession, which still persisted at the time of my fieldwork (Kawanishi 2001; Kuttner and Posen 2001; Porter et al. 2000). Because of the long-term recession, the demand for clothing stagnated and cheap products eroded the quality-clothing market (Buhyong Lee 2005; Kyeong Lee 2004). The weak consumer market also changed the business practices of Japanese retailers and buyers. Retailers suffering from shrinking profit margins preferred buyers who could fulfill small orders in a faster and cheaper way. Responding to the demand of retailers, buyers began to place more rush orders with contract factories while cutting the price they paid. At the level of the contract factories, the changes were translated into the need to cut production costs. Because Nawon was firmly integrated into the global production chain, the management of the factory had to compete with other garment factories to secure buyers' orders. The competition often became intense because the buyers squeezed the unit price of products. The buyers constantly changed their business relationships with contract factories, searching for the factory that offered the lowest per-unit cost. That only made Nawon's management desperately seek to reduce production costs by all means possible.

Management's imperative to reduce production costs brought changes to the factory regime. At Nawon, management responded to the buyers' price-squeezing by reducing labor costs. To achieve this goal, it first replaced the Korean managers with the Korean-Chinese interpreters. This change led to a new form of factory regime that relied on a collaborative relationship between the Korean managers and the Korean-Chinese interpreters on the shop floor. Later, to further cut labor costs, management decided to replace many Korean-Chinese staff on the shop floor with Han-Chinese workers. The creation of a Han-Chinese staff destabilized the factory regime that was based on the collaboration between Koreans and Korean-Chinese, which made management search for new managerial resources to maintain its control of the new Han-Chinese staff.

The transforming factory regime at Nawon also reveals how management took advantage of the specific political and economic conditions of the two countries, China and South Korea. On the shop floor, management made full use of the ethnic division between Korean-Chinese and Han-Chinese to consolidate its control over labor. Management gradually abandoned its initial preference for Korean-Chinese as it gained confidence in its ability to control the shop floor without their support. Instead of a Korean-Chinese staff, which was expensive, management increasingly relied on Han-Chinese staff on the shop floor. The industrial trainee program in South Korea highlights how management used the economic gap between the two countries to maintain its control of Han-Chinese workers.[2] The program reinforced the factory regime at Nawon by making the Han-Chinese workers dream of a better future guaranteed by "Korean money." To qualify for the program, many workers tried to be more obedient to management and gradually joined the group of pro-management workers. The new developments on the shop floor finally led to the creation of a charismatic-paternalist factory regime at Nawon, the end result of complex interactions between managerial patronage, the strong leadership of the Korean plant manager, and Han-Chinese workers' hope for a better future. My discussion begins with management's attempt to establish authoritarian control on the shop floor.

TABLE 5-1. Organization of Shop-Floor Staff, 1996

	Positions	Number	Ethnicity	Gender	Number
Cutting Section	Section leader	1	Korean	Male	7
	Senior cutter(s)	1	Korean		
	Assistant cutter(s)	5	Korean-Chinese		
Sewing Section	Section leader	1	Korean	Male	14
	Section deputy-leader	1	Korean	Female	
	Line leader(s)	2	Korean	Male: 1 Female: 1	
		10	Korean-Chinese	Male	
Finishing Section	Section leader	1	Korean	Male	3
	Section deputy leader(s)	2	Korean: 1 Korean-Chinese: 1	Male	
Mechanical Department	Senior technician(s)	1	Korean	Male	7
	Junior technician(s)	6	Korean-Chinese	Male	
Total					31

Source: Author

AN AUTHORITARIAN FACTORY REGIME AND THE POLITICS OF ETHNICITY

During the first three years from 1994 to 1996, the hierarchy on the shop floor was characterized by a South Korean monopoly of every top staff position. Company statistics in 1996 clearly show the near monopoly of shop-floor authority (see Table 5-1).

On the shop floor, Korean-Chinese interpreters occupied more than 70 percent of the staff positions. Because the Korean managers taught newly hired Han-Chinese workers the "A to Z" of making clothes, management needed more Korean-Chinese interpreters on the shop floor than in the office. As mentioned in Chapter Three, management considered Korean-Chinese more reliable as local assistants than Han-Chinese. In fact, during the first three years of its operation in China, management did not allow Han-Chinese to take any managerial staff positions. It worried that Han-Chinese staff might destabilize the shop floor by taking advantage of their "ethnic connection" with the large number of rank-and-file Han-Chinese workers.[3]

The Korean-Chinese dominance in numbers, however, was only superficial, because the Korean managers occupied all key staff positions on the shop floor. During the early period, Korean-Chinese did not have any position that required special knowledge of garment production, such as senior tailor and sewing-section leader. Instead, they took only supplementary positions such as tailor assistant and finishing section deputy leader. The seven Korean-Chinese line leaders in the sewing section may have been exceptions, because those positions normally came with the authority to make independent decisions on minor issues. The Korean-Chinese line leaders, however, were not allowed to pass any garment with minor defects along the production line without a Korean managers' personal inspection. Every single step of garment production, in other words, was under the powerful control of the Korean managerial staff on the shop floor.

Management's justification for its authoritarian control of the shop floor was the Korean-Chinese interpreters' lack of shop-floor experience. Unlike the Korean-Chinese in the factory office, the management argued, the Korean-Chinese on the shop floor had neither knowledge of garment production nor experience in shop-floor management. Therefore, the Korean managers insisted that they should teach the interpreters the know-how of shop-floor control as well as the technical knowledge of garment production. "We didn't give the Korean-Chinese employees any authority on the shop floor," a Korean executive at Nawon Korea said, "until we felt confident that they had enough knowledge and experience when it comes to shop-floor management."

The Korean-Chinese lack of shop-floor experience and technical knowledge, however, was not the only reason for the South Korean monopoly of shop-floor authority. The managers expressed their concern about ethnic tension between Han-Chinese and Korean-Chinese, which they thought originated from the deep-rooted Sino-centrism of Han-Chinese: "Han-Chinese are the dominant ethnic group in China," a senior Korean manager said, "and for that reason they tend to look down on other ethnic groups." According to him, the deep-rooted ethnic feeling of superiority made it hard for the Han-Chinese workers to accept the authority of the Korean-Chinese on the shop floor because it directly violated the Sino-centric order.[4] The Korean managers thought that if they had allowed the Korean-Chinese interpreters to exercise discretion in managing the Han-Chinese workers, the workers' dissatisfaction would have increased to a dangerous level. "The Han-Chinese workers would have felt it very hard to accept the Korean-Chinese authority," a senior Korean manager said, "if they had come to know the Korean-Chinese interpreters' lack of technical knowledge and managerial know-how." That was why, during the first year of Nawon's operation in China, its management ordered the Korean-Chinese staff on the shop floor to hide their ethnic identity and behave like Koreans. Considering deep-rooted Sino-centrism, management believed that this unusual managerial policy could reduce the possibility of ethnic conflict on the shop floor and help the Korean-Chinese to consolidate their control of the Han-Chinese workers.

The Korean managers' statements about ethnic animosity were not simply justifications for their monopoly of shop-floor authority. In daily operations on the shop floor, management observed the potential for labor unrest that might be ignited by the Korean-Chinese staff's control of the Han-Chinese workers. The Han-Chinese workers often expressed their resentment of the Korean-Chinese managerial staff. During my fieldwork in the factory, they often asserted that their Korean-Chinese supervisors did not deserve such a privileged status. "It's like a windfall," a Han-Chinese worker argued. "They're able to speak Korean because they happened to be born as Korean-Chinese." Management hoped that it could prevent the latent ethnic tension from escalating into open conflict by strictly limiting the Korean-Chinese to the role of simple assistants.

THE CREATION OF A COLLABORATIVE FACTORY REGIME

Promoting Korean-Chinese

In the spring of 1997, a faxed document from Nawon Korea signaled a change in the original structure of the factory regime. In the document, Nawon Korea announced that it would decrease the number of Korean managers on the shop floor as part of an effort to cut production costs. Its key buyers' demand to cut prices was behind the decision: "By all means possible, we have to meet their new price guidelines," Nawon Korea wrote in the document. "If not, we will lose our key buyers to other factories." The document also noted that decreasing the "pricey" Korean workforce would significantly reduce labor costs, and eventually help Nawon to survive the fierce price competition with other garment factories. According to a company financial report, the average monthly wage of a Korean-Chinese interpreter on the shop floor was only 1,470 yuan, while that of a Korean manager was 16,666 yuan (Management of Nawon 2002). In the same document, Nawon Korea also made it clear that reducing the number of Korean managers should be a long-term goal that eventually would leave only a few Korean managers on the shop floor.

Shortly after an initial announcement of layoffs, Nawon Korea informed Nawon that it had decided to dismiss four out of the nine expatriate Korean managers on the shop floor. The decision was a severe blow to the existing factory regime that depended on the Korean monopoly of shop-floor authority. It was perfectly clear to the management of Nawon that the remaining five managers could not handle all the daily inquiries from the intermediary Korean-Chinese managerial staff. Management had no choice but to make changes to the existing hierarchical structure of the shop floor.

Following Nawon Korea's notice, the management at Nawon announced that it would transfer part of its managerial authority to the Korean-Chinese interpreters. With the reduced number of Korean managerial staff, management could no longer maintain the factory regime based on the Korean managers' near monopoly of shop-floor authority. In fact, the Korean managers at Nawon initially did not welcome the change because they were worried that the transfer of authority would increase the Han-Chinese workers' ethnic grievance against the Korean-Chinese interpreters. The managers, however, eventually concluded that, for Nawon to survive in the face of increasingly tough competition with other garment factories, the layoff was inevitable. They believed that with the recent improvements in the methods of labor control and discipline, they would be able to control the shop floor even with a reduced number of Koreans. "We knew that the decision [of the transfer of authority] was more or less hasty," a Korean manager recalled, "but we also believed that we had gained enough ability and local knowledge to handle the new situation." As analyzed in Chapter Four, management's increased know-how in controlling local Chinese labor further lessened its unease about the possible negative effects of the change.

The changed composition of the shop-floor managerial staff demonstrates the partial transfer of authority to the Korean-Chinese interpreters (see Table 5-2). There was no change in the number of the interpreters on the shop floor (twenty-two). The promotion of Korean-Chinese to key staff positions, however, reflected their enhanced authority on the shop floor. Although Koreans still held every section-leader position, Korean-Chinese now occupied several key positions such as senior tailor, junior technician, and line leader of the sewing section.

The promotion of Korean-Chinese in early 1997 was not a nominal change in their positions. It came with a real transfer of authority once monopolized by Koreans. Management taught the Korean-Chinese some high-level skills of garment production, such as making pattern templates and programming embroidery machines. The two senior tailor positions in the cutting section highlighted the transfer of authority from Koreans to Korean-Chinese. Even under the highly standardized system of industrial garment production, the job of senior tailor still requires a high level of individual skills. In particular, a tailor's ability to make pattern templates identical to the specifications is the most valued individual skill. This skill marks the first and the most important process in garment production, because any difference between the templates and the specifications will lead to high defect rates and eventually result in buyers' making claims for losses.[5] Before the transfer, the Korean managers regarded template-making skills as one of the key sources of their authority and did not allow the Korean-Chinese interpreters in the cutting section to acquire it. A senior Korean manager at Nawon Korea recognized the power potential of tailoring skills because he had worked as a senior tailor at Nawon:

> At first, the Korean-Chinese assistants thought that they could easily fig-ure out how to make [sample] templates. However, whenever they made templates by themselves, they found that they could never make theirs exactly match the specifications. Of course not! To acquire top-level tai-loring skills they would have to spend the same or even more time than

TABLE 5-2. Organization of Shop-Floor Staff, 1997

	Positions	Number	Ethnicity	Gender	Number
Cutting Section	Section leader	1	Korean	Male	
	Senior cutter(s)	2	Korean-		5
	Assistant cutter(s)	2	Chinese	Male	
Sewing Section	Section leader	1	Korean	Male	
	Section deputy-leader	1	Korean	Female	14
	Line leader(s)	12	Korean-Chinese	Male: 10 Female: 2	
Finishing Section	Section leader	1	Korean	Male	
	Section deputy leader(s)	2	Korean-Chinese	Male	11
	Group junior leader(s)	8	Han-Chinese	Female	
Mechanical Department	Senior technician	1	Korean	Male	
	Junior technician(s)	4	Korean-Chinese	Male	5
Total					35

Source: Author

> I did in learning the skill. In addition, they need a good mentor to teach them the skill. When they realized that they couldn't make their templates no better than clumsy copies, they even dared to ask me to teach them the skill. Why should I? I never taught them about the skill in any easy way.

By transferring the technique of making pattern templates, management made it clear that the Korean-Chinese interpreters had become full members of the shop-floor managerial staff. Although Koreans still held the key positions of section leader and senior technician, management gradually handed over important duties to Korean-Chinese. This followed the original plan of Nawon Korea that it would in the end reduce the Korean managers' role on the shop floor to the minimum, and leave them responsible for only the final check of each production procedure. In addition to the transfer of authority, management gave new benefits to the Korean-Chinese interpreters on the shop floor that it had previously offered only to the white-collar workers in the factory office. For example, management substantially increased the wages of the Korean-Chinese on the shop floor, to the same level of the white-collar workers in the office. Management also upgraded the amenities in the Korean-Chinese living quarters, another sign of the changing status of the Korean-Chinese in the workshop.

The Korean-Chinese interpreters on the shop floor quickly understood the meaning of their promotion. They knew that their new positions with real authority would raise their status over that of the Han-Chinese workers. For that reason, they tried hard to secure the key positions such as senior tailor and senior technician. These positions were important to the Korean-Chinese interpreters because they symbolized high-level skills in garment production and machine maintenance, and thus would support their newly acquired authority. Whenever one of the positions became vacant, the Korean-Chinese interpreters promptly found another Korean-Chinese and recommended him to management. "We should never allow Han-Chinese to take over the positions," a Korean-Chinese interpreter said. "They're the symbols of our ethnic pride and superiority over the Han-Chinese in this factory."

The new authority of the Korean-Chinese on the shop floor greatly strengthened their ethnic consciousness. The Korean-Chinese staff frequently expressed their strong feeling of superiority to Han-Chinese. For example, when Han-Chinese workers made mistakes in production procedures, they often complained that the workers were slow, stupid, and insubordinate. Their frequent complaints reflected the tense situation of the workshop where the small group of Korean-Chinese interpreters had to supervise a large number of Han-Chinese workers. The high stress of labor supervision greatly enhanced Korean-Chinese ethnic consciousness that had originated from their memory of Han-Chinese ethnic discrimination against them. The interpreters argued that, as an ethnic minority, they had seen how the Han-Chinese took the social and economic initiative and assumed their central status in Chinese society. "Han-Chinese always despise Korean-Chinese," a Korean-Chinese interpreter said, "because they believe they're superior to us." The deep-rooted feeling of ethnic discrimination led the Korean-Chinese staff to view the Han-Chinese workers' reaction to their supervision with deep suspicion. They believed that the Han-Chinese workers had little reason to be obedient to them.

"It would be really hard for the workers to accept our control," another Korean-Chinese interpreter argued, "because we're minorities." With this suspicion, they tended to regard even the slightest sign of disruption on the floor as an expression of Han-Chinese insubordination and disloyalty.

The collaborative relationship between the Korean managers and the Korean-Chinese interpreters created a new type of factory regime on the shop floor. This regime was different from its predecessor because it was based not on the Korean managers' near monopoly of shop-floor authority but on authority shared between the Koreans and the Korean-Chinese. With the reduced number of Korean managerial staff, it was inevitable that management would allow the Korean-Chinese interpreters to participate in managing the shop floor. The term "collaboration," however, should be used with some reservation. It was apparent that, under the new factory regime, the Korean-Chinese interpreters had more room to make decisions. They felt this was a real change from the previous structure of shop-floor management under which they had to consult Korean managers about every workshop matter. Under the new regime, however, the Korean-Chinese interpreters still had to be very cautious so as not to infringe on the authority of the Korean managers. The interpreters tried to avoid even the slightest chance of confrontation with the Korean managers because they were worried that would give management a bad impression of them and might result in their loss of management's favor. The collaborative relationship between the Korean managers and the Korean-Chinese interpreters remained hierarchal inasmuch as the interpreters could exercise authority to the extent that they recognized management's ultimate authority.

POLITICAL INACTION OF THE HAN-CHINESE WORKERS

The making of the "Korean dream"

The promotion of the Korean-Chinese in early 1997 also had a negative effect on management's control of labor. The promotion increased the Han-Chinese workers' dissatisfaction with management because it included no Han-Chinese. Actually, there were some nominal changes in favor of the Han-Chinese. With the Korean-Chinese promotion, management also promoted some Han-Chinese workers to group leader positions in the finishing section, positions that were newly created at the time (Table 5-2). Few Han-Chinese workers, however, thought of this as a real change. Unlike the Korean-Chinese staff, the group leaders had no real authority to make their own decisions. Management ordered them to consult their Korean-Chinese superiors about any problem in production procedures. It believed that it was too early to give authority to the Han-Chinese: "If we had promoted Han-Chinese workers at the same time as the Korean-Chinese promotion," a senior Korean manager said, "it would have weakened the Korean-Chinese authority and eventually created tensions and conflicts between the two groups." Management thought that it should not promote Han-Chinese until the new factory regime based on the collaborative relationship between Korean management and Korean-Chinese interpreters became stable. Management's lingering concern about Han-Chinese ethnic animosity toward Korean-Chinese played a key role in the decision.[6]

At first, the Han-Chinese workers did not directly express their discontent with the promotion of the Korean-Chinese. Managerial memos at that time showed that there was not much change in product defect rates and the number of worker disputes. This implied that the Han-Chinese workers initially accepted the enhanced authority of the Korean-Chinese staff. "When the Korean-Chinese got the new authority," a senior Han-Chinese worker remembered, "we instantly realized that they became a real part of management." The Han-Chinese workers believed that they now had to obey the commands of the Korean-Chinese interpreters because they assumed the same authority as the former Korean staff, including the power to punish wrongdoings in the workshop.

It did not take a long time, however, for management to notice the Han-Chinese workers' growing discontent with their Korean-Chinese supervisors. Management was primarily concerned about the growing number of complaints from the machine operators in the sewing section, the most important workforce on the shop floor. Many operators felt that the recent promotion was totally unfair because they believed they had more skills and know-how in garment production than the Korean-Chinese interpreters. They also thought that the interpreters got their authority thanks to their "flattery" of the Korean managers. "While we were doing the endless stitching on the dusty shop floor," a line leader of the sewing section argued, "the Korean-Chinese giggled with the Koreans." Around late summer of 1997, management felt a great deal of pressure to check the Han-Chinese workers' growing discontent. During the summer, managerial meeting memos wrote about "little events" related to the Han-Chinese workers' growing discontent. One of the memos reported that, in the dark street outside the factory, some "unknown numbers" of the Han-Chinese workers fled after taunting the Korean-Chinese staff at a distance. On the shop floor, Han-Chinese workers still did not show any open defiance of their Korean-Chinese supervisors. However, the "little events" outside the factory clearly indicated their growing discontent with the Korean-Chinese staff.

Management could not find an easy solution to the growing discontent. Going back to the previous authoritarian factory regime might have been the best option, because it would scale back the authority of the Korean-Chinese staff and thus get rid of the source of the Han-Chinese workers' discontent. Management was not able to choose that option, however, because Nawon Korea made it very clear that it would never increase the number of Korean staff again. Finally, in a joint meeting of all the Korean managers at Nawon and Nawon Korea, an executive of Nawon Korea proposed an industrial trainee program as a solution to the Han-Chinese workers' growing discontent. According to the initial plan for the program, Nawon Korea expected that the program would decrease the workers' discontent by giving selected workers "not only higher wages . . . but also the rare chance to experience the better [standard of] living and culture of Korea." In the same document, Nawon Korea promised that the wages of an industrial trainee would be about 60 percent of what Korean employees got in the mother factory. That would be about three times more than that of the workers at Nawon. Nawon Korea expected that a program with such "exceptional benefits" would make the Han-Chinese workers more obedient, or, at least less defiant, because it would certainly create a lot of competition among workers to get the limited positions.[7]

For management, the industrial trainee program had the extra advantage of reducing the production costs of the mother factory in South Korea. In late July 1997, Nawon Korea completed the automation of the production lines of the mother factory to increase profit margins. The automation, however, could not completely remove all human labor because garment production, by its nature, always requires a certain involvement of human hands in the production procedures (Blumenberg and Ong 1994; Hill 1994). Nawon Korea was afraid that hiring expensive South Korean workers would only reduce the advantages created by the automation. Nawon Korea hoped to significantly reduce labor costs by bringing in "dirt-cheap" Chinese workers as industrial trainees.[8]

In an internal document titled "Selection Criteria for Industrial Trainees," Nawon Korea stated that all of the incoming industrial trainees should be women and should be in the sewing section. In addition, it made it clear that workers with longer careers at Nawon be given priority in getting the chance to work in Korea. The three criteria reveal what Nawon Korea intended to get from the program. The first criterion reflected management's belief that women workers were much easier to control than male workers. The Korean managers of Nawon Korea and Nawon shared a strong belief that male workers, by their nature, were more inclined to engage in disruptive behavior such as face-to-face confrontations and strikes. The second criterion reflected management's preference for skilled labor. Bringing skilled Han-Chinese workers to the mother factory would shorten the time needed to retrain the workers for the new workshop situation in Korea. Inviting skilled labor of Nawon would also facilitate the transfer of the "modern" manufacturing techniques of Korea to Nawon. After the two-year industrial trainee program in the mother factory, they thought, the trainees would contribute to improving product quality in the branch factory. Finally, Nawon Korea included the last criterion to retain skilled workers at Nawon. The number of trainees, twenty-two, was quite small considering the large number of machine operators in the sewing section. Because of the small number of trainees, workers had to wait for two to five years to get a chance to go to Korea. Management anticipated that the long waiting list would lower turnover rates in the sewing section and help the company retain the workers most crucial in garment production.

The Korean managers at Nawon, however, felt it hard to accept the second criterion. They believed that Nawon Korea's plan to exclude the cutting and the finishing sections from the program would only aggravate the workers' discontent in those sections. After discussions, Nawon Korea acknowledged the potential risk of the original plan and agreed to include eight workers from the two sections. However, even with the revised program, Nawon Korea still maintained its skilled-worker-first principle. As Table 5-3 shows, Nawon Korea insisted that industrial trainees from the

TABLE 5-3. Assignment Plan of Industrial Trainees, 1997

Section	Positions	Number
Cutting section	Cutter	2
	Counter	1
Sewing section	Operator	22
Finishing section	Inspector	2
	Ironing worker	3
Total		30

Source: Author

two sections should come from positions such as cutters, inspectors, and ironers, all of which entail at least a small bit of skill.

At the beginning, management thought that it would be difficult to select trainees because many Han-Chinese workers would apply for the small number of positions. "Just think about the huge wage difference between the mother factory and Nawon," a senior Korean manager said. "We expected the big Korean money would attract many workers."[9] Contrary to their expectations, however, the actual number of applicants was only 32, slightly more than the number of open positions. Managers at Nawon realized that many workers had not applied because they feared life in an unknown country. Several workers said that they had intended to apply but eventually could not, because their parents did not like the idea of them "going abroad." In the end, management sent to Korea only twenty workers who met the selection criteria. They did not have enough time to go through another round of application procedures.

It did not take long, however, for management to see changes in the Han-Chinese workers' attitude toward the trainee program. Their initial reluctance dramatically gave way to great enthusiasm after the early return of four trainees to China in 1998. The four trainees wanted to terminate their traineeship early because they could not adjust to the new living environment of the mother factory, especially the "spicy Korean food." After a short break in their hometowns, the four ex-trainees resumed their jobs at Nawon. Management wanted to retain the workers because they had acquired some degree of the advanced skills from their job experience in the mother factory.

Shortly after they resumed their jobs, the four former trainees and their life in South Korea became hot topics of conversation among the Han-Chinese workers. For many of them, this was the very first time to see people who had lived in a foreign country for such a long period. In fact, none of the workers had ever traveled overseas. The ex-trainees often talked about warm showers, well-heated dormitory rooms, "exotic" Korean food, and occasional sightseeing in South Korean cities and tourist attractions. Somewhat exaggerated, the stories caused the Han-Chinese workers at Nawon to dream about the better living and working conditions in South Korea, which sharply contrasted with the poor conditions at Nawon. The stories of the former trainees became so popular that, even at the time of my fieldwork in 2003, many of the senior workers still remembered what the four ex-trainees had talked about.

However, what most impressed the Han-Chinese workers was not the fancy part of the stories. The workers were literally shocked and deeply impressed by the large amount of money that the trainees had brought from Korea. A senior Han-Chinese worker said:

> 19,000 yuan for only one year's work! At Nawon, I just earned 8,000 for the same period. They earned such a lot even though they seldom worked overtime. In South Korea, they went to the factory at 8:30 a.m. and came back to their dormitory at 5:30 p.m. No more overtime, just relaxation! While they were idling in the warm dorm rooms in Korea, here we had to work overtime until 11 p.m. . . . After much of the drudgery on the shop floor, I just earned such a small amount of money! How could they make such big money while working so little?[10]

The workers could not exactly understand what made for such a huge wage difference between South Korea and China. However, they clearly noted how the "Korean money" changed their fellow workers' lives. The story of Xuemei, who had been to South Korea as one of the first group of industrial trainees, was the most popular example of the "Korean dream." She easily got the chance to be in the first group of trainees thanks to her position as a machine operator and the small number of applicants. After the full two-year trainee program in South Korea, she came back to Nawon with 40,000 yuan. Later, she married a local resident of Qingdao, a junior manager of a dye factory near Nawon. In addition to her newly purchased home in a brand-new apartment complex, she gained permanent residence status through her husband's good connections to an official of the municipal government. Many workers believed that, without her Korean money, she could not have changed her fate as a "small-peasant woman." The workers became very eager to go to South Korea as they saw how the trainee program and Korean money brought dramatic changes to their fellow workers.

The industrial trainee program contributed to management's control of labor because it reduced the Han-Chinese workers' discontent and created a pro-management group among them. As the program gained popularity, workers began to compete with one another for the limited number of trainee positions. The competition intensified when the workers saw the long and growing waiting list of the workers qualified for the trainee positions.[11] Some workers began to think that they could increase their chances of going to Korea earlier if they demonstrated good work performance. "Everyone believed that the trainee program would change one's fortune," a senior worker remembered. "That's why many became determined to do everything that they could to please management."

Management was very satisfied that most of the pro-management workers came from the sewing section. The machine operators had most resented the promotion of the Korean-Chinese. Their discontent might have grown into a serious threat to management because they were the largest and the most important workforce on the shop floor. Now the operators believed that it made more sense to cooperate with management because they received the largest quotas of the highly coveted trainee positions. "It didn't matter whether they were Koreans or Korean-Chinese," a machine operator said. "They made records of my work performance and reported them to management." The Han-Chinese workers' changed attitude toward the Korean-Chinese staff was reflected in their improved work performance. The changes among the sewing-section workers indicated that management had secured its authority on the shop floor, which had been threatened by the Han-Chinese workers' growing discontent with the promotion of the Korean-Chinese. This achievement made management more confident about its ability to control the Han-Chinese workers. "Insofar as there was a chance to go to Korea," a Korean executive of Nawon Korea argued, "Han-Chinese workers would try hard to behave like 'model workers' instead of making useless complaints about the management."[12]

Emerging schisms among the Han-Chinese workers

The industrial trainee program further contributed to management's labor control by unexpectedly creating a new schism among the Han-Chinese workers. As the program continued, several workers in the cutting and the finishing sections began to express their dissatisfaction with the workers in the sewing section. At the center of the discontent was the growing number of ex-trainees in the sewing section. Since the return of the first group of trainees from Korea, rumors about the close relationship between ex-trainees (many of whom were in the sewing section) and the Korean managers had spread on the shop floor. As the number of ex-trainees increased, it became a common scene on the shop floor that the ex-trainees had brief conversations with the Korean managers in Korean. Occasionally, the ex-trainees used simple Korean expressions such as *"Nae* [Yes]," *"Aniyo* [No]," *"Araseoyo* [I got it]" to assure the managers that they understood their instructions. Using the simple Korean expressions that they had learned in South Korea, the ex-trainees might have tried to establish and maintain close relationships with the Korean managers and show off their Korean to other workers. The workers in the cutting and the finishing sections, however, viewed such behavior as unnecessary flattery or, even worse, "flirting." They suspected that the ex-trainees tried to get something extra from the managers by using their shallow knowledge of Korean.

At first, the trainee program increased the non-sewing-section workers' discontent with management because it only gave very small quotas to the two sections. "Just five positions to our section!" a worker in the finishing section complained. "I can't go to Korea even if I wait for eight years." The workers, however, knew very well that they had no power to change the program that heavily favored the sewing section. They thought that management was not much concerned about their discontent because it did not care much about the workers in the two sections, who only had low-level skills. Management, they believed, considered them more dispensable than those in the sewing section. "Management wouldn't care about us even if we leave the factory tomorrow," a worker in the cutting section said. "It's easy to find young girls who can do our simple jobs." The workers in the two sections concluded that it was futile to express their discontent with the trainee program. The acute feeling of powerlessness diverted their negative feeling to the lucky workers who had been to Korea.

The sewing-section workers' feeling of entitlement aggravated the non-sewing-section workers' discontent. The ex-trainees, mostly in the sewing section, thought that they were different from the workers who had never been to Korea. They often talked about their experience in the mother factory and how "Korean money" had changed their life. The practice of storytelling gradually made the sewing-section workers yearn for the bright future guaranteed by the trainee program. Their high expectation to join the trainee program developed into a feeling of difference. In the sewing section, even the workers who had not been to Korea thought that in the near future they would go to Korea and change their fate as "poor peasant girls" through "Korean money." The workers in the cutting and the finishing sections pointed out the "arrogant" attitudes of the sewing-section workers. According to them, when they were hired, there was no difference between them and those in the sewing section: "Everything was just pure luck," a worker in the finishing section argued. "They were country bumpkins just like us. They happened to be in the sewing section and happened to go to Korea. They have no right to look down on us."

In late February 2000, the growing inter-section antagonism finally exploded. It was in the middle of a high-order season and Han-Chinese workers had been working on all-night overtime for three consecutive days. Management was pushing them hard to finish a rush order that had to be shipped out the next day. While most workers were exhausted, the machine operators felt especially fatigued. The rush-ordered garments had different stitching patterns and it took extra time to finish them. The operators finally felt relieved when they saw no fabric left in the cutting section. That meant that they would finish their jobs in no more than three hours. They were disappointed, however, when the finishing section inspectors began to send defective garments back to the sewing section. The inspectors detected problems such as misaligned stitch lines and lost stitches in many of garments that the operators had just finished.

Fixing was quite a vexing job for the machine operators. It always disrupted their normal operations and extended their work hours. If their daily tasks included four different styles of garments, the operators had to change machine settings three times according to the different sewing specifications. For example, if their next task required stitches with different thicknesses, colors, or needle pitch, they had to change the thread and adjust the machine settings. Sometimes the changes needed the help of technicians from the mechanical department and that further slowed down the work pace and extended the machine operators' work hours. The machine operators felt fixing jobs highly stressful because most such jobs included multiple styles of garments and always came during the last few hours before an order was shipped.

Late that night in February 2000, the operators' initial feeling of disappointment about the returned garments soon changed into deep frustration. They realized that the number of defective garments was so large that they had to work even until the next morning. A senior Han-Chinese worker who worked as an operator that night still had a clear memory of the following event:

> We were extremely tired from the three-day all-night work. I saw several operators half asleep sitting in front of their machines. . . . We agreed that there were garments that could not pass the original criteria of quality check. However, if we had done our best to make every piece of garment perfect we could not have finished the order in time. The inspectors of the finishing section also knew this very well. They could have classified some of the defective garment as quality products if they had really cared about our difficult situation. To the contrary, they inspected the garments too strictly and returned many to us. . . . They *intentionally* kept us working much longer than what we had expected [emphasis by the interviewee].

Deeply frustrated with the sheer number of returned garments, an operator raised her hand and asked her Korean-Chinese line leader to come. Although she tried hard to explain to him that the finishing section workers "framed up" their section, it only infuriated the line leader. He did not care as much about the possibility of framing up as he did about the large number of rejected garments. "First, you should have done your job correctly!" he shouted at her and went back to his position. With the unsympathetic response from their line leader, the operators could not but continue with the fixing.

It was already past 3 a.m. when the operators heaved a sigh of relief when they had almost finished off the fixing job. If the inspectors of the finishing section had not returned garments as defective for a second time, they might have left the workshop. The sewing-section workers, however, finally ran out of patience when they saw the finishing-section counters again returning the garments that they just had sent to them. Changcui, who was one of the twelve sewing-section counters that night, remembered that the finishing section counters sent back almost half of the garments. "It was simply outrageous," she recalled, "that they returned so many garments. Usually they classified only about 5 percent of the once-returned garments as defective."

While the puzzled workers in the sewing section were trying to figure out what really went wrong to cause the mountain of returned garments, they heard a loud smashing sound from the end of their production line bordering on the finishing section. In the tense silence after the loud noise, they saw Haiyun, a sewing-section counter, fiercely staring at a finishing-section counter. It was she who made the loud noise by throwing her statistics record on a worktable of the finishing section. The Korean-Chinese line leaders promptly ran to Haiyun and took her out of the workshop. Management ordered that, as collective punishment for the disturbance, workers in the two sections would have to remain on the shop floor until 6 a.m. In addition, management announced that it would not pay for the overtime hours put in that night.

Management tried to prevent inter-section conflict by all means possible because it would seriously disturb normal production operations. Three days after the inter-section conflict, management announced its decision to punish every worker involved in the conflict. It imposed a one-hundred-yuan fine on all workers in leader positions of the two sections for failing to prevent the conflict. Haiyun, the sewing-section counter who directly caused the disruption, was hit with a hefty two-hundred-yuan penalty. A week later, the management at Nawon finally dismissed her upon Nawon Korea's strong request for a more severe punishment. Two days after management's notice of dismissal, she left the factory and none of her friends saw her off.

The unprecedented outbreak of inter-section conflict enhanced the sewing-section workers' feeling of difference from the workers in the other two sections. Before the event, their feeling of difference remained rather vague and was not expressed in any noticeable way. The confrontation between the two workers, however, made many workers in the sewing section believe that the workers in the other two sections had some kind of ill will against them. The ill will, several sewing-section workers argued, was close to jealousy that was created by management's preferential treatment of the sewing section. It was out of jealousy, they contended, that the inspectors of the finishing section returned such a large number of garments as defective and kept them working.

The sewing-section workers' changed view of the workers in the other two sections indicated a new schism emerging among the Han-Chinese workers. On the one hand, the workers in the cutting and the finishing sections developed their ill will against the sewing-section workers because they received management's preferential treatment. On the other hand, the sewing-section workers gradually changed into a pro-management group because they believed that their exclusive corporate benefits such as the high priority in the trainee program would guarantee them a better future. The sewing-section workers' pro-management turn significantly weakened solidarity among workers, because they were the largest group of workers on the shop floor and their jobs were most crucial to the normal operation of the workshop.

THE EMERGENCE OF A CHARISMATIC-PATERNALIST FACTORY REGIME

Creating a Han-Chinese managerial staff

The new factory regime based on the collaborative relationship between Koreans and Korean-Chinese had its own vulnerability. Just like the preceding factory regime, it was affected by changes in the global chain of garment production. Since the winter of 1999, Nawon Korea observed ever-growing competition among contract factories. Above all, a growing number of new Chinese factories intensified the competition by offering per-unit production costs lower than those of Nawon. "To maintain our business relationship with buyers," the executive director of Nawon Korea argued, "we should always keep our prices competitive, at least close to what is offered by the new Chinese factories." Again, Nawon Korea chose to reduce labor costs as a quick and relatively easy method to maintain its competitiveness. At this time, the reduction targeted not Korean managers but the Korean-Chinese staff on the shop floor. Nawon Korea justified the Korean-Chinese layoffs by the large wage difference between the Korean-Chinese and the Han-Chinese employees. According to an internal report on wage payments at that time, the average wage of a Korean-Chinese interpreter on the shop floor was almost three times larger than that of a Han-Chinese worker. The layoff plan, however, eventually changed the existing factory regime based on the collaboration between the Korean management and the Korean-Chinese interpreters, as management sought support from the Han-Chinese workers on the shop floor.

The factory regime was also internally vulnerable. From the very beginning, its stability largely depended on the Han-Chinese workers' support of the Korean-Chinese staff. The industrial trainee program seemed to secure crucial support when it created a group of pro-management Han-Chinese workers in the sewing section. However, the Han-Chinese workers' support of the Korean-Chinese staff was fundamentally weak because they did not deem authority wielded by the Korean-Chinese the same as that of the Korean managers. They thought that they would just endure the Korean-Chinese control since management backed the Korean-Chinese on the shop floor.

The collaborative factory regime became increasingly unstable as a growing number of Han-Chinese workers—most of whom were ex-trainees—expressed their disrespect for Korean-Chinese managerial staff. During the late spring and the early summer of 2000, several managerial memos reported subtle but negative changes in the Han-Chinese workers' attitudes toward their Korean-Chinese superiors. Their challenge of the authority of the Korean-Chinese did not take any form of direct confrontation that would only incur management's punishment. Instead, the Han-Chinese workers chose to gradually undermine the legitimacy of the Korean-Chinese order by means of official channels. On the shop floor, they asked detailed questions about the instructions given by their Korean-Chinese superiors to confirm whether the instructions were really relevant to resolving specific problems in the production procedures. For example, a Han-Chinese ex-trainee challenged her Korean-Chinese line leader by arguing that he intentionally allowed a bunch of imperfect garments to pass through the production line. She brought the case to the Korean managers and finally won the case as management decided that the garments should be returned to the sewing section for fixing.

Such a bold move against the authority of the Korean-Chinese was based on the Han-Chinese workers' growing confidence in their knowledge of and skill in garment production. The ex-trainees in particular firmly believed that they were sufficiently qualified for the intermediary managerial positions Korean-Chinese interpreters held. "After learning advanced skills in the mother factory in South Korea," an ex-trainee argued, "we felt that there was no more way for management to justify the Korean-Chinese monopoly." Some ex-trainees even argued that they had more professional qualifications for the managerial positions than their Korean-Chinese superiors because they had learned the most advanced production skills in Korea. The Han-Chinese challenge to the Korean-Chinese was an ironic result of the industrial trainee program: initially introduced to create pro-management Han-Chinese workers and consolidate the factory regime based on a collaboration between Koreans and Korean-Chinese, the program in the end undermined the regime.

The double-sided pressure from Nawon Korea and the Han-Chinese workers convinced management of the difficulty of maintaining the existing hierarchy on the shop floor. Management especially worried that the Han-Chinese workers' challenge to the Korean-Chinese staff would eventually destabilize the entire shop floor operation, because ex-trainees were at the center of the challenge. "They are the core of the skilled labor in our factory," a Korean manager said. "If we had let their discontent grow, it would have had a really bad impact on the entire operation of the workshop." At the same time, the managers felt it was very hard to challenge Nawon Korea's plan to reduce the number of Korean-Chinese managerial staff on the shop floor. It was not simply a matter of following the decisions of the headquarters. As expatriate managers who spent most of their time in China, they acutely felt the reality of intensifying competition with other garment factories. If they failed to reduce labor costs, other factories, with their low production costs, would soon have the edge over Nawon.

After several discussions with Nawon Korea, the management at Nawon finally complied with the plan to reduce the number of Korean-Chinese managerial staff on the shop floor. In late summer 2000, management announced it was replacing twelve Korean-Chinese line leaders of the sewing section with Han-Chinese workers. This replacement continued until the end of the year, by which time Han-Chinese finally accounted for almost 80 percent of the shop-floor managerial staff. The change left only five out of thirty-one staff positions held by Korean-Chinese. The creation of a Han-Chinese managerial staff, however, did not lead to an overall transfer of managerial authority from Korean-Chinese to Han-Chinese. Management maintained a certain power balance between the two ethnic groups by allowing Korean-Chinese to keep several key positions in the workshop, such as senior tailors and technicians.[13]

The changes in the personnel composition on the shop floor satisfied most Han-Chinese workers, particularly the Han-Chinese managerial staff, all of whom were ex-trainees. "I felt so happy with the promotion," Han-Chinese finishing section leader said, "because I didn't need to take orders from the Korean-Chinese any more!" What made them even more satisfied was management's decision to raise their monthly wage close to the level of that of the Korean-Chinese. This decision brought a noticeable change to their lives. With their wages more than double the average wage of the rank-and-file workers, the new Han-Chinese managerial staff could enjoy more comfortable living and occasional shopping and dining out in downtown Qingdao. Though less enthusiastic, the rank-and-file workers also agreed that the promotion of the Han-Chinese was a good decision. They expected that their new Han-Chinese superiors would be better than the Korean-Chinese ones. Several workers said that some Korean-Chinese staff were excessively strict because they used their commanding status to express their ethnic animosity against Han-Chinese. They even argued that the Han-Chinese staff would make good leaders because they spoke correct Chinese: "Sometimes it's hard to understand what Korean-Chinese say in Chinese," a Han-Chinese worker argued, "because they didn't learn Chinese as their mother language."

Management felt relieved to observe the positive effects of the Han-Chinese promotion. At first, management was afraid that the rapid increase in the number of Han-Chinese managerial staff might weaken its control of the shop floor. Several Korean managers who were in their mid- or late-fifties were skeptical about the obedience of the new Han-Chinese staff because they still worried about allegedly deep-rooted Han-Chinese defiance. In contrast, the new Han-Chinese staff expressed their overall satisfaction with the change, which brought them real authority on the shop floor and significantly increased wages. The rank-and-file workers' positive view of the Han-Chinese promotion was an extra bonus for management. It seemed apparent to management that the workers preferred being controlled by managerial staff with the same ethnicity.

The dream of "decent wages" and Han-Chinese workers' faith in management

The promotion of Han-Chinese in 2000 brought some visible changes to the shop floor. The new Han-Chinese staff began to attend the daily managerial meeting that had before been open only to the Korean managers and the Korean-Chinese managerial staff. The Han-Chinese participation in the meeting indicated that management now viewed them not as targets of its labor control but as assistants of the shop-floor management. However, management wondered whether it could really rely on the Han-Chinese staff to the same degree as it had on the Korean-Chinese interpreters. "All in all," a Korean manager argued, "they are Chinese. They could never be a part of the Korean nation." The Han-Chinese staff's inability to talk with Korean managers without the interpretation of Korean-Chinese confirmed management's belief in the hard-to-change ethnic difference. Management's deep-rooted suspicion of Han-Chinese caused it to maintain some of its discriminatory treatment of its Han-Chinese employees. Even after their promotion, for example, the Han-Chinese managerial staff continued to live in the factory dormitories with the rank-and-file workers. They lived under the same restrictions of nighttime curfew and the limited use of electric appliances in their rooms. The Han-Chinese staff's unchanged living conditions sharply contrasted with the benefits that management had given to the Korean-Chinese managerial staff, especially their relatively desirable living quarters.

Surprisingly, most of the Han-Chinese managerial staff did not care much about management's discriminatory treatment. Instead, many of them said that they were satisfied with their current jobs at Nawon because management had rarely failed to pay their wages on time. "As long as I can receive my wages on time," a group leader of the finishing section said, "I don't care about the small benefits." The idea of "wages first" was also widely shared by the rank-and-file workers. Just like the Han-Chinese staff, they were very concerned about the timing and amount of their monthly pay. The Han-Chinese workers' concern about their wages was clearly expressed in a common scene every payday. On paydays, many workers were busy calculating the exact amount of their forthcoming wages, referring to their handwritten memos of their overtime hours.

The deep concern about the on-time payment of wages explains why most Han-Chinese employees on the shop floor felt satisfied with management. Needless to say, earning a wage is the most important reason workers go to their workplaces every workday. At Nawon, however, there was something special in the Han-Chinese workers' concern about their wages. The workers often mentioned the on-time payment of "decent" wages as the main reason they worked in the factory. By the word "decent" the workers meant that their wages should exceed the basic wage at least by 30 percent. At Nawon, the Han-Chinese workers wages consisted of two parts, basic and overtime wages. The basic wage was fixed because it was calculated based on the workers' normal work hours (from 8 a.m. to 5 p.m.). The amount of overtime wage was calculated according to the number of work hours worked after 6 p.m. This of course meant that their actual wages varied according to the length of overtime.

The Han-Chinese workers' monthly pay showed a big difference between the low-order and the high-order seasons. According to the annual payroll statistics of the factory, the workers earned the largest portion of their annual income during the high-order seasons. In the factory, a worker's basic wage constituted less than 60 percent of her total income. She earned more than 40 percent of her annual wages from overtime, which accounted for only 25 percent of her total work hours. The difference came from the pay rate structure that applied a higher pay rate to overtime hours. Han-Chinese workers well understood the correlation between the length of overtime and the amount of their wages. If they had only worked regular hours, their wages would have been far less than the "decent" amount.

The wide fluctuation in wages also explains why the Han-Chinese workers regarded overtime as a necessary evil. They felt extremely tired after working overtime for three or four weeks. Several days of all-night overtime were the most difficult part. The workers believed that all-night overtime simply "ate up" their health because they had to work literally day and night with only two or three hours of rest a day. Whenever they felt extremely exhausted from the endless overtime, Han-Chinese workers said the following sentence as if it were a mantra—"The more overtime we do, the more money we make." The hardship of overtime would only be rewarded by the on-time payment of "decent" wages. Using the expression of Han-Chinese workers, money was their "blood."

Management was also concerned about the widely fluctuating wages because it believed that such a large fluctuation would undermine the stability of the workshop. During the high-order seasons, management received an overwhelming volume of orders, often exceeding the maximum production capacity of Nawon. During such times, the Korean managers often complained that they would not be able to fulfill orders on time even if they made the workers work all day and night. The excessive overtime made the workers extremely fatigued and sensitive. In contrast, during the low-order seasons, especially when Nawon Korea could not secure enough orders from its key buyers, management sometimes did not have enough work to keep all production lines operating. The low volume of orders not only led to less overtime and smaller wages but could also increase the worker's discontent with management. During the low-order seasons, the Korean managers at Nawon often tried to find subcontract orders from other garment factories or third-party buyers. They had to secure a certain volume of orders to pay their workers "decent" wages, which would prevent the workers' discontent from growing to an alarming level.

The managerial necessity to secure subcontract orders brought significant uncertainties to the factory's operations. First of all, there was no guarantee that management could secure enough subcontract orders. As the prefix "sub" implies, subcontract orders were not on the official documentation of the original contract between a factory and a buyer. The orders were created by the management of the original contract factory that unexpectedly received orders far in excess of its production capacity. Subcontract orders also came from factories that experienced problems in their workshop and thus could not fulfill their orders in time. In the two cases, the troubled management of the factory divided the original order and gave parts of the order to other factories: it would be much better for them to subcontract the order and complete it than to pay heavy penalties to buyers for incomplete orders. Because of the unofficial nature of these arrangements, however, there were virtually no official criteria for subcontract decisions. Instead, having close relationships with the management of other factories was often believed to be the key to getting subcontract orders.

The payroll statistics of Nawon showed that the management of the factory was good at getting subcontract orders. Despite some seasonal fluctuations in workers' wages, the wage difference between the high- and the low-order seasons was much smaller than that of other, nearby garment factories. The exceptional ability of management to secure subcontract orders gradually made the Han-Chinese workers trust management. Their trust became stronger as they observed that the management of nearby factories repeatedly failed to guarantee their workers a fair amount of wages. A Han-Chinese worker in the sewing section said:

> The management of nearby factories often fail to pay wages to their workers on time. Their wages are also lower than ours. You can never know how miserable workers feel if they can't get their money after they worked overtime day and night. . . . We're lucky to have management that gives us decent wages on time.

The stark difference in the feeling—the miserable feeling of the workers in nearby factories and the feeling of trust in management among the workers at Nawon—is one of the reasons why neighboring factories suffered from a series of labor disputes since the mid-1990s. At that time, Nawon did not experience any serious labor dispute such as a sit-in or absenteeism. In addition, the workers of neighboring factories had a higher turnover rate than those at Nawon, which also reflected the difference in the workers' feelings.

Referring to the workers' "trust" in management does not mean that it completely removed their uneasy feeling under the close labor supervision or their discontent with management's discriminatory treatment. Despite all of their ill feelings and discontent, however, the Han-Chinese workers at Nawon still believed that their management properly administered the factory. When they talked about the proper management of their factory, none of the workers mentioned their poor working conditions or discriminatory corporate benefits. Instead, they regarded the on-time payment of "decent" wages as the most important reason for staying at Nawon.

A charismatic-paternalist factory regime

Plant manager Bak was at the center of the Han-Chinese workers' belief in management. Bak had two contrasting characteristics. On the one hand, as a labor supervisor he was authoritarian. On the other hand, he made an effort to pay the workers' "decent" wages. At Nawon, he had played a key role in introducing powerful labor-controlling measures. For example, in 1994 he proposed that management put the plant manager's desk on the shop floor to resolve the persisting peeping problem.[14] When he became the plant manager of Nawon in 1996, he even required the Korean managers to stay in the workshop as long as they could. He made himself a model, spending most of his work hours on the shop floor. He also insisted on personally checking key manufacturing processes such as pattern-template making and product packaging. Whenever he found defective garments that had passed through the production lines, he instantly scolded the managerial staff and imposed fines on them. Because of his authoritarian management style Han-Chinese workers nicknamed him "The emperor of Nawon." Many Han-Chinese workers said that they even held their breath when they felt his watchful eyes on them.

However, the Han-Chinese workers did not always regard the plant manager as an authoritarian figure. Occasionally they said that he had a "caring" or "benevolent" personality hidden under his domineering appearance. The seemingly contradictory view of the plant manager arose from his exceptional ability to get a large volume of subcontract orders during the low-order seasons. He found the orders through his close connections with the management of other garment factories in Qingdao. He very well understood that subcontract decisions heavily depended on personal connections and trust among the managers of different factories. During the low-order seasons, he was busy phoning other factories and asking about subcontract orders. Sometimes he invited managers of other factories to private drinking sessions to facilitate the subcontracting process.

The role of plant manager Bak became crucial in integrating the Han-Chinese staff into the managerial body on the shop floor. Now with a reduced number of Korean-Chinese interpreters, management believed it should firmly integrate the new Han-Chinese staff into the existing managerial body on the shop floor. The task was particularly challenging because, since its first day of operations in China, management had regarded Han-Chinese employees as the objects of control, not as a part of management. The plant manager eased the integrating process because he won the Han-Chinese workers' trust. Many Han-Chinese workers at Nawon thought that the plant manager's extraordinary effort to secure subcontract orders was largely responsible for their "decent" wages. Though the plant manager was tough on workers in the workshop, many of them believed that his strict labor control would ultimately benefit the workers themselves. A finishing section work group leader said:

> Sometimes we wished he had been less strict with us. But if he had been really generous to us, our factory would have fallen into disorder and it

would've damaged his reputation as a plant manager . . . [and] it would have certainly undercut his ability to get subcontract orders.

The workers accepted his strict labor control as a sheer inevitability of factory life because "decent" wages were more important than anything else. "As long as the plant manager supervises our workshop, we can rest assured": this was a paraphrase of Mao Zedong's famous words that Han-Chinese workers often used. In the bitter political struggles during the 1970s, the "Great Helmsman" of China used the words to express his strong belief in one of the top party leaders.[15] The paraphrase nicely reflected how much they trusted the plant manager's ability to properly administer the factory and thus bring them "decent" wages.

Management's need to meet its payroll, however, cannot explain every aspect of Bak's effort to get subcontract orders. In general, management always needs a certain volume of orders to generate enough profits to pay wages and maintain the production facilities. However, the plant manager's effort to get subcontract orders was unusual. He always tried to secure orders that exceeded the amount required by management. Behind his unusual effort there was a deep-rooted paternalistic concern about the Han-Chinese workers. This sprang from his unique view of the workers, whom he considered having characteristics similar to those of the Korean women workers in his memory. In several meetings with me, Bak said that he very well understood what brought the young Chinese women to Nawon and made them work day and night:

> Many Han-Chinese workers endure the drudgery of factory jobs not only for their own sake but also for the good of their parents. They believe they should help their aging parents because, when they get married, they'll have to leave home and live apart from their parents.[16]

In an interview, Bak said that he strived to get a large volume of orders because he deeply sympathized with the Han-Chinese workers' "self-sacrificing" behavior. His "deep understanding," however, was not based on any actual knowledge of the Han-Chinese workers. As a high-ranking manager, he had no personal relationship with the workers. Although he spent much of his work time on the shop floor, his interactions with the workers, including the Han-Chinese managerial staff, remained formal. His belief in the effectiveness of strict labor control, his limited Chinese language, and his busy schedule kept him from knowing the personal background of individual workers.

Instead, Bak often said that, among the Han-Chinese workers at Nawon, he saw the images of Korean women workers whom he had met twenty to thirty years earlier at garment factories in South Korea. Ironically, it was this memory that justified the poor living conditions in the factory dormitories and the discriminatory policies against the Han-Chinese workers. In the same memory, however, the plant manager found the basis for his sympathy with the Han-Chinese workers. "The Han-Chinese workers in the factory are just like the Korean workers I knew," the plant manager declared, "who had saved much of their income to support their poor and aging parents."[17] The memory of Korean women workers in the past created his belief in the similarities between the two groups who, he thought, shared the same motivation to work: a sense of duty to the family.

There was a subtle and more personal reason behind the plant manager's unusual effort to get subcontract orders. At Nawon, other Korean managers also believed that Han-Chinese workers on the shop floor were somewhat similar to the Korean workers of the past. Their understanding, however, did not lead them to seek more subcontract orders. Bak was the only manager on the staff at Nawon who tried to find orders and pay Han-Chinese workers' "decent" wages. He once said that the Han-Chinese workers reminded him of his elder sister, who had worked as a machine operator at a garment factory in South Korea during the 1970s. He remembered that his sister "wasted" the prime of her youth at a sweatshop in Korea to support her family. Her sacrifice had a special meaning for him because she saved a large portion of her wages for his college education. In his eyes, the young Han-Chinese women workers at Nawon bore the same burden of supporting their families. Stories about several Han-Chinese workers' exceptional self-sacrifice confirmed his belief in the similarities between his sister and the workers at Nawon: "I was deeply moved," he once confessed, "when I heard about the story of a worker who gave her debit card to her brother. . . . She simply let him use her savings for his school expenses."

The plant manager's emotional view of the Han-Chinese workers created an important labor-controlling effect as it intertwined with the workers' subtle and personalized feelings about the manager. These feelings were based on their bittersweet memories of him. The memories, mostly related to his unexpected generosity, were gradually formulated through their everyday experience with him during their long-term employment at Nawon. A work group leader in the finishing section, for example, clearly remembered the unexpected moment when she had a personalized feeling about the manager:

> One day I miscalculated the stock of a rush ordered product and it eventually delayed the order shipment. When the Korean-Chinese section leader found out my mistake, he immediately reported it to the plant manager. . . . When the Korean-Chinese leader brought me to the office, I was already in tears fearing severe punishment. To my surprise, the plant manager asked me in a low and soft voice whether I knew what went wrong. When I barely said yes, he kept silent for a while. Not a single word at all! After the silence that I felt lasted forever, he sighed heavily and said that he would never forgive me again if I made the same mistake. He ordered me to return to the shop floor and correct the errors in the statistics. He didn't punish me for that mistake.

Han-Chinese workers who had received similar favors from him shared a sentiment that was close to the feeling of indebtedness. "I was really shocked," another worker with a similar experience said, "that he didn't punish me. His decision was really unexpected considering his strict managerial style." Because the favors were highly unexpected, the workers were even more impressed by his generosity and his "humane" side.

A surprising move of the plant manager strengthened the Han-Chinese workers' belief in his "humane" side. One of the foreign buyers suddenly informed Nawon Korea that he could not pay on time for the garments he had received due to unexpectedly weak sales. That in turn greatly delayed the payment of the wages of the Han-Chinese workers at Nawon because at that time Nawon Korea did not have enough cash to meet the payroll.

The Han-Chinese workers, who were deeply frustrated by the delayed payment, heard that the plant manager borrowed money from a local bank on his personal account. "We were really impressed by him," a Han-Chinese line leader said. "He paid our salary using his own money. . . . No other Korean manager would do that." The plant manager's occasional expressions of concern about the Han-Chinese workers gradually created a unique idea among the workers. Many thought that the plant manager had a certain "humane feeling" (C. *renqing*).[18] By those words, the workers meant he was compassionate and caring. Several Han-Chinese managerial staff even compared the plant manager with their fathers. "The plant manager rarely smiled at us," one of the managerial staff said, "just as my father back in the countryside rarely smiles." Although her father was strict with her and rarely expressed his "tender loving care," she said that he really cared for her deep in his heart. She argued that she knew that the plant manager cared for workers, even though he never said a single word to indicate that. Just as her father was tender and caring deep in his heart, she said, the plant manager looked after the workers with his unusual effort to get subcontract orders.

In the end, a new factory regime emerged from the interwoven memories and feelings of management and labor. This regime was charismatic-paternalist, with both the charismatic leadership of the plant manager and the subtle paternalistic relationships between the plant manager and the Han-Chinese workers. My definition of the emerging factory regime as charismatic follows the analysis of Max Weber (1968 [1956]: 241–45). Charismatic authority, according to Weber, relies on exceptional qualities of an individual who exercises strong leadership of a group or organization. The qualities include an individual's physical, intellectual, and moral prowess, which cause the members of a group to acknowledge his authority and thus follow his orders.[19] The new factory regime at Nawon heavily depended on the strong individual leadership of the plant manager, who had exceptional abilities to handle the tense situation in the workshop. His high competence in securing a large volume of subcontract orders in particular induced the Han-Chinese workers to acknowledge and follow his authoritarian style of labor control.

The patronizing role of management and the workers' view of management as caring added a paternalist nature to the factory regime. Paternalist relations between management and labor are not uncommon in multinational corporations. Ong (1987) analyzes how the Japanese managers of a multinational factory in Malaysia advocated the virtues of corporate familism and emphasized management's caring role of Malaysian women workers. Drori (2000) also shows that Jewish managers frequently used the rhetoric of a patriarchal household head to justify their authoritarian control of Arab women workers. Unlike these two cases in which management adopted overtly paternalistic language, the Korean management at Nawon did not use paternalist rhetoric in any explicit way. The plant manager never used the term "family" or "father" either in official meetings or on the everyday shop floor. "Our factory is just a sweatshop," the manager once said. "Who would believe that we're a family?" The paternalist nature of the factory regime was only subtly implied in the plant manager's attitude toward the Han-Chinese workers. The subtlety, however, does not mean that the effect of the paternalist control was less powerful at Nawon. In the factory, the subtle but multilayered emotions and memories between management and labor were inextricably intertwined with the material benefits of a "decent" wage and, as a result, strengthened the factory regime.

Furthermore, the factory regime at Nawon had a highly personalized character. As implied by the term "charismatic," the factory regime observed at Nawon heavily depended on an individual, plant manager Bak. Han-Chinese workers' casual comments on management well reflect its personalized character. When the workers talked about management, they often used "the plant manager" or "he" instead of the abstract expressions such as company or management. They used the latter expressions only to the Korean executives and visiting managers from Nawon Korea. Han-Chinese workers' individualized view of management contrasted with local employees' common view of their foreign supervisors as banal agents of corporate interest who lack individual personalities (for example, Ong 1987; Drori 2000; Fuller 2009).

Inside the established factory regime, however, the potential for a future crisis was already brewing. Ironically, the new factory regime had its own vulnerability created by one of its key elements that supported its whole structure: the charismatic leadership of the plant manager. As much as the factory regime relied on this charismatic individual, even a slight change in his circumstances could have a serious impact on its operation and structure. The crisis came in a really unexpected way, with Bak's sudden and mysterious death.

SIX

Pitfalls of Globalization

Local Connections and Their Impact on the Factory Regime

MULTINATIONAL CORPORATIONS AND GLOBAL-LOCAL COLLABORATION

Over time, the collaboration between foreign management and local government officials grew and influenced the factory regime at Nawon. Multinational corporations, as agents of global capitalism, are closely connected to local organizations of their current locations, such as local governments and surrounding communities. They especially need the local government's timely support to ensure smooth local operations, which eventually results in growing collaboration between the two. Ironically, the ever-increasing demands for greater flexibility and effectiveness in globalized production make it more critical for transnational capital to be successfully embedded in local spaces within a short time (Harvey 1982: 398–405; Sassen 2000: 218–19). The need for timely embedding prompts multinational corporations to seek local "partners" such as local government officials. The growing collaboration between the global and the local contradicts the common image of multinational corporations as highly mobile and dominant in their relations with the local people and community. According to the common image, multinational corporations, with their large-scale investment projects and great economic resources, bring significant changes to local communities as well as to the physical landscapes of a particular locale (Reich 2007). The actual situation in multinational corporations, however, in some ways departs from the image of free-flowing transnational capital and its overwhelming power over the local.

At Nawon, local-level Chinese government officials and the multinational management from South Korea developed a collaborative relationship as they found a shared interest in the uninterrupted operation of the factory. The Chinese government officials offered many benefits to Nawon to facilitate its relocation because they needed foreign capital investment to develop the local economy. These benefits included extra tax reductions, low electricity and water rates, loose customs control, connivance at labor-code violations, and, most importantly, recruitment services to provide cheap Chinese labor for the factory. Management responded to the benefits with some "special" gifts to the officials. The continuing exchange of benefits became the key element of the local officials' growing collaboration with the foreign management.

Under the constant pressure to cut production costs, the management of Nawon considered the local officials' services highly crucial to the success of its business in China. Provincial and county government officials, for example, organized the Korean managers' business trip to Pingshan County and helped them find cheap labor in its remote farming villages. Grassroots local officials provided a more direct service to management. Shortly after Nawon began its operations, the officials of nearby Fuyang village assumed the responsibility of supervising the Han-Chinese workers' living outside the factory. As mentioned in Chapter Two, the officials managed the factory dormitories and administered the nighttime curfew throughout dormitories. It is a common practice of local Chinese governments to join foreign management in controlling workers, especially when the workers are mostly nonresidents coming from the remote countryside (Chan 1998a; Ching Kwan Lee 1998a: 109–36; Pun 2004: 30). The joint labor control exercised by management and the village officials reveals a common tendency of multinational corporations to work with authoritarian local political regimes to secure uninterrupted production (Sen 2006: 145).

At Nawon, however, the term "collaboration" cannot explain every aspect of the relationship between management and local officials. Despite its reliance on local officials for the factory's operations, management kept a distance from the officials and limited their role in managing the factory. Management still had a deep suspicion of "backward" China. During most of the 1990s, management viewed China and its people as located at the early stages of economic and social development. The village officials were not exempt from this assumption. This deep-rooted conviction led to an unofficial managerial principle of "independent management" that strictly limited local officials' intervention in factory management. Under this principle, management only asked officials to supervise the Han-Chinese workers' dormitories, which were located *outside* the main factory premises.

Falling profits, the decreasing number of Korean and Korean-Chinese managerial staff, and deteriorating factory facilities, however, eventually led management to compromise the principle of independent management. Under the worsening conditions, management increased its reliance on the local officials' unofficial support, allowing them to strengthen their influence in the workshop. This inevitably created a new mechanism of labor control that operated through a network of local-level surveillance (Chan 1998a, 2001; Ching Kwan Lee 1998a). The local-level surveillance was powerful because it resorted to the unofficial alliance between the village officials and a local gang, called "the merger of the black and the white" in China (Yunxiang Yan 2003: 27). The triangular relationship among the foreign management, the village officials, and the street gang demonstrates a particular form of global-local collaboration in a post-socialist political situation whereby criminal organizations forge alliances with local government officials (Nike et al. 1995; Pine 1996).

Rising tensions within the global-local collaboration eventually led to the collapse of the existing factory regime at Nawon. Management's growing reliance on the "special" support from the local power holders strengthened their influence over the factory's operations. When the influence grew to an alarming level, management attempted to restore the principle of independent management. The growing tension between the foreign management and the local power holders culminated in the sudden death of plant manager Bak in a mysterious car accident. Management was unable to find the exact cause of his death because it neither had observed the accident scene nor found vital clues about his death. Meanwhile, rumors of a local conspiracy against management only deepened its worries about the influence of the local power holders. The accident fundamentally transformed the existing global-local collaboration in the factory, eroding the collusion between the foreign management and the village officials. My discussion begins with the local Chinese government officials' supporting role in labor management at Nawon.

DEVELOPING GLOBAL-LOCAL COLLABORATION

Local government and labor control

Local-level Chinese government officials played an active part in the successful launching of Nawon. For example, it was the village head, Hong, who accompanied Korean managers to Pingshan County and helped them to find cheap labor. During the short business trip to Pingshan, he persuaded the Pingshan government officials to advertise the new job opportunities at Nawon through official channels such as village bulletin boards. His close relationship with the magistrate of Pingshan County made the public advertisement possible: the village head and the county magistrate were "war buddies" from the Korean War (1950–1953). Ironically, they fought in the war as members of the People's Liberation Army, "to fight against the American imperialists and their puppet, the South Korean government."[1] Four decades after the war, the former Communist warriors were seeking an investment by a South Korean firm to develop the local economy.

The management at Nawon credited the village head with the successful result of the first recruitment. Without his close relationship with the Pingshan government, it would have been impossible to secure enough Han-Chinese workers to fill the shop floor. At that time, many young women in Pingshan were reluctant to go to Nawon because they had no acquaintance who had ever worked at a foreign factory located in such a distant city as Qingdao. When the local government advertised the jobs on the government bulletin boards, they felt that it would be safe to apply for the jobs. "After seeing the advertisement on the bulletin boards," a Han-Chinese worker recalled, "we concluded that our local government guaranteed the safety of the jobs." To further assure the residents, the officials of Pingshan even announced the jobs using the village loudspeakers, which had been used as a mass mobilization method during the "socialist revolution" of the 1960s and the 1970s.

The Pingshan County government's unusual favor was just a part of the support provided by local-level government officials. As mentioned earlier, shortly after Nawon began operations, the officials of nearby Fuyang village joined in the supervision of labor at the factory. During the early years of the factory, management suffered from a lack of experience in controlling Han-Chinese labor. While struggling to discipline the newly hired workers fresh from the countryside, management realized that the officials of Fuyang village could control the workers much better than could Korean managers. "Just as we well understand the Korean-Chinese," a Korean manager said, "the village officials know the Han-Chinese workers much better than we do."

At the same time, however, management was highly cautious in determining the exact manner of village officials' involvement in labor supervision. Concerned with the possible negative influence of "backward" Chinese officials, management decided to limit their participation to the administration of factory dormitories. A senior Korean manager at Nawon Korea said:

> The village officials can't understand what factory management really means. How can they? They've been Communist Party cadres for more than half of their lives and thus have virtually no idea of a capitalist economy. In this sense, they're not that much different from the workers from the countryside. . . . It would be good if they only control the Han-Chinese workers in the dormitories. The village officials would have a really bad influence on our factory if they intervene in the shop-floor management.

As mentioned in Chapter Two, the village officials welcomed management's request for help. The officials knew very well how Nawon, one of nineteen multinational corporations in the region, could greatly contribute to the development of their village by generating extra tax revenue. The village officials willingly participated in the labor management of Nawon also because they viewed the large group of migrant workers as a potential threat to public security. In their eyes, it made little difference that most of the workers at Nawon were young and unmarried women who were supposedly more docile and easier to control than male workers. "That they are young girls doesn't make any big difference," a security officer said. "They have the same peasant nature. They're unruly, uncultured . . . they're potential troublemakers."

The village officials' administration of the factory dormitories created a new mechanism of labor control operating at the local-community level.

The controlling mechanism was highly effective because it ran through the network between village residents and the officials, taking full advantage of the local residents' prejudice against migrant workers. In fact, the village residents became an active arm of the local surveillance mechanism by occupying the administrative positions of the dormitories.

GIFT EXCHANGE AND GROWING LOCAL INFLUENCE

Although management transferred the administration of the factory dormitories to the village government, it never allowed the village officials to interfere with the main factory operations. This limit originated from management's principle of independent management. Several developments after the Han-Chinese promotion in 1997, however, made it very difficult for management to maintain this principle: the depletion of managerial resources, especially the reduced number of Korean and Korea-Chinese managerial staff, aging production facilities, and deteriorating financial stability caused by small production profits.

Despite the diminished resources, management had successfully maintained its authority on the shop floor. As discussed earlier, the industrial trainee program and the Han-Chinese promotion created pro-management workers on the shop floor. This was reinforced by the charismatic-paternalist factory regime. Management, however, felt that it could not entirely rely on the new Han-Chinese managerial staff. Again, suspicion of the Han-Chinese staff was rooted in management's belief of the cultural difference between Koreans and Han-Chinese. Management assumed that it could not entirely trust Han-Chinese staff who did not share any "culture" with Koreans. Despite the creation of a pro-management Han-Chinese staff, management was still afraid of the possibility that they would side with the rank-and-file workers, who were also Han-Chinese. In order to prevent a possible collaboration, management finally turned to the village officials. Management's about-face came from its newly acquired local knowledge of the deep division between locals and nonlocal "migrants": "Both are Han-Chinese," a Korean manager said, "but the villagers treat the Han-Chinese workers in our factory just like foreigners."

The aging facilities of Nawon further expedited the compromise in the principle of independent management. After a decade of operations in China, the factory suffered from increasing invariable costs, mainly created by the need for frequent maintenance of its worn-out production equipment. Deteriorating working and living conditions of the factory also bothered management. As mentioned in Chapter Two, management did not care too much about the Han-Chinese workers' poor working and living conditions. Management did not deny that the conditions were poor but argued that they were at least not worse than those of many other factories. However, the arrival of new garment factories with a better living and working environment led management to feel the necessity of improving the employees' working and living conditions.

Since 1999, management had discussed improvements to its facilities with Nawon Korea, focusing on upgrading the sewing and cutting machines and installing an efficient ventilation system. Management finally concluded that it could not afford the upgrades because neither Nawon Korea nor Nawon had sufficient financial resources. In order to win the stiff competition with other garment factories, Nawon Korea had no choice but to accept buyers' "price squeezing" and offer low per-unit prices. The result was a gradual undermining of its financial stability. With the small margins, the management at Nawon sometimes felt it difficult to maintain, let alone improve, the existing production facilities. "With the small profits," plant manager Bak once complained, "we can barely meet the monthly payroll of the Han-Chinese workers. . . . Virtually nothing remains after that." Though his statement somewhat exaggerated the factory's weak financial condition, it reflected the growing difficulty in sustaining operations on the shop floor with the company's meager profits.

In addition, the aging facilities made management vulnerable to the government's periodic inspections of the factory. Since the late 1990s, the Chinese central government had gradually tightened its monitoring of the working conditions in multinational corporations, which had been criticized as the "world's sweatshops" by major Western media (for example, Ash 2002; Kahn 2003).[2] Responding to the changes in the central government's policy, the municipal government of Qingdao implemented a new "sudden inspections" program. This gave the officials of the district government the authority to randomly inspect factories with no prior notice. After the first round of the sudden inspections, the management at Nawon received a citation and paid a fine for violating government standards on shop-floor safety. The inspection and the citation surprised management because it was the first time that the district government carried out inspections without prior notice. Before the policy change, the government had published its inspection schedules in advance and given management time to prepare.

The sudden inspections gave the village officials of Fuyang a rare chance to directly intervene in the management of the factory. For the Korean managers, who still did not know how to deal with the next round of sudden inspections, the village officials notified them of the next scheduled inspection. Thanks to this unexpected favor, management was able to prepare for the next "sudden" inspection. Whatever the motive of the move, village officials' unusual favor changed management's attitude toward them. As village officials continued to offer this favor, management, first suspicious of officials, gradually came to regard them as reliable business partners.

Other unofficial favors of village officials strengthened the collaborative relationship. Village officials helped management make acquaintances inside the district government. Having good connections with the district government was potentially important for management because it had comprehensive responsibilities for legal measures that could directly affect the operations of multinational factories. Village officials invited several district government officials and senior Korean managers of Nawon Korea to private dinners, which were paid for by Nawon Korea.

Due to its unofficial nature, it was hard to confirm the benefits that management received through its newly developing network among high-ranking officials. Only through the Korean-Chinese office workers could I get a hint about the importance of the unofficial benefits. Thanks to the new network, the office workers said, they could expedite customs clearance procedures by directly calling a customs office official. Many orders given to Nawon called for materials such as high-quality fabrics and exotic buttons that had to be imported from other countries. The customs office with jurisdiction over the greater Qingdao region was notorious for its slow clearance speed. For this reason, shortening the customs clearance time became critical for many multinational corporations in fulfilling rush orders. Thanks to its newly developing network with high-ranking officials, the customs office gave Nawon priority over other factories. Korean-Chinese workers also said that they were amazed when their factory had electricity while neighboring factories suffered from power cuts. The rapidly growing demand for electricity, created mostly by the large number of factories, put enormous pressure on the region's power grid. This occasionally resulted in power outages, which caused serious problems for many factories. The office workers asserted that Nawon got priority in the limited supply of power thanks to its special relationship with some important figures in the district office.

As the village officials continued to offer special benefits to Nawon, the Korean managers felt pressure to return their favor. As Marcel Mauss pointed out, gifts are never free (1990 [1922]). Management knew that it had to give gifts back to the village officials in order to maintain its "friendly" relationship. Shortly after the first private dinner with officials from the district government, management discussed how it could return the village officials' favor. It decided to hire a close relative of the village head to work in the personnel affairs division. This was not an easy decision. At first, the expatriate managers at Nawon were very reluctant to compromise the principle of independent management. They worried that it would be hard to contain the village officials' influence once they took part in management of the shop floor. The president of Nawon Korea, however, argued that they should hire the village head's relative. His close personal relationship with the village head and concern about his business network in China (established with the help of the village head) made him view the special hiring in a different way. The president thought that the benefits would be greater than the potential risks. In particular, he expected that the recruitment would reinforce management's labor control by creating a de facto village government's presence on the shop floor. "Han-Chinese workers know that the village officials are tough," the president insisted in a meeting with the expatriate managers. "The recruitment of a relative of the village head will enhance our labor control on the shop floor." In the end, the expatriate managers agreed.

At first, the recruitment made both management and the village officials happy. Though not entirely convinced that it was a good idea, the expatriate managers at Nawon observed that, after the recruitment, petty pilfering by the Han-Chinese workers greatly decreased. Small discrepancies in quantities between input materials and output products had always bothered management. The Korean managers believed that the discrepancies were caused by "bad apples" among the workers. "When an order includes fashionable garments," a Korean manager said, "we have to be really careful to prevent pilfering." To eliminate the problem, management once ordered that every worker had to go through a personal body check at the factory main gate. However, management soon realized that it was nearly impossible to eradicate the practice. The Han-Chinese inspection staff came from Pingshan, the hometown of the rank-and-file workers. "It was hard for them to be really strict with the bad elements among the workers," a Korean manager said, "because they were their friends or sisters from the same village." Management thought that the village head's close relative, the new head of the personnel affairs division, contributed to the decrease.

The village head also seemed to be satisfied with the recruitment of his relative. He continued to provide the schedules for factory inspections and helped the president of Nawon Korea to expand his local network among local government officials. According to a Korean-Chinese interpreter, the president kept expanding his business network to include high-level officials in the district government. Behind his vigorous networking was always the village head's active support. Every time he visited China, the president was busy having private dinners with high-level local officials, and the village head and several of his close acquaintances accompanied the president most of the time. Everything indicated that the village head was satisfied with the recruitment of his close relative.

The close relationship between the village head and the president of Nawon Korea was sometimes expressed in real gifts. In the early winter of 2000, the Han-Chinese workers were surprised to see the village head arriving at the factory in a shiny brand-new car imported from South Korea. For the rank-and-file workers at Nawon, the car (with a market price of over 400,000 yuan) was prohibitively expensive: "We can never make that much money," a Han-Chinese worker said, "even if we continue to work day and night."[3] They suspected that the brand-new car was also far beyond what the village head could afford. As a grassroots government official, he only received a meager salary from the government. Rumors about his new car spread quickly in the workshop. No Han-Chinese worker believed that he purchased the car with his own money. They suspected that the car was a gift from the president of Nawon Korea, who wanted to return favors from the village head.[4]

The conspicuous gift from the president of Nawon Korea confirmed the Han-Chinese workers' suspicions about his close relationship with the village head. The workers believed that, in case of a labor dispute on the shop floor, the village officials, including the village head, would side with management. They were worried that any kind of protest against management would incur the pro-management village officials' wrath. The Han-Chinese workers' distrust of the village officials' pro-management attitude only deepened their "collective inaction," their submissive attitude toward management's authority. Another widespread rumor—that the village head called the president "elder brother"—only further reduced the likelihood of the Han-Chinese workers taking collective action. "In times of trouble," a worker cynically said, "the younger brother [the village head] should help his elder brother [the president of Nawon Korea]."

Several studies report that, in cases of labor disputes, migrant workers find it difficult to find shelter in local government. Local officials are often reluctant to intervene and protect workers' interests because they feel they have shared interests with management (Solinger 1995; Chan 1998a, 2001). Local officials tend to regard workers as objects of control, while trying to keep an amicable relationship with management. The Han-Chinese workers' situation at Nawon was perhaps worse than the reported cases, because the village head, the local supporter of the Nawon Korea's president, had a strong influence over the entire village. Thanks to his decade-long public career as the village head and lifelong residence in the village, he had established a strong position in the local community. His influence over the village community was so powerful that even the party secretary and the public security bureau of the village consulted him about village affairs. With the pro-management village head, the Fuyang village government functioned as a local agent in support of the factory regime at Nawon.

Tripartite collusion

In the late 1990s and the early 2000s, thugs and bullies increased their influence over many local towns and villages in China. During this period, the central government reduced financial support to local-level governments and urged local-level officials to search for financial resources to maintain their organizations. Some officials took advantage of the state's "retreat" from local government and used their public authority to advance their personal interests. Criminal organizations established relationships with corrupt local government officials and increased their unofficial influence over local communities and government offices (He 1998; Sun 1999; Yunxiang Yan 2003). High-ranking officials of the Chinese Communist Party denounced the vicious collusion between local officials and criminal organizations and warned that both homegrown and overseas gangsters were infiltrating government organizations at various levels. In the worst cases, some local officials even operated undercover units to better liaise with criminal syndicates (*Guojia shiwu* 2006; Mulvenon 2006). This "merger of the black and the white" (C. *hei bai he liu*) whereby criminal organizations (black) are allied with local government officials (white) to promote their common illegal interests, is especially widespread in northern China (He 1998: 282–319). In this region, gangsters even took positions in state agencies and the legal system, thus ensuring a durable influence within the government (Sun 1999: 39).

In Fuyang village, a local gang exerted its influence in the form of threats against the Han-Chinese migrant workers in multinational factories. The workers of Nawon remembered that, particularly during the early years of the factory, the village gang randomly threatened them on the streets. The workers feared the gang and would not venture outside after sunset. During my fieldwork, the gang threat was still a popular topic of conversation among the workers. They talked a lot about wrongdoings committed by the gang. A Han-Chinese worker told me about the usual way the gang harassed women migrant workers:

> If a worker walks along the dark street at night, local thugs quickly appear from nowhere. They surround her, teasing or cursing, then steal all her belongings. If she's lucky, they will stop at that point. However, if she has really bad luck, she may suffer from their [sexual] harassment. Two years ago, a worker in the sewing section became a victim of harassment. . . . The incident made the worker so scared . . . she lost her ability to speak for almost a full day.

At Nawon, almost thirty workers had experienced direct or indirect gang threats. None of them, however, had ever reported the threats to the pubic security office of the village. They said that they *could not* do so because they suspected that there might be a "very special" relationship between the gang and the village officials. Their suspicion was based on a widespread rumor that the secret leader of the village gang was the village head's second son. Considering the village head's powerful influence over the village government, the workers thought that bringing their cases to the public security bureau would be a waste of time. Several workers even suspected that such an action might bring retaliation from the gang.

As the village gang began to threaten them more purposefully and deliberately, the Han-Chinese workers' suspicion gradually changed into a conviction that there was a special relationship between the gang and the village officials. During the early period of Nawon, the gang threat was random and did not seem to have any specific targets. Workers said that most of their previous encounters with the gang did not develop into any serious situation: the tough guys said some sexually disparaging comments, snatched their valuables, and then let them go. After management recruited the village head's relative to manage the personnel department, however, the gang threat began to take a purposeful and calculated pattern. The new division head implemented much enhanced body inspections to decrease the workers' petty pilfering. This, however, increased the Han-Chinese workers waiting time for the inspection and made them feel very tired. The village gang selectively threatened the workers who had openly complained of the new head of the personnel affairs division. Many workers thought that the pinpoint mode of the gang's threats had proved a close connection between the local gang and the village head.

The Han-Chinese workers did not think that the expatriate Korean managers at Nawon were directly involved with the gang threats. A distinctive division of business between the expatriate managers at Nawon and the executives at Nawon Korea contributed to the Han-Chinese workers' trust in the expatriate managers. It was the president of Nawon Korea who attended all the private meetings with the local government officials. The president kept most of his business meetings confidential and the expatriate Korean managers at Nawon did not know about the details of his meetings. The division of business between Nawon and Nawon Korea gave the Han-Chinese workers the impression that the expatriate managers were different from those at Nawon Korea. The workers knew that the Korean managers of their factory participated in the decision to recruit the village head's relative. At the same time, however, the workers did not notice any change in the expatriate managers' attitudes on the shop floor. Despite the increasingly close relationship between the president of Nawon Korea and the village head, the Han-Chinese workers felt that the

Korean managers at Nawon treated them just as they always had done. Most of all, plant manager Bak continued to make the same effort to get the subcontract orders that would lead to "decent" wages.

The unique work division within management channeled the Han-Chinese workers' criticism to the president of Nawon Korea. Considering his close relationship with the village head, the workers believed that the president played a key role in hiring the village head's relative. His lack of relationship with the Han-Chinese workers also contributed to their negative view of him. "The president only cares about networking," a Han-Chinese line leader said. "He couldn't remember the name of a single [Han-Chinese] member of the managerial staff." Other Han-Chinese staff even ridiculed his scanty knowledge of actual garment production. In contrast, many Han-Chinese workers appreciated the fact that the expatriate Korean managers—especially plant manager Bak—knew the fundamentals of making garments and spent a lot of time in the workshop. Most importantly, workers believed that the expatriate managers understood the importance of "decent" wages. Their positive view of the expatriate managers helped the management at Nawon maintain its control of the shop floor despite changes detrimental to the workers such as the hiring of the village head's relative, the enhanced body inspections, and the growing gang threat.

The Han-Chinese workers' belief in the difference between the expatriate managers at Nawon and the president of Nawon Korea was not completely mistaken. As mentioned earlier, the expatriate managers and the president of Nawon Korea originally disagreed over the special recruitment of the village head's relative. The expatriate managers hesitated because they were worried about the potential negative effect on the shop floor. The president of Nawon Korea also acknowledged that the recruitment might adversely affect the principle of independent management. However, he regarded the recruitment as a small and inevitable managerial cost necessary to maintain "smooth operations" in the village. The president also believed that it would bring an extra labor-controlling effect because the shop floor presence of the village head's relative would enhance management's control of labor. The disagreement among the Korean managerial staff seemed to be resolved when the recruitment brought the anticipated labor-controlling effect. However, the village gang closely cooperated with the village head's relative and surreptitiously joined the deepening collaboration between management and the village officials. This heralded an emerging tripartite collusion between the foreign management, the village officials, and the local gang.

The emerging tripartite collusion supports the general argument that multinational corporations often work with authoritarian local political regimes to secure efficient and uninterrupted local operations (Sen 2006: 145). The collusion also shows a particular form of global-local collaboration in a post-socialist context. In many post-socialist countries, the rapid transition from a socialist to a capitalist system created an unprecedented degree of social disorder and economic dislocation. The lack of a universal policy on tax exemptions and unclear criteria for privatization further aggravated the troubled situation. This allowed criminal organizations to pursue their unlawful interests by siding with corrupt officials (Ledeneva 1998; Swain 1996). In post-socialist China, many government officials have taken advantage of the relative scarcity of transparent rules about proper economic transactions and decision-making procedures. They sometimes establish secret connections with local criminal organizations to solidify their status in the local political landscape (Kwong 1997; Levy 1995; Liu 1983). The developments at Nawon demonstrate how the connection between criminal organizations and corrupt government officials can contribute to foreign management's control of local labor. In the case of Nawon, however, the labor-controlling effects of the new recruitment did not last long.

THE END OF THE CHARISMATIC-PATERNALIST FACTORY REGIME

Increasing tension between management and the local power holders

After the first special recruitment, management hired several more relatives of village officials. Its original plan was to strictly limit the number of local residents among its employees. Many Korean managers, especially the expatriate managers at Nawon, were worried about the potential negative effect of such hiring. They argued that the special recruitment should be a one-time event. Nawon's management eventually had to change the initial plan as the village officials persistently demanded additional hiring. The officials viewed the special recruitment as management's proper return of their favors. The village head's personal request to the president of Nawon

Korea to hire more of his relatives sparked another heated debate within management. Hiring acquaintances of the village officials, the expatriate managers argued, would excessively increase local influence and eventually force management to compromise its principle of independent management. After a long debate, management finally decided to accept the village head's request. Management's deepening reliance on his special favors made it extremely hard to refuse the request. The personal relationship between the president of Nawon Korea and the village head also contributed to the decision. The president knew that he could never have had such an extensive local network without the village head's assistance.

For a while, the new recruitment seemed to contribute to management's control of labor by creating a new schism among the workers. The Korean managers observed that there were virtually no personal interactions between the workers of Fuyang village and the migrant workers from Pingshan. The fact that the local workers commuted from their homes in Fuyang village greatly reduced their chance of interacting with the workers from Pingshan, who lived in the dormitories. The social distance between the two groups was so wide that they even did not share dining tables in the factory canteen. "I don't want to eat with them," a local worker said, "because of the migrant workers' rancid body odor." The local workers spoke their local Qingdao dialect among themselves, which deepened the schism between the two groups. The workers from Pingshan often said that the local workers from Fuyang village intentionally spoke in their dialect when they wanted to speak ill of their nonlocal coworkers. The local workers' close relationship with the village head further widened the distance between the local and the migrant workers. The workers from Pingshan became more reluctant to interact with the local workers after they learned that many of them were relatives of the village head: "The local workers may be secret agents of the village head," a Han-Chinese worker from Pingshan argued. "They may report what we said on the shop floor to him." Thus, all the new developments on the shop floor indicated that the additional recruitment of the Fuyang village residents created a new schism based on the different regional origins of the Han-Chinese workers, which in the end weakened the potential for the workers' solidarity.

The Korean managers at Nawon, however, soon noticed the negative effects of the recruitment. Around the end of 2001, petty pilfering that had dramatically decreased right after the new recruitment began to increase again. A rumor had it that the new workers from Fuyang pressured the migrant workers from Pingshan to steal garments for them, alluding to their "special" connection with the village head. During my fieldwork, I also observed the village head's sister in the personnel affairs division making a similar request to the workers on the shop floor. Many nonlocal workers said that they had stolen some garments and given them to her. They argued that they could not reject her requests. "She's the village head's sister," a Han-Chinese worker in the finishing section said. "We were really afraid of her retaliating if we refused her demands."

Though pilfering was one of its top concerns, management did not try to crack down on it. The Korean managers suspected that the recent outbreak of pilfering was closely related to the local workers. Management, however, decided to ignore the reemergence of this shady practice at least for a while. The managers reluctantly made this decision because they could not find hard evidence of the local workers' involvement in pilfering. "The Han-Chinese workers would not step forward as witnesses," a Korean manager said, "because they were worried about the village head and the gang behind him." The president of Nawon Korea's special relationship with the village head also played a key role in the connivance. He was afraid that punishing the local workers might harm his amicable relationship with the village head. The president believed that the punishment could be a blow to the village head's "face" and damage his reputation, and, consequently, endanger management's relationship with him. He also maintained that the benefits created by the presence of local workers on the shop floor still outweighed the disadvantages.

An unexpected failure to fulfill an order, however, caused management to change its approach to the pilfering. Because of unexpectedly high consumer demand, a regular Japanese buyer placed a rush reorder for five styles of garments that Nawon had made two months earlier. The buyer wanted Nawon to fulfill the order as soon as possible so that it could meet the demand before the end of the season. Management felt confident that it could fulfill the order on time. Nawon still had the remainder of fabric and accessories from the original order. Because rush reorders are common in the garment industry, it is a widespread practice to keep materials of previous orders for a while. Management also believed that the workers could make the garments faster than usual because they still remembered the detailed production procedures from the first time. "Just two months had passed after the first order," plant manager Bak said. "The workers still remembered the detailed specifications of the garments." Management's belief that it could fulfill the order on time was so strong that the plant manager even made a phone call to the Japanese buyer to reassure him.

A report from the materials department completely destroyed management's confidence. Jihwan, the Korean-Chinese in charge of the materials statistics, went to the factory warehouse to check the quantity of raw materials needed for the rush order. What he found there was an apparent discrepancy between the numbers in the statistics book and the actual quantity of fabric. "At first, I couldn't believe my eyes," he said. "I repeatedly checked the amount of fabric and it became clear that we didn't have enough materials to complete the order." Management was deeply embarrassed by the discrepancy. In the past, most discrepancies happened on the shop floor and they were only related to small-scale pilfering. What happened in the warehouse was a brazen smuggling of expensive fabric from the factory. Because management had to reorder fabric, the order shipment was significantly delayed. Plant manager Bak had to ask the Japanese buyer to give him more time to fulfill the order.

After the incident, management concluded that there must be some connection between the workers on the shop floor and "bad elements" outside. "The scale of the pilfering was unprecedented," a Korean manager said. "It could never have been possible without coordination between factory insiders and outsiders." Management suspected that the newly hired workers from Fuyang village had some connections with the village gang. "The local workers are at one end of the criminal network," a Korean manager argued. "It's easy for them to establish connections with the gang because they're from the same village." Among the local workers, management pointed to Jiang in the materials department as the internal accomplice of the smuggling. The testimony of two Han-Chinese workers supported the suspicion. "Although it was dark," one of the two witnesses said, "I could recognize Jiang . . . he seemed to be throwing bolts of fabric over the factory wall."

Despite their strong belief in Jiang's collusion with the village gang, the Korean managers realized that it was difficult to punish him. The two workers who had witnessed Jiang's misconduct refused to testify against him. It was a well-known fact that Jiang was one of the village head's relatives. The witnesses were worried that their testimony against Jiang would endanger them. Jiang was also believed to have a close relationship with the "tough guys" of Fuyang village. Several workers said that they saw him mixing with gang members on the streets of downtown Qingdao. "If I testify against him," the other witness said fearfully, "the village thugs, his close friends, will *kill* me" (emphasis by the interviewee). Management also found it hard to prove Jiang's involvement in the smuggling. The Korean managers seriously worried that the village head would be deeply embarrassed if they publicly denounced Jiang with no hard evidence of his involvement. In the end, instead of officially punishing Jiang, the plant manager personally met with him. When he admonished Jiang about the rumors about him, Jiang completely denied the allegation.

Just about a month later, a similar theft case from the warehouse was noticed. The Korean managers were deeply perplexed by the theft, because it did not leave even a single clue. The perfect theft only reinforced the managers' belief that there was collusion between the village gang and the local workers of Fuyang village. But without any hard evidence, management could not take any strong action. The Korean managers at Nawon even considered asking the village head for help. "Considering his special connection to the village gang," a Korean manager said, "he probably knows who did it." The manager was aware of the rumor that the village head's son was the leader of the local gangsters. The president of Nawon Korea, however, objected to the idea. "There's no evidence," he said, "that the village head has connections with the gang . . . it's all just rumors." The president even denied the rumor that the village head's son was deeply involved with the gang. "It's a matter of his family," he continued. "I can't ask him such a rude question about whether he knows the mastermind behind the thefts." He was afraid that any unfounded claims against the village head's relatives would damage his close relationship with the village head and thus undermine his local network.

The persistent theft unexpectedly created a schism among the Korean management. While the expatriate managers insisted that management should implement strong measures to check local influence, the president was very reluctant to take any step that might affect his expanding local network. After a long discussion, management decided that it would no longer question the possible connection between the village head and the theft. Instead, it decided to enhance the existing nighttime surveillance of the main factory premises by hiring two nonlocal men who would be in charge of a nighttime patrol. The expatriate managers at Nawon grumbled about the modest resolution to the persistent problem of pilfering. They argued that this solution could never stop the pilfering because it failed to remove its fundamental source: the group of workers from Fuyang village.

Death of the plant manager

In the early summer of 2002, the management at Nawon finally set up an unofficial plan to restore its principle of independent management. First, management collected the factory warehouse keys from the materials department. The managers called the department a "den of the pilfering criminals" because it had a large number of local workers. Management suspected that the local workers in the department were intimately involved in the theft cases. With this change, management would directly control the troubling department as well as the stock of raw materials. It also established a new hiring standard to check the growing local influence. The new standard stipulated that all new workers should not have any local background. The managers at Nawon believed that this new requirement would gradually reduce the number of local workers in the factory and decrease the local influence on the shop floor. They argued that the gradual change would not hurt their existing relationship with the village officials. The president of Nawon Korea finally approved the plan, because he also felt that management should check the local influence on the shop floor, which had grown to an alarming level.[5]

The new plan, however, was suspended in July 2002 after a completely unexpected accident. Shortly after 6 a.m., the phone in the financial manager's room started ringing. "It sounded quite ominous," financial manager Moon recalled, "because I had rarely received calls so early in the morning." His sense of foreboding was warranted. An official of the public security bureau informed him about a fatal car accident. Around 4 a.m., a police patrol found a damaged car on the side of a highway to the city. What they found inside was the dead body of a middle-aged man. With the car's license plate, they traced the owner of the car and finally called the manager. At a local morgue, the financial manager saw the lifeless body of plant manager Bak. According to the police report, he was killed when his car was rear-ended by a heavy truck, a common occurrence on the streets of the industrial areas in and around Qingdao. The police could find neither the hit-and-run truck nor its driver.

Plant manager Bak's tragic death brought fundamental changes to the Korean management at Nawon. His death signaled the collapse of the charismatic-paternalist factory regime. The regime could no longer be sustained without his strong leadership and paternalistic concern for the workers. Because there was no other manager who had the same charismatic qualities and concern for the workers, management gradually lost the Han-Chinese workers' trust. His death also fundamentally changed management's view of the configuration of local power. After the plant manager's funeral, the Korean managers at Nawon and Nawon Korea tried to find the real cause of the accident. Whom had he met with during his last several hours? Why did the local police clean up the accident scene before the Korean managers came to see it?

Their suspicions about the ultimate cause of the plant manager's death deepened as a Korean manager of a nearby factory argued that he saw the deceased plant manager in a downtown restaurant. He testified that, the night before the accident, he saw the plant manager drinking with several people who looked like "Chinese tough guys." After discussion, the Korean managers at Nawon and Nawon Korea reached a tentative conclusion that the village gang might be behind Bak's death. The managers suspected that the deceased plant manager had gone out for a meeting with the village gang to negotiate about the recent theft cases. During the meeting, they probably got into a heated argument about the thefts and management's recent anti-theft measures such as its direct control of the materials department and the new recruitment standards. The Korean managers at Nawon and Nawon Korea argued that the gang would have resented the measures, because they mainly targeted workers from Fuyang village. The fatal car accident might have been the result of the quarrel: the deceased manager refused some excessive demands of the gang and the gang tried to intimidate him by tailgating his car. "The gang may have not intended to kill him," a Korean manager said. "They may have just tried to threaten him. . . . The plan went really bad with the fatal car accident."

The conclusion, however, remained no more than a plausible story of the tragedy. Though management felt certain that the village gang was deeply involved in the plant manager's death, it could not take any official move. Just like the recent theft cases, management lacked hard evidence of the village gang's involvement. Despite rampant rumors about the gang's involvement, management could find none who would testify about the case. In addition to the lack of evidence, the Korean managers' fear of the village gang made it more difficult for them to take concrete action. A Korean manager confessed that, after the plant manager's death, he became very wary of the dark streets outside the factory: "From time to time, I feel the village gang watching me from a remote corner. . . . They may suddenly come out of nowhere and threaten me just as they did the deceased plant manager." Thus the Korean managers' shared feeling of helplessness over Bak's death developed into fear of the village gang. What made the managers more uneasy was their suspicion about a possible connection between the public security bureau and the gang. They believed that the public security bureau hastily cleaned up the accident scene to cover up the real cause of the plant manager's death. From the tragic death of the plant manager and subsequent developments, management realized that it had gotten deeply ensnarled in the net of the local power holders.

A POWER SHIFT FROM THE GLOBAL TO THE LOCAL?

Management's ultimate inability to stop the worsening pilfering problem reveals an unexpected consequence of global-local collaboration, a shifting power relationship between foreign management and local power holders. At the beginning, the Nawon management had the initiative in virtually every matter concerning the factory. In their relationship with the foreign management, the village officials functioned as its able local assistants. They served the needs of management, supporting management's search for cheap labor and its administration of the factory dormitories. The relationship gradually changed, however, as management increasingly depended on the village officials' unofficial and secret services. Intensifying price competition, aging factory facilities, and enhanced government inspections of the factory made it inevitable that management would seek the village official's "special" favors.

Management gradually compromised its principle of independent management as it hired the village officials' relatives. Management regarded the hiring as its returning a favor. With the compromise, however, the local power holders surreptitiously increased their influence in the factory. The increasing number of thefts and their growing size reflected the local power holders' deepening influence in the corporation. Management could not effectively cope with the problem because the expatriate managers at Nawon and the president of Nawon Korea approached the problem differently. While the managers weighed the immediate negative impact on their shop-floor management, the president cared more about the village head's key role in expanding his business network in China. The lack of hard evidence for the relationship between the local employees and the pilfering sustained the different views within management, making it unable to check the growing local influence on the shop floor. To the migrant workers on the shop floor, the inaction of the divided management only seemed to confirm the rumors about the secret connections among the local employees, the village officials, and the local gang. The migrant workers' fear of the village gang's retaliation thwarted management's attempt to uncover the mastermind behind the organized thefts. The rumors about the close relationship between the gang and the village officials kept the Han-Chinese migrant workers from testifying about the wrongdoings of the local employees.

Unlike the popular image of multinational corporations dominating local communities with their enormous economic and political power, the reality at Nawon was that management needed the local officials' timely support in order to ensure smooth local operations. At first, management tried hard to maintain its principle of independent management by minimizing local intervention in the factory. Like most foreign managements that consider local people and their communities "backward," the management of Nawon believed that local intervention in the factory would harm its operations. But both macro- and micro-level changes such as intensifying price competition, declining corporate profitability, and aging factory facilities hampered management's effort to sustain the principle. When the Nawon management unwillingly compromised the principle and allowed local officials to increase their influence on the shop floor, the global-local collaboration developed in a new direction. At Nawon, the secret liaison between village officials and the local gang transformed the collaboration into a tripartite collusion, where the criminal organization threatened the migrant workers through its connection with officials. The collusion reveals how a particular post-socialist political condition, the infiltration of criminal organization into government, created a distinctive form of global-local collaboration.

The shift in the power relationship between the global and the local, however, did not empower every group of people that belonged to the local. At Nawon, the Han-Chinese migrant workers from Pingshan remained the most underprivileged. In fact, their status in the factory and in the local community further deteriorated because they were subjected to the local power holders' arbitrary power in addition to management's labor control. The migrant workers' precarious situation demonstrates how local power holders' growing desire for greater political influence can bring down dire consequences on underprivileged people, especially when power holders' political ambition meets with multinational capital's incessant demand for higher labor productivity. In the local community of Qingdao, the "empowerment of the local" (Hall 1997: 187) did not seem to have any liberating effect on the most underprivileged group of local people.

SEVEN

Clash of the Global and the Local

The sudden death of the plant manager delivered a shattering blow to the Nawon management. Suffering from declining profitability and diminishing financial resources, management had heavily depended on his managerial ability and strong leadership. Since the establishment of the charismatic-paternalist factory regime around 1997, Bak had been the most important figure in management. The executives at Nawon Korea thought that they could no longer maintain the existing managerial principles and practices at Nawon because with the death of Bak they lost the firm's core management figure and could not find a suitable replacement.[1]

Nawon Korea began to search for a new plant manager by analyzing what had caused the collapse of plant manager Bak's factory regime. The executives of Nawon Korea concluded that all the problems originated from "too much localization" and the local power holders' excessive interference in factory management. To reduce the local influence, they planned to reverse the localization process and restore the principle of independent management. To achieve the goal, Nawon Korea brought a Korean manager from a garment factory in Guatemala as the new plant manager of Nawon. The executives at Nawon Korea expected that the new plant manager could achieve the goal by making use of advanced managerial know-how that he had acquired on the "more global" shop floor in Guatemala. The executives thought that the proximity of Guatemalan factories to the United States, allegedly the most globalized country in the world, and their experience of fulfilling orders from that country made them more globalized than the factories in China. However, the new plant manager's "global" managerial know-how and labor-controlling methods created new tension between him and the Han-Chinese workers. He ignored the managerial practices and principles of the previous management, criticizing the workers for their inefficiency and backwardness. The Han-Chinese workers felt embarrassed and then became angry when the new management greatly increased the intensity of labor on the shop floor while disregarding their expectation of a "decent" wage.

The new developments at Nawon show how a certain mode of globalization can increase tensions and conflicts when it imposes particular cultural concepts and norms on local people while ignoring existing local-level concepts and norms (Barber 1995: 3–20; Schaeffer 1997: 263–319). The workplace of multinational corporations can become a space of tension and conflicts when foreign management forces local labor to follow its "culture" while not paying proper attention to the "culture" of local labor.[2] The plant manager violated the shared cultural code between the previous management and the workers. Instead, it sought higher labor intensity, reduced the workers' overtime pay, and ignored the importance of ensuring "decent" wages. The new plant manager's impersonal view of the workers brought the tension to a new level. In the end, the "global" management's sheer ignorance of the "culture" on the shop floor unexpectedly empowered the Han-Chinese workers and provoked them to launch a floor-wide strike.

THE NEW PLANT MANAGER FROM GUATEMALA AND A "HIGHER LEVEL OF GLOBALIZATION"

The executives at Nawon Korea sought to reduce the local influence over Nawon by making its management "more global." They imagined that a new "global" management would operate under "universal and rational principles of production, labor supervision, and employee evaluation."[3]

Though the executives wanted to restore the principle of independent management, they also acknowledged that the local officials were still indispensable parts of their business. They believed that they should maintain their relationship with the village head as long as he continued to provide official and unofficial support for Nawon. The two contradictory objectives placed them face to face with a difficult-to-resolve dilemma. They were well aware of how their previous move to reduce local influence irritated the local power holders. Every measure to reduce local influence, they thought, should be deliberately implemented in such a way as not to provoke strong reactions from the local power holders, especially from the village gang. With this consideration, management decided to retain the local employees from Fuyang village. In fact, the tragic accident that befell plant manager Bak made management more suspicious of the local employees' secret connections with the gang. At the same time, however, management understood how a hastily made decision, such as laying off local employees, could result in dire consequences. Reducing local influence was its top priority. It had to be done, however, in a deliberate way.

After a long discussion, Nawon Korea found a solution to the dilemma in the Chinese government's discourse on globalization. As the Chinese government sought full membership in the World Trade Organization (WTO) in 2001, it launched a series of nationwide globalization campaigns calling on corporations and their employees to be prepared for global-scale competition (Kipnis 2007; Wang and Guo 2002; Editorial 2003; Hairong Yan 2003). Many Chinese corporations revamped their organization and business practices to meet global standards. The popular discourse of global standards often meant more professional, efficient, and transparent practices in corporate management that corresponded to the standards of the allegedly most advanced corporate management in the West (Wei 2006; Luo 2008).

The executives of Nawon Korea believed that incorporating the Chinese government's rhetoric of globalization into their attempt to restore "independent management" could reduce the risk of a violent reaction among the local power holders. It would be hard for the village officials to object to future changes if the changes looked as if they conformed to the government's call for globalization. With this consideration, Nawon Korea announced that the new management at Nawon would eliminate all the past managerial practices that were "unofficial, private, and opaque" and introduce "more global, objective and scientific principles."[4] This was not the first time that Nawon Korea emphasized its advanced and modern characteristics, contrasting them with backward and underdeveloped local, "Chinese" practices. During its early years in China, management regarded its methods of labor surveillance and discipline as modern and advanced, and believed they would effectively transform allegedly backward Han-Chinese workers into the model industrial workers. Ironically, at this time, Nawon Korea justified the future changes in the management at Nawon by referring to the globalization rhetoric of the Chinese government that it once regarded as the key symbol of "Communist" backwardness.

Finally, in September 2002, the executives at Nawon Korea announced that the company would appoint a South Korean named Jo as the plant manager. The announcement emphasized his "global" career. He had worked as a plant manager in Latin American garment factories and the executives of Nawon Korea considered those factories "more global and advanced" in production technologies and labor management than factories in China.[5] Why did Nawon Korea view the Latin American garment factories as more globalized than those in China? What originally brought the new plant manager to the remote garment factories in Latin America? The "global" career of the new plant manager was closely intertwined with the globalizing history of the Korean garment industry.

Since the mid-1980s, many Korean garment factories left Korea and moved to Latin America. This was a strategic move to cope with rapidly increasing wages, active Korean labor unionism, and restrictive trade quotas set by GATT (KOFOTI 1990, 1992; Lee and Song 1994; Park and Park 1989; Song 1989).[6] After their relocation to Latin America, many Korean garment factories quickly became accustomed to the highly competitive contract market of the region. They gained credit for successfully fulfilling a large volume of rush orders from big retail companies based in the United States, such as Gap, K-Mart, Levi's, OP, and Phillips-Van Heusen (Bonacich et al. 1994; Sklair 1989; Personal interview with Jo, 2002). While meeting the buyers' demand for prompt delivery of large-volume orders, however, many Korean garment factories became notorious for their oppressive practices of labor control, which included arbitrary dismissal, labor-code manipulation, and threats of harsh punishment of defiant workers (Peterson 1992, 1994).[7]

The personal career of plant manager Jo reflects the globalization of the Korean garment industry. Throughout his career, he moved from one country to another following the relocation of Korean garment factories and gained hands-on experience in different multinational workshops. His first job was a junior cutter in a joint-invested multinational garment factory in South Korea. After changing companies several times for higher wages and better treatment, he finally settled at Nawon Korea as a senior manager in 1985. Thanks to his outstanding ability to manage the shop floor, he became the plant manager of Nawon Korea in 1990. In 1993, he led the expedition team of Korean managers to Qingdao and Pingshan and briefly took the role of the interim plant manager of Nawon. In 1995, he accepted a Korean multinational corporation's offer of the plant manager position at a garment factory in Honduras. After that, he served as plant manager for Korean garment factories in Guatemala and Honduras.

Jo's career spanning multiple countries brought him a reputation as a "global" manager who, by definition, would be effective immediately upon his arrival at any factory anywhere in the world (Fuller 2009: 72). The executives at Nawon Korea believed that as the new plant manager he could restore management's authority in a short time, using his global know-how gained in supervising factories in different geographical locations. They also noted that he briefly served as the interim plant manager at Nawon: "Plant manager Jo supervised Nawon during one of the most difficult periods of its history," a senior executive at Nawon Korea said. "Together with his career in Latin America, that should certainly help him to take a full charge of the troubled factory."

Nawon Korea's belief in Jo's "more global" management practices further justified the new appointment. The executives at Nawon Korea hoped that the new plant manager would easily restore "independent management" by using the highly authoritarian management style that he had acquired through his career in *maquila* factories.[8] They believed that the new management should steer clear of the "unofficial, private, and opaque" nature of the former management. The former management of the late plant manager was also authoritarian. However, as we have noted, it was at the same time paternalistic, since it was based on his personal concern for the Han-Chinese workers. The executives at Nawon Korea considered Jo's impersonal approach to the workers more compatible with "global" standards than the previous management's personal and paternalist approach.

The new plant manager also believed that he should remove personal elements from managerial practices and reduce the influence of unofficial connections on the shop floor. He declared that management's personal concern with the rank-and-file workers was not only unnecessary but also harmful to effective factory management. This strong belief was based on his experience in *maquila* factories:

> The management of Guatemalan factories usually hires thousands of workers to fulfill a large volume of orders within a short period of time. In that situation, to have personal concern for the ordinary workers is impossible and could do harm to management. . . . Workers will not obey management if they know management has human blood and feelings. I believe management's relationship to labor should remain impersonal. It should be based on objective rules of rewards and punishments.

Mr. Jo, however, was very cautious about changing managerial practices and organizations at Nawon. He was well aware of what happened to the former plant manager, Bak. Jo was worried about the local power holders' violent reaction to the changes that he would make, particularly his attempt to reduce their influence on the factory. "It would be a suicidal attempt," Jo said, "if I make any decision to remove their influence overnight." Instead of any sudden and overall change that might induce the local power holders' resistance, he chose to start with the restructuring of shop-floor organization. "The changes on the shop floor must seem purely a matter of production," he argued. "They would least attract the local power holders' attention." He also planned to adopt the slogan of "global" restructuring to reduce the risk of strong reactions from the power holders.

Although initially limited to the shop floor, the plan for "global" restructuring ultimately aimed at reducing the local influence on management. The plant manager suspected that there was a local conspiracy against management, operating through a secret network between the village gang and some "bad elements" among the Han-Chinese workers. He expected that the restructuring would cut these secret ties. Jo highlighted that the shop floor of Nawon should be run with a tighter production schedule, stricter rules of punishment, and a more rational and impersonal relationship between management and labor. He firmly believed that his restructuring would decrease the local power holders' influence on factory management.

Jo's unique understanding of globalization processes made him confident in the success of his new plan. He believed that the garment factories in Latin America are at a more advanced stage of globalization than their Chinese counterparts. In private conversations, he often said that the managerial principles of Guatemalan factories should be the standard for Nawon's management, because such a standard met the demands of American buyers, who had the highest expectations of product quality and on-time order fulfillment. Jo often used the word "America" as a reference to the most advanced, scientific, and universal standards in the garment industry. He thought that the relatively "backward" factories in China should follow the model. "The validity of existing managerial practices of Nawon," he argued, "should be evaluated on the basis of their compatibility with global, American standards." Based on his belief in the allegedly advanced nature of the Guatemalan managerial practices, the new plant manager disregarded the existing managerial practices at Nawon, especially those established under Bak's leadership. He thought that he could restore managerial authority by introducing objective principles of rewards and punishment, devoid of any personal concern or paternalist care for the workers.

In the summer of 2001, Jo finally announced his first project of "global" restructuring. The project aimed to increase labor productivity by applying the "global standard" shop-floor structure to Nawon. He first focused on the work-group structure of the finishing section. As discussed in Chapter Four, under the previous management, the shop floor was organized into the two production systems, the hand-off and the flexible work-group. Because different styles of garments required different amounts of sewing, the production lines in the sewing section had different work speeds, and the finishing-section workers moved from one worktable to another according to the changing workloads coming from the sewing section. As analyzed in Chapter Four, management had been concerned with the frequent moving of the finishing-section workers. The previous management tried to resolve the issue of "foot-dragging" by increasing the overall work speed, but did not change the work-group system. The new plant manager, however, wanted to make fundamental changes to the system by applying his "global" standards:

> I know that there's a need for group work in the finishing section. But
> I think that the cost of confusion during position changes is too much.

> Look! Can't you see the idle workers in the section? They are taking advantage of the loopholes in the work-group system. You know, under that system, it's really hard to check individual workers' productivity. That's why the work-group system generally has low productivity.

He suspected that the previous system could breed a sense of solidarity and freedom among the section workers. Under the work-group system, workers who finished their work quotas early moved to other worktables and helped other workers to finish their workloads. The workers felt somewhat relieved from the tense situation on the shop floor when they moved from one worktable to another. Jo firmly believed that his new management should eliminate these moments of freedom, brief as they were.

According to his globalization project, the new plant manager first dissolved the "backward and chaotic" work groups. He regrouped them into twelve units, each aligned with the twelve production lines of the sewing section. He ordered the workers to stay at their individual work positions. Then he appointed a senior worker in each unit to be the unit leader and ordered her to check individual workers' work progress and report three times a day. Finally, he strictly prohibited workers from leaving their positions without permission from both the unit and the section leaders. With this new requirement, the plant manager intended to reduce individual workers' "unnecessary" movements.

The new unit system, as expected, enhanced management's labor control and increased labor productivity. After the restructuring, management could easily notice the difference in the work performance of units in the finishing section. The plant manager frequently criticized the leaders of slow work units and praised unit leaders who had achieved production goals on time. Units that completed their work quotas had to leave the shop floor even when other units in the section were still working. He thought that the acknowledgment of different performance among units would boost labor productivity and improve labor control. At the same time, he announced that management would give some bonuses to the unit with the highest labor productivity. In contrast, the workers of the unit with the lowest productivity would receive negative work evaluations, which could jeopardize the renewal of their labor contracts. "The new [work-unit] system is good for management," he once said. "It means order, effectiveness, and speed. Don't you feel thrilled at the orderly production scene?"

The finishing-section workers soon realized that the unit system fundamentally changed their work routine. Their work speed had increased because now they had to keep pace with the fast work speed of the production lines in the sewing section. The unit leaders closely watched and recorded individual workers' job performance and reported it to management. This apparently reinforced management's control of labor. "Under the previous [work-group] system, we could change our work speed a little," a senior worker of the finishing section said. "Now it's almost impossible because the unit leaders watch our work progress and report it to the plant manager." With the individualized statistics, management could easily punish "lazy" individual workers.

The restructuring of the finishing section instantly enhanced productivity. After only one week of its implementation, statistics showed that the finishing section workers did their jobs faster. The plant manager was very excited to see that the overtime of the section decreased by 15 percent from its average before the reorganization. This resulted in a big savings in labor costs. Jo's report about the reduced overtime pleased Nawon Korea, which was under constant pressure to cut production costs. Encouraged by Nawon Korea's high evaluation of the changes in the finishing section, Jo pushed forward with his "global" restructuring.

As the second measure of his "global" management, the plant manager implemented a new rule about workers' procedures for exiting from the shop floor. According to the existing exit procedures, after work hours, all workers on the shop floor were expected to stop their jobs at the same time. After cleaning up their workspace, they began to exit from the workshop in a sequential manner, beginning with the cutting section. After observing this practice, the plant manager argued that he found many workers stopped or slowed down their work "well before" their section leaders ordered them to do so. He argued that, combined with the clean-up time (approximately ten minutes), the total time spent before the workers' actual exit from the shop floor amounted to fifteen to twenty minutes. The greatest time "wasted" in the exit procedure occurred in the finishing section, he said, because the workers there were at the end of the production line and thus left the shop floor last. "It's a total waste," he argued. "I can't believe that our company still pays workers for the time they simply idle away waiting for their turn to leave."

Plant manager Jo's new rule on exit procedures revealed that the main target of his global restructuring was in fact to maximize labor productivity by squeezing even the smallest fraction of time from workers. Under the new exit rule, workers stopped their jobs and left the shop floor according to different time schedules. First, two out of the twelve production lines stopped their tasks and started their clean-up routine. When they finished the clean-up and began to leave the shop floor, the workers of the next two production lines began their clean-up routine. Thus under the new sequential order of exiting, some workers kept working while others were leaving the shop floor. Among the workers on the shop floor, those in the last two production lines had to work longer than others. Their extra work time might amount to as much as twenty minutes, for which they received no extra pay.

With the overall restructuring of the shop floor and the enhancement of managerial authority, the new plant manager also intended to check the local influence on the shop floor. Though he introduced the changes under the slogan of globalization, he believed that they ultimately would serve as a stern warning to the local power holders and the "bad" workers in the workshop. The new exit rules and the work-group system clearly showed that the new plant manager was very much interested in every move of the workers on the shop floor. Most of all, the frequent and detailed statistics of individual worker's work progress clearly revealed who might be a "model" worker and who might not. Jo once argued that the two changes would reduce the number and the scale of pilfering incidents, which he regarded as an indicator of the local power holders' influence on Nawon. In fact, the factory statistics after the changes showed a sharp decline in the incidence of pilfering, which supported Jo's belief in the effectiveness of his "global" management in restricting the local power holders' influence.

INCREASING TENSION ON THE SHOP FLOOR

"Global" management and workers' growing discontent

The Han-Chinese workers' discontent with the new plant manager grew apace with the enhanced productivity brought by his "global" restructuring. The growing discontent was caused by the increased work speed and the new methods of labor control. However, what made the workers most frustrated was the plant manager's intention of decreasing overtime. They believed that the new plant manager sent them a clear message with all the changes that he made on the shop floor: "He's never happy to see us working overtime," a sewing-section operator complained. "He believes that we slow down our work on purpose to make more money [from overtime]." As mentioned in Chapter Five, overtime was critical for the Han-Chinese workers to earn a "decent wage." If they worked only the normal work hours, their average monthly incomes would fall by 30 or sometimes even 40 percent. The resulting amount was far from what they considered "decent."[9] Furthermore, it was in late August, the very beginning of a low-order season, that the plant manager began to push hard his global managerial principles and practices. Many workers feared that the decreased overtime would certainly result in dismally small wages.

Jo's reluctance to find extra orders during the low-order season in 2002 only confirmed the Han-Chinese workers' dire predictions. Unlike Bak, the new plant manager made little effort to find extra orders. He may have felt it difficult to get subcontract orders because they were often only available through close personal connections with other factories. The late plant manager Bak had good connections thanks to his long-term stay in China. However, Jo did not have a network because he had just arrived at Nawon from Guatemala. His reluctance to make the effort to find orders also originated from the managerial style he had acquired during his long stay in Latin America. The management of *maquila* factories tended to regard workers as simply objects of control. It neither paid much attention to workers' "humane side" nor tried to build any personal relationship with them. Though Jo agreed that a certain amount of subcontract orders was necessary for the basic operations of the factory, he did not see any good reason to get orders beyond those that were essential to keep the factory running.

The fact that the *maquila* factories in Guatemala could easily dismiss workers (Peterson 1992, 1994) further contributed to plant manager Jo's view of the Han-Chinese workers not as individuals but as an aggregate. He once proudly remembered how easy it was in Guatemala to fire "troublemakers." According to the practice that he called "three strikes and you're out," he could terminate workers after giving them a "red card" three times. This unique practice contributed to establishing the managerial dictatorship on the shop floor of Guatemalan factories and enhanced management's impersonal view of workers (Peterson 1994: 282). To plant manager Jo, who shared the same view, it was only a strange and totally unnecessary practice for management to try to find extra orders to secure a certain amount of wages *for* the workers. He firmly believed that the seasonal fluctuations in the volume of orders were just as natural as the changes in market supply and demand. He argued that there should be no reason for management to make the effort to secure extra subcontract orders.

The shop-floor situation of Nawon, however, was very different from what the plant manager understood. Firing a worker was not as easy as in the *maquila* factories. In principle, the Chinese labor law prohibits arbitrary termination of employment. A termination is considered arbitrary if it is due neither to the end of a labor contract (renewed annually) nor to a worker's serious misconduct. Though management can take advantage of the ambiguity in the expression of "serious misconduct," firing a worker for no apparent reason may cause the government to intervene. In fact, the labor law made the management at Nawon cautious about ending a worker's employment. During its decade-long operation in China, management fired not more than ten workers for violating factory regulations.

What most distinguished the shop-floor situation at Nawon from that of the *maquila* factories, however, was the relationship between workers and management. At Nawon, under the late plant manager's leadership, emotional and moral ties between workers and management had been key supports of the factory regime. Plant manager Jo almost completely ignored the potential importance of these ties because he was supremely confident of the superiority of his "global" management. He insisted that the former management had failed because it relied on the backward local characteristics, including its unnecessary concern for the Han-Chinese workers as well as its excessive reliance on the village officials.

Mounting tension between two Korean managers

The "global" management of plant manager Jo also worsened his relationship with the financial manager, Moon. Jo believed that Moon's managerial practices were not compatible with his "global" management because they were similar to those of the deceased plant manager. Under the previous management, the former plant manager, Bak, often relied on

Moon's assistance. During the high-order seasons, for example, Bak had asked Moon to take over some of his duties such as sample inspections and preparations for buyers' visits. Thanks to his successful performance as his assistant, Moon won the plant manager's strong trust. Bak even said that he felt closer to Moon than to his own brothers in Korea. Through his close relationship with Bak, Moon gradually learned the plant manager's managerial know-how and distinctive style of labor management, including his personal concern for workers and unusual effort to get subcontract orders.

Jo believed that Moon's personal concern for the Han-Chinese workers was detrimental to his management. From his managerial perspective, similar to that of the *maquila* factories, any personal relationship between workers and management was unnecessary and in fact potentially harmful to effective labor control. As his "global" management achieved the expected results, Jo further believed that Moon's managerial style, which was "too close to workers," was no longer necessary. Moreover, when he observed that Moon gradually gained the Han-Chinese workers' support, the new manager began to regard Moon as a real liability. Jo came to recognize that some Han-Chinese workers considered Moon a symbol of the kind of "ideal" management that they were accustomed to under the deceased plant manager's leadership. "Insofar as the workers see a better alternative on the shop floor," Jo once said, "it'll be difficult for me to establish strong managerial authority."

In fact, many Han-Chinese workers thought that Moon was better than the new plant manager in many ways, especially at managing the shop floor and the workers. They said that his successful tenure as the interim plant manager following Bak's sudden death confirmed that belief. "Manager Moon knows what he ought to do as a plant manager," a Han-Chinese worker argued. "That's why there was no big problem in our factory when he was the interim plant manager." The Han-Chinese workers also gave him high credit for his effort to find subcontract orders during the low-order season of 2002. That effort, workers believed, proved that he understood the importance of "decent" wages to them. It further distinguished Moon from the new plant manager. "First of all," a Han-Chinese worker said, "Manager Moon takes care of us while Old Jo only tries to squeeze out labor." She called the plant manager "old" Jo, a pejorative, expressing her deep discontent with him. Han-Chinese workers' discontent with plant manager Jo rapidly grew as they contrasted him with "able and caring" financial manager Moon.

The Han-Chinese workers' growing sympathy with financial manager Moon led Jo to seek an extreme "solution." He decided to remove Moon from Nawon. Despite all of the differences, it might have been better for him to find a way to cooperate with Moon: he had the know-how about doing business in China that the new plant manager did not have. Jo, however, felt that retaining Moon at Nawon was much more of a liability than the potential benefit that he might get from Moon's continued presence in the factory. The plant manager believed that, by removing Moon, he could more easily establish his "global" management on the shop floor. If he could successfully remove Moon from Nawon, it would show his supreme authority in the factory and eliminate the Han-Chinese workers' hope for an alternative management.

With that in mind, Jo deliberately spread a rumor about the financial manager. The rumor had it that Moon had embezzled money from Nawon using his position as financial manager. In the multinational factories in and around Qingdao, it was not uncommon to hear stories about expatriate managers who "played with" corporate money, taking advantage of the remote and relatively lax supervision of their headquarters in Korea. That was why, from the very beginning of Nawon, Nawon Korea stipulated that the plant manager should closely check on whether the financial manager was properly administering factory funds and report to the headquarters on the result of the checking. During Bak's tenure, rumors of embezzlement circulated at Nawon Korea from time to time and they were related to Bak's close relationship with Moon. "The two were too close to each other," a senior executive of Nawon Korea said. "Such a close relationship may have prevented the plant manager from strictly checking Moon's performance." Plant manager Jo attempted to take advantage of Nawon Korea's suspicions about Moon. He sent a secret report to Nawon Korea, charging that the financial manager had misused corporate funds.

Jo's first attempt to remove Moon, however, was not successful. The executives of Nawon Korea investigated the case for two weeks and decided that they would not punish Moon for the alleged embezzlement. After a closed communication with plant manager Jo, they concluded that they could not find any decisive evidence of wrongdoing, especially the kind of wrongdoing alleged in Jo's secret report. Behind the decision was Nawon

Korea's ambivalent view of the financial manager. The decision did not mean that Moon was completely cleared. On the contrary, Jo's secret report rekindled Nawon Korea's doubts about Moon, specifically regarding the profits generated by subcontract orders. Because most subcontract orders did not come through Nawon Korea, no one in the corporate headquarters knew the exact order amounts that Nawon had received from garment factories in China. Due to the opaque practices of subcontracts, Nawon Korea believed, it was easy for Moon to "play with" the money. They suspected that he may have reported falsely on the profits earned from the subcontract orders. At the same time, however, Nawon Korea also well understood that Moon was the only expatriate Korean manager at Nawon who had sufficient local experience to manage their troubled branch factory. Considering all things, the executives of Nawon Korea decided to keep Moon at Nawon.

The failure of his first attempt to remove Moon did not discourage Jo. At this time, he tried to keep Moon from participating in management of the shop floor. According to the original principles of factory hierarchy, Moon, as financial manager, would not be allowed to supervise the shop floor. Only the plant manager has the authority to control the workshop. Deceased plant manager Bak, however, had allowed Moon to take part in the shop-floor management because he needed Moon's help during the busy high-order seasons. Under the former management, when Bak was not on the shop floor, the Han-Chinese workers often consulted Moon about production-related problems. The practice continued even after Jo became the new plant manager. At first, Jo was not much concerned about the practice because he was not familiar with the shop-floor situation of Nawon and needed Moon's occasional assistance. However, as he became more confident in his control of the shop floor, Jo began to consider the practice unnecessary. Finally, in early September of 2002, Jo ordered that every managerial staff on the shop floor should not consult with Moon about production-related questions. He justified the order in the name of reestablishing the original principles of factory hierarchy and complying with "global" methods of management: "It's a simple matter," he said. "The financial manager has no authority to deal with affairs on the shop floor. It only disturbs the otherwise streamlined flow of top-down authority."

While most of the Han-Chinese workers obeyed the plant manager's order, several Han-Chinese managerial staff kept asking Moon for his advice on shop-floor issues. Their seemingly defiant behavior resulted from their simple and practical need to get quick answers about problems on the shop floor: "The plant manager was not in the workshop when I needed a quick response from him," a Han-Chinese managerial staff said. "I couldn't waste time just waiting for him to return." However, the continued practice of seeking Moon's advice deeply upset Jo. "The Han-Chinese workers ignore my order in front of my face," he resentfully complained. "Sooner or later I'll correct their bad habits."

It did not take long before the plant manager finally vented his anger on the Han-Chinese managerial staff who continued to consult with Moon. One day in early October, the finishing section folders were trimming garments before putting them into plastic bags, thus finishing a period of overtime that had lasted for two weeks. At that time, the unit leaders noticed that their workers were extremely tired. They asked the finishing section leader Chen if they could let the workers trim the remaining garments while sitting on the floor. Chen allowed the workers to do so. "I believed it would be perfectly fine," she said. "The former management [of the deceased manager Bak] allowed us to work sitting on the floor when we were extremely exhausted." Section leader Chen did not inform the plant manager of her decision because, under the former management, the section leaders could change the workers' work posture at their own discretion.

Her decision provoked plant manager Jo's fierce anger. When he came back from a dinner with foreign buyers and saw the workers sitting on the floor, he shouted out in Korean: "What the hell are you doing? Is the shop floor your living room? Is there any factory in the world where workers make money while sitting on the floor?" At the moment, the Han-Chinese workers did not understand why the plant manager was shouting. There happened to be no Korean-Chinese interpreter near the plant manager. "Though we knew he was really angry," a finishing section folder remembered, "we couldn't figure out exactly what made him so mad." Bewildered workers stayed sitting, which infuriated the plant manager. Only after Jo repeatedly sat down and stood up several times to nonverbally deliver his message, did they realize that he was angry because of their work posture.

Shortly after the incident, Jo ordered all managerial staff of the finishing section to gather in front of his desk in the middle of the shop floor. When

Sumin, the Korean-Chinese senior cutter, was ready to interpret for him, the plant manager began to chastise the Han-Chinese staff. His harsh reproach on the shop floor embarrassed and humiliated the staff. It was their first time to be rebuked in front of the rank-and-file workers. Perplexed by the unexpected situation, section leader Chen tried to vindicate her decision: "I ordered the workers to sit. It had been our routine established by the former plant manager." Her comment about the former management only further provoked Jo's anger: "I don't care what plant manager Bak said before!" he shouted at her. "He's dead and now I'm the plant manager who orders what you should do!" When he belittled the deceased manager, the whole shop floor fell into a heavy silence.

TOWARD A STRIKE

The Han-Chinese workers' nostalgic memory of the former management

The plant manager's outburst sent a clear message to everybody on the shop floor: he would not tolerate any challenge to his authority, especially when it was based on the practices or principles of the former management. Many Han-Chinese workers said that, with the incident, they realized his determination to remove all the elements of the former management. "Did you see how the plant manager reacted to Chen [the finishing section leader]?" a Han-Chinese worker said. "We should be really careful not to be the target of his anger." The incident, which earned the plant manager the nickname of "Fierce Jo," seemed to enhance his shop-floor authority. After that, the Han-Chinese managerial staff waited for the plant manager at his desk when he was absent from the shop floor. They no longer consulted with financial manager Moon when they could not find the plant manager.

However, Jo soon faced strong opposition from the Han-Chinese workers. It was the "global" managerial practices he introduced that triggered the opposition. Workers clearly realized that his management was more exploitative than that of its predecessors. The overall restructuring of the workshop and the new exit rules demonstrated that he was obsessed with creating even the most minute methods of increasing productivity. What most frustrated the workers was his indifference to their expectation of "decent" wages. They argued that the indifference explained why he did not make any sincere effort to get subcontract orders. In October 2002, the workers received dismal wages, the lowest since 1997.[10] That was the result of the small volume of subcontract orders as well as reduced overtime.

As their dissatisfaction with the current management grew, the Han-Chinese workers increasingly cherished the memory of the former management. Their nostalgia for the former management did not mean that the workers felt the former management was much less authoritarian than the current one. Many workers still remembered how the late plant manager closely supervised them on the shop floor. However, plant manager Jo's total ignoring of the importance of "decent" wages and his obsessive quest for high labor productivity made the workers reflect more on the positive aspects of the former management. "Old Jo does nothing!" a senior worker exclaimed. "The only thing he can do is to sit behind his desk. . . . Oh, here's another. He shouts at us for no reason during his shop-floor inspections." Oftentimes, their criticism of Jo was followed by nostalgic comments on the deceased plant manager's unusual effort to find subcontract orders and his personal concern for the workers.

A fresh rumor from the factory main office intensified the Han-Chinese workers' discontent. According to the rumor, Nawon Korea had finally decided to dismiss Moon as financial manager and had begun an unofficial search for a replacement. Jo's secret report of Moon's alleged embezzlement fueled Nawon Korea's doubts about Moon. In fact, such a rumor was not completely new to the workers. Even during the time of plant manager Bak, they had heard rumors about the impending dismissal of both Bak and Moon. As mentioned in Chapter Six, the two expatriate managers had often disagreed with the president of Nawon Korea over the growing local influence on the factory. Their tense relationship with the president contributed to the rumors. At that time, however, the rumor proved to be false.

As for the new rumor, at first most of the Han-Chinese workers did not take it seriously. They believed that it would turn out to be no more true than the past rumors had been. However, when several workers in the finishing section revealed the plant manager's "dirty frame-up" of the financial manager, their thinking about the rumor completely changed. According to the finishing-section workers, when they were working overtime to pack rush-ordered garments, the plant manager secretly ordered them to pack defective products together with normal ones. The garments were part of a subcontract order that Moon got through his connection with a local garment factory.

The workers were afraid that the defective garments would certainly damage Moon's reputation among the local garment factories and make it much more difficult for him to get subcontract orders.

Many Han-Chinese workers suspected there might be some correlation between the recent rumor and the plant manager's secret order to pack defective garments. They thought that the plant manager, through his secret order, intended to undermine Moon's reputation and destabilize his employment status. The Han-Chinese workers' concern quickly developed into further idealization of the former management. "All the bad things came with Old Jo," a unit leader of the finishing section bitterly said. "It would have been much better if financial manager Moon had become the plant manager, instead of Old Jo." Workers were mainly concerned about the rumor because Moon was the only Korean manager at Nawon who was familiar with the practices and principles of the former management. The workers were quite certain that, without Moon, the entire factory would fall under the control of plant manager Jo and they would have to face tighter surveillance, greater labor intensity, and, most of all, decreased wages.

This dire prediction finally drove several Han-Chinese managerial staff to attempt to mobilize the workers for a collective action. "To keep the financial manager in our factory," a line leader in the sewing section said, "we should do something for him." At first, they planned to send an open letter in the name of the entire Han-Chinese workforce on the shop floor. The letter would request Nawon Korea to reconsider its decision to replace Moon. They soon realized, however, that it was very difficult to get workers' signatures. Even the workers who eagerly joined the drive for the open letter hesitated to put their names on it. They feared that Nawon Korea would reject the appeal and punish the participants. Though they were concerned about Moon, their fear of management's retaliation was stronger than their wish for the letter's success. The well-known rumor about the village gang as the mastermind behind plant manager Bak's death further discouraged workers from putting their names on the open letter. "The gang even killed the plant manager," a line leader of the sewing section said. "It'd be a piece of cake for them to do bad things to us." Workers heard that the relationship between the gang and management became estranged after Bak's death. However, they said that that did not mean the gang would not interfere in issues concerning their factory. They were worried that the gang would not tolerate any form of labor dispute on the shop floor because it eventually would weaken their influence on the workers.

A (pro-management) strike

On a normal work day in early November 2002, the Han-Chinese workers finally emerged from their political inaction. That morning, plant manager Jo started his day by eating breakfast in the factory dining hall. After breakfast, he went to the main office and had a cup of coffee served by a Korean-Chinese office worker. Everything seemed fine until people in the office noticed the unusual silence at the main gate of the factory. It was about 7:40 a.m. and the gate should have been crowded with Han-Chinese workers waiting for their turn to enter the gate. People in the office, however, did not hear the usual sound of the workers' chatting. Then, Sumin, the Korean-Chinese senior cutter, broke the uneasy silence by jumping into the office. He was holding a piece of large white paper in his hand that he found on the outside wall of the main factory building:

> Our beloved sisters!
> We ask your participation in our cause to protest against plant manager Jo. Since he became the plant manager, many problems have occurred. Our factory made less and less profit and product quality has deteriorated. All that has happened clearly demonstrates that the plant manager cannot properly administer our factory. . . . He treats us in a really bad manner. . . . For the sake of our factory, we should unite and oppose his tyranny. Any traitor to our cause should be punished in the name of our solidarity.

When he finished hearing the content of the wall poster (C. *dazibao*) through Sumin's interpretation, Jo exploded in rage. Burning with anger, he almost could not speak: "How . . . how dare they challenge me like that?!" He almost ran out of the office to find the striking workers and fight with them. Only after the Korean-Chinese office workers stopped him several times from going out of the office did Jo relent, collapsing on his chair. The strike completely shattered his confidence that the Han-Chinese workers were gradually acquiescing to his authority. It also destroyed his wishful expectation that Nawon Korea would soon dismiss financial manager Moon.[11]

Management notified the local government of the strike after its attempt to persuade the workers to return to the shop floor failed. About two hours later, officials from the labor and the public security bureaus arrived at Nawon. They considered the strike fairly moderate compared to other, serious labor disputes which involved blocking or occupying factories. At Nawon, the workers simply refused to go to work and remained gathered in the small space between the dormitory buildings. At first, the officials vainly tried to get closer to the workers by walking through the main gate. But the officials could not open the steel gate because evidently the workers had blocked the keyhole with a hard object. They did not try to forcibly enter the dormitories, worrying that that might spark a strong reaction from the workers. Instead, they tried to find the leaders of the strike and directly talk to them. But no worker stepped forward even after the officials' repeated requests.

The officials, having now run out of patience, finally decided to follow the "due procedures" set out in government regulations. They ordered the workers to gather in front of the main gate and announced that management had the right to file lawsuits against individual workers if they refused to stop the "illegal" strike and return to the shop floor. The strike was plainly illegal, they argued, because the workers did not take the legal course of grievance reconciliation before they refused to go to work: "Raise your hand," an official from the public security bureau shouted at the workers, "if you would like to face a lawsuit and pay a heavy penalty!" The workers returned to the open space between the factory dormitories and engaged in discussions. After about ten minutes, they began to return to their dorm rooms. Neither management nor the officials knew what their return meant.

To the surprise of management and the officials, around 2 p.m. of the same day, the Han-Chinese workers came back to the shop floor and resumed their work. Management felt relieved by the workers' early return because it had been worried that they would continue the strike until the local government decided to intervene. The intervention might require management to take time-consuming and often costly legal steps to resolve the incident. The Han-Chinese workers' early return also meant that management did not need to fire a large number of them, which would significantly disrupt the normal production schedule. Before the end of the day, all the production lines had resumed normal operations without a single interruption. The only difference from the routine was plant manager Jo's absence from the shop floor.

The strike demonstrates the Han-Chinese workers' potential to protest against the highly exploitative "global" management and the local gang. Most of all, it shows how, in launching the strike, the workers appropriated the spatial division originally designed by management. As mentioned in Chapter Two, management enhanced its control of labor by building the Han-Chinese workers' dormitories completely separate from the main factory site. The two checkpoints and the heavy steel gate of the dormitories restricted the workers' movement and their access to the main factory area. The workers took advantage of that and maintained the spatial division by locking up the steel gate. During the strike, no one was able to get the gate open because of the hard object that completely blocked its keyhole. This small but decisive event during the strike indicated the hidden vulnerability of management's labor control, which was revealed by the Han-Chinese workers' subversive use of the spatial division. It also shows the double-sided effect of the workers' collective living in factory dormitories, which contributed both to management's labor control and to the workers' resistance potential (Pun and Smith 2007: 41–43).

The spontaneity of the strike also reflects the Han-Chinese workers' deliberate strategy to avoid possible retaliation from the village gang. The workers clearly observed how the fear of the gang thwarted their initial plan to write an open letter to Nawon Korea. The strike with no visible leaders made it very difficult for the gang to retaliate against the organizers. Finally, the strike minimized the possibility of the gang's interference by excluding the local workers from Fuyang village. The local workers did not have even a single clue about the strike. In the morning of the strike, they came to the factory from their village homes and were completely surprised to see the workers on strike behind the closed gate. After the strike, several workers from Pingshan said that they did not give the local workers any prior notice of the strike because they suspected the local workers had secret connections with the gang.

The strike exemplifies the "rightful resistance" of farmers and migrant workers in contemporary Chinese society (O'Brien 1996). In the process of rapid social and economic change, farmers and migrant workers, poor and undereducated, have suffered from various forms of discrimination and unfair treatment. Many farmers have received insufficient compensation for their land confiscated by local government officials for new sites of factories, power plants, and residential buildings. Migrant workers often suffer from the nonpayment of wages while local government officials show little interest in their predicament. Their protests against unfair treatment and insufficient compensation often are met with threats from gangs with the tacit approval of local officials (for example, Chan 1998a, 2001; Jing 1999; O'Brien 2006; Pun 2005). Under this harsh situation, farmers and migrant workers have gradually developed a strategy of resistance that appropriates the very discourses of the powerful. Instead of resisting in a way that would imply an outright negation of the existing power structure, underprivileged people have incorporated discourses of the powerful— such as the government's slogan of "serve the people" or several lines from the Chinese labor law—into their resistance.[12] With this adaptation, they tactfully organize their resistance and reduce the risk of retaliation from corrupt local officials.

The Han-Chinese workers' strike at Nawon exhibits features of "rightful resistance." It was resistance because the workers collectively refused to go to work and asked for the removal of plant manager Jo. At the same time, the strike was "rightful." The workers argued that they mobilized the strike both for management and for themselves. In the wall poster, they claimed that the strike was in the interests of the entire company, suffering as it was from the new plant manager's improper administration of the shop floor. Their resistance never denied the hierarchical difference between management and labor. By appealing to the executives at Nawon Korea for Jo's removal, the workers acknowledged the company headquarters' prime authority. What the workers wanted was simply "proper" management.

The strike, at the same time, revealed the Han-Chinese workers' limited understanding of the structural mechanism behind "global" management. In a broad context, the strike resulted from the macro-level changes in the global chain of garment production, including the fierce price competition among contract factories and the long-term recession in overseas consumer markets. Plant manager Jo's obsession with labor-squeezing methods reflected the increasingly exploitative nature of the global garment industry as well as his uncompromising personal character. The strike, however, did not target the global mechanism of labor squeezing. Instead, the Han-Chinese workers thought that Jo's *personal* inability and defects caused all the recent problems at Nawon. In their nostalgic recollection of deceased plant manager Bak, the workers often described their relationship with him as more personal and human than entirely economic and contractual. In contrast, the workers described Jo as an ill-tempered individual who was hardly concerned about them. For them, the structural factors were far beyond their everyday reality of the workshop. They believed that all the negative developments in the factory would disappear by removing plant manager Jo—the individual who came from Guatemala, bringing all the bad things with him.

ULTIMATE LOCALIZATION OF A FOREIGN MANAGEMENT?

About one month after the strike, Nawon Korea announced that plant manager Jo would leave Nawon and take up the position of plant manager at the mother factory in South Korea. Nawon Korea, with the announcement, emphasized that the change was not related to the strike. According to their official explanation, it was due to the mother factory's need for a new plant manager to replace the old one, who was retiring. Jo would be an ideal match for the position, Nawon Korea said, because he had served as a plant manager of the mother factory and was familiar with its shop-floor situation. Few at Nawon, however, believed the explanation. Most employees at Nawon—both Korean-Chinese and Han-Chinese— suspected that Nawon Korea, with the unexpectedly early position change, had rebuked Jo. He apparently failed to achieve his managerial objective of establishing a "global" management. "Nawon Korea purposefully did not use the word dismissal," a Korean-Chinese interpreter argued, "because they were afraid it might give an impression to the Han-Chinese workers that they accepted the workers' call to replace the plant manager."

In fact, the decision reflected Nawon Korea's acknowledgment of the ultimate failure of "global" management. The strike deeply shocked the executives at Nawon Korea because they never anticipated it. They had been satisfied with the enhanced labor productivity and the reduced overtime under the new management. The executives even regarded these early achievements as signs of the plant manager's consolidating power on the shop floor. The strike shattered this belief and forced them to accept that the attempt to transplant a "global" management from Guatemala had failed. Some executives at Nawon Korea even said that their experiment with "global" management was more than a simple failure, because it caused the unprecedented workers' strike. They concluded that "global" management only inflicted additional damage on the weakened managerial authority on the shop floor.

The ultimate failure of "global" management placed Nawon Korea in a deep dilemma: who could be the next plant manager, taking the difficult role of undoing all of the fresh damage done to managerial authority? Could this be achieved with another, probably more extreme version of "global" management? If so, how could another "global" plant manager avoid the resistance of the Han-Chinese workers who now might be more confident in their ability to resist? Or would it be better to step back from "global" management? In the end, the executives at Nawon Korea concluded that any further push toward a higher level of globalization would only provoke the workers to protest. After heated discussions about the future management at Nawon, Nawon Korea appointed financial manager Moon as the new plant manager. The decision indicated that Nawon Korea had reversed its policy on a higher level of globalization, at least for a while returning to the previous managerial principles under the deceased plant manager, Bak. "Since Manager Moon was close to the deceased plant manager," a senior executive at Nawon Korea said, "he should be able to restore management's authority within a short time." He added that the Han-Chinese workers "should be happy" with the decision.

As expected, Moon, as the new plant manager, restored managerial authority over the shop floor within a short time. Within two weeks of his appointment, management saw some positive changes in the workshop. The hourly output increased to its pre-strike level and the product defect rate significantly dropped. Management also said that there was no report of worker misconduct on the shop floor. This kind of tranquility was highly unusual in a factory that had recently experienced a floor-wide strike. The fast restoration of the shop-floor routine largely resulted from the Han-Chinese workers' high expectations of the new plant manager. The new plant manager, Moon, many workers thought, would meet their expectations of management because he had been close to the deceased manager and familiar with his managerial principles and practices. "Just like plant manager Bak," a senior Han-Chinese worker said, "Moon *understands* what we're really concerned about" (emphasis by the interviewee).

Moon knew what the Han-Chinese workers expected from his management. "They trust me," he once said, "because they think that I understand what they work for." He also knew, however, that the Han-Chinese workers' support was conditional. It would disappear if he failed to meet their expectations of "decent" wages and paternalistic treatment. To meet the workers' expectations, first he undid the changes brought by his predecessor's "global" management. He abolished the unit system and reestablished the work-group system in the finishing section. He also restored the Han-Chinese staff's authority by allowing them to resolve minor issues on the shop floor at their own discretion. Finally, he abandoned the exit rule introduced by Jo. These moves reinforced the workers' conviction that Moon's managerial principles would be different from Jo's "global" management.

The Han-Chinese workers gladly accepted the changes. The rank-and-file workers welcomed the resumption of the exit rules as they had existed under Bak's management because they had been deeply embarrassed with the labor-squeezing effect of the manager Jo's exit rule. The Han-Chinese staff were also delighted with the restoration of their authority on minor issues on the shop floor. They had felt humiliated by the near-dictatorial managerial style of Jo, who ordered them to report even minor changes on the shop floor to him. Interestingly, few workers regarded the restoration as management's concession to them. Instead, they thought that the changes meant that management had returned to the "good old days" that had existed under Bak's leadership. Many workers thought that the restoration, which came with Moon's appointment as the plant manager, would bring back the "good" management in their memory. The return of "good" management, they expected, would once again guarantee them "decent" wages.

Plant manager Moon, however, could not restore every element of Bak's management. For one thing, Moon did not have the kind of charisma Bak had.[13] To make matters worse, Nawon Korea was suffering from a deteriorating financial situation and could not provide any support for the new plant manager. In 2003, two Japanese buyers unexpectedly informed the corporation that they would terminate their decade-long business relations with Nawon Korea. Increasing labor costs and Nawon Korea's inability to upgrade production facilities explained the loss of key buyers. Since the mid-1990s, workers' yearly average income in Shandong Province had increased by more than 10 percent each year.[14] Recently opened factories with plenty of capital maintained their competitiveness by installing efficient, labor-saving production equipment. Such factories attracted buyers with their competitive prices guaranteed by the highly automated production lines. Nawon Korea could not provide the necessary upgrade for the aging facilities at Nawon because it did not have sufficient financial resources. This eventually created a vicious cycle of rising production costs and a decreasing volume of orders, which further undercut Nawon Korea's financial situation.

In view of his lack of charisma and Nawon Korea's financial inability to support Nawon, plant manager Moon sought other resources to consolidate his managerial authority. He never regarded the village officials as a potential resource because he suspected that they were closely related to plant manager Bak's death. Instead, he tried to win support from the Han-Chinese workers, especially from those on the shop floor. As the number of expatriate Korean managers and Korean-Chinese interpreters had been greatly reduced, the Han-Chinese staff on the shop floor became the main mediators between management and the rank-and-file workers. It was crucial, therefore, for Moon to win their support. Moon more aggressively sought the Han-Chinese staff's support when he learned that they had organized the strike to retain him in the factory.

With his effort to win the Han-Chinese workers' support, plant manager Moon also intended to reduce the local power holders' influence on the factory. As the closest Korean manager to deceased manager Bak, he strongly suspected the Han-Chinese workers from Fuyang village of conspiring with the local gang to steal materials from the workshop. He believed that the petty theft eventually caused Bak's death when he tried to stop the stealing by breaking the gang's connections within the factory. In a private conversation with me, Moon said that he could check the gang's influence on the shop floor in a relatively safe way, by establishing a close relationship with the nonlocal Han-Chinese managerial staff. At Nawon, except for the finishing section leader, all high-ranking Han-Chinese managerial staff on the shop floor came from Pingshan. They bitterly resented the local employees from Fuyang village because many of them, sometimes even some rank-and-file workers, tended to disregard their authority as managerial staff. "Local workers look down on us deep in their heart," a Han-Chinese line leader from Pingshan said. "They only pretended to obey our orders." The rumor about a possible connection between the local workers and the gang only increased the nonlocal workers' dislike of the local workers. Moon believed that he could enhance his control of the workshop and reduce the local influence by winning the support of the nonlocal Han-Chinese staff.

First, to gain greater support from the Han-Chinese staff, Moon scheduled an after-work drinking session with them. Since the early period of Nawon, the Korean managers and the Korean-Chinese interpreters had occasional after-hour gatherings at a nearby tavern. Management arranged them to lessen the tension on the shop floor and maintain a good relationship with the interpreters. The practice was abolished by the former plant manager Jo, who thought that it would only blur the distinction between management and labor and damage his impersonal and "global" management. Moon resumed the drinking sessions and invited some Han-Chinese staff as well as Korean-Chinese interpreters. The new inclusion pleased the Han-Chinese staff. "We were really excited," a sewing-section line leader said, "because it was our first time to join the session. It had been open only to the Korean-Chinese interpreters."

About an hour after the beginning of the first drinking session, something unexpected happened. After having several glasses of beer, many participants felt somewhat drunk. Amid the hustle and bustle of the tavern, the Korean-Chinese interpreters and the Han-Chinese staff urged Moon to talk about how he felt when he became the new plant manager. After refusing several times, Moon rose from his seat. He seemed drunk after consuming strong liquor offered by the attending staff:

> I'm not a Korean "bastard" but a Chinese "gentleman." Why? I've already spent eight years in China and I've worked with you all that time. As you very well know, last year I visited Korea just one time, for six days only. . . . The Korean executives at Nawon Korea don't know China. Do you know any of them who remembers your name? They come, lodge in luxury downtown hotels only for several days, and then go back to Korea. How can they know the freezing cold of the shop floor in winter, how can they know the steaming heat of the factory in summer? . . . Now that I'm in charge of the whole factory, you can seek my help in case of trouble. . . . Cheers!

Although he did not speak in fluent Chinese, the term "bastard" that Moon used to refer to the executives at Nawon Korea surprised all those present. Among them, the Han-Chinese staff were shocked by his strong criticism of the Korean executives. None of them had ever imagined them being called "bastards" in such an official occasion. His strong remark shocked the staff also because they thought that Moon would eventually take sides with Nawon Korea. Although he "understood" the workers and had a human feeling toward them, Moon, as plant manager, was still a member of management. At the drinking session, Moon contrasted his hardworking image on the shop floor with the image of Korean executives who stayed in downtown hotels during their occasional factory visits. With the contrast, he boasted about his moral superiority over the executives and his closeness to the Han-Chinese workers.

His surprising comment about the executives at Nawon Korea made many Han-Chinese staff trust the plant manager even more. They believed in the genuineness of his statement because he made the comment while risking Nawon Korea's possible punishment for disobedience. The Han-Chinese workers' growing distrust of the executives at Nawon Korea also contributed to their trust in Moon. A Han-Chinese worker told me of an episode to point out their lack of sincerity:

> One day, a Korean executive unexpectedly visited our factory canteen. Entering the canteen, the executive briefly frowned to see how crowded it was. Then he asked us to give him one of the steamed buns [C. *mantou*] on the table. He put a small piece of the bun in his mouth and chewed. All of a sudden, he smiled at us and said in clumsy Chinese: "It is really tasty." His comment amazed us because we thought that he couldn't speak Chinese. . . . Anyway, we were happy to see him eating a bun. We had never imagined that he would dare to eat the crappy canteen food. . . . We were deeply disappointed, however, when we saw him dumping the remaining bun on his way back to the factory office.

Plant manager Moon's surprising statement at the drinking session not only made the Han-Chinese workers feel closer to him. It also strengthened their support of the new management, because it resonated with their negative view of headquarters. Workers considered the executives of Nawon Korea distant from the sweaty workshop and lacking sincerity. In contrast, they believed that Moon was close to their life of toil and more sincere in his relationship with them than the executives.

Though Moon inherited many features of Bak's management, he did not have the deceased manager's charisma. Therefore, he resorted to open expressions of paternalism and loosening factory regulations to gain the Han-Chinese workers' support. He often emphasized his role as a caring manager who was concerned about the workers. In several drinking sessions with the Han-Chinese staff, he also mentioned that he was the only Korean manager who understood the detailed situation of the factory and thus could create "decent" wages for the workers. He further sought the workers' support by rarely using extreme measures against them. For example, he stopped applying the rules of collective punishment and practicing the morning exercise. The plant manager argued that they were no longer useful because the Han-Chinese workers well understood the regulations and the spirit of collectivism. "The workers do what they should do," he argued, "because they are thoroughly accustomed to the rules and practices." In addition, he gave the Han-Chinese staff more comprehensive authority on the shop floor, allowing them to resolve by themselves a larger number of production-related issues.

CONCLUSION: THE LIMITS OF GLOBALIZATION

All the developments at Nawon after plant manager Bak's death clearly show how a certain mode of globalization can heighten discontent at the local level and eventually provoke a backlash against the globalizing process. In the multinational Nawon factory, the term "global" concealed the exploitative and impersonal nature of the new management. Plant manager Jo justified his obsession with labor-squeezing methods in the name of globalization, which in fact were based on his personal experience of the highly authoritarian management of *maquila* factories. Believing in the superiority and universal applicability of his "global" management, he ignored the significance of "decent" wages for the Han-Chinese workers and failed to express proper concern for them. That heightened the Han-Chinese workers' discontent with his management and eventually triggered the unprecedented workers' strike.

The strike demonstrates that a unilateral mode of globalization inadvertently contributes to creating critical local assessments of the very process, especially when it violates existing local ideas of the proper and moral order of things and behaviors. The common view of multinational corporations assumes that they, using their overwhelming economic and political resources, can impose their own values and practices on local employees regardless of the latter's existing values and practices.

The ultimate failure of "global" management at Nawon corrects the overly triumphant view of multinational corporations and highlights the importance of local values and practices to their "smooth" operations. The strike, however, did not mean that the Han-Chinese workers changed the fundamental mechanism of the global chain of garment production, such as its constant demand for reducing lead time and production costs. After the strike, the Han-Chinese workers observed some positive changes on the shop floor, such as the end of Jo's "global" management, the enhanced authority of the Han-Chinese staff, and the limited use of extreme methods of punishment and labor control. However, "good" management and the positive changes on the shop floor were subject to the impersonal mechanisms of a global industry. Workers lacked effective means to restrain that industry and, in fact, with any change in the global industry they might lose whatever little they had achieved.

My study highlights a little-studied aspect of "localization" in multinational corporations, the growing significance of local values in actual corporate management. In many management studies, the term "localization" means a significant participation of local staff in management (Shanghai Asset Inc. 2005; Shin 1993). However, many foreign managements believe that, to localize, they first have to transform the local employees' consciousness, making their "parochial" values and ideas more compatible with the "global" or "universal" standards of multinational corporations (Lawrence and Yeh 1994; Doeringer et al. 1998; Fuller 2009). The decade-long changes in the management of Nawon correspond to "localization." At Nawon, both the Korean-Chinese and the Han-Chinese employees had been promoted to managerial staff positions, gradually replacing the expatriate Korean managers. Management's consistent effort to transform the Han-Chinese workers' "peasant" consciousness also shows that the management was concerned about deeper-level changes in its local employees.

Localization at Nawon took a different direction when plant manager Moon attempted to consolidate his shop floor authority by gaining the support of the Han-Chinese workers. According to the common managerial idea of "localization," management highly values local employees only when they sacrifice their local values. In order to be promoted, they must behave and think like "global" employees. In the process of transformation, foreign management must keep its status as the guarantor and the missionary of global values and standards. At Nawon, however, localization proceeded in a different way, as the management actively incorporated key local values that had originated from the Han-Chinese workers' personal and collective experience on the shop floor and in their rural hometowns. Diminishing support from its headquarters and the local power holders' infiltration into the factory induced management to make this change. A moral contract between management and labor became more important as plant manager Moon increasingly appealed to the Han-Chinese workers' expectation of "ideal" management embedded in local ideas of paternalist leadership and moral obligation.

EIGHT

Globalizing Capital and the Bleak Future of Chinese Workers

Multinational corporations (MNCs) are places where the dynamic relationship between the global and the local are configured, bringing social and economic changes to the local communities involved in MNCs' operations. Responding to the imperatives of capital to reduce lead time and cut production costs, MNCs try to find ideal places for profit maximization. The relocation of South Korean corporations to China clearly shows how capital incessantly moves from one place to another according to the changing business conditions of specific locations. However, contrary to the overly triumphant image of a global capitalism that "compels all nations to adopt its mode of production" (Marx and Engels 1992 [1848]: 22), MNCs cannot impose their organizational principles and managerial practices on local people in a unilateral manner. Instead, operations in a new location always need support from the local, because MNCs require a stable and timely supply of local infrastructure, business-related services, and, most of all, cheap labor. MNCs' demand for local operations meets with local government's desire for developing its economy, which eventually creates not a unilateral but a collaborative relationship between the two.

At Nawon, local politics and the histories of China and South Korea complicated the formation of a multinational management and its methods of labor control. The management at Nawon was a historical creation of the rapid industrialization of South Korea, which was also a consequence of globalizing capitalism. The process was characterized by many years of military government, an authoritarian work culture, and large-scale foreign investments in the country. At the beginning of its operations in China, Nawon's management assumed itself to be the messenger of the highly efficient production technologies and managerial know-how of advanced industrialism. The basic architecture of the factory buildings and the organization of the shop floor reflected the "universal" know-how and principles of advanced industrialism. Just like other foreign managements that view local labor as backward and undisciplined, Nawon's management considered the Chinese workers on the shop floor to be still locked in the values and practices of underdeveloped farming villages. Especially during the early period of its operations in China, management assumed its superiority to Chinese labor, believing in its advanced position in the unilinear process of modernization.

Behind its facade as an agent of advanced industrialism, however, the Nawon management retained characteristics that cannot be explained by the universalist discourse. For example, management divided the living and working spaces according to the ethnicity of its employees and discriminated in its treatment of them on the same basis. These divisions and discrimination originated from management's arbitrary understanding of national and ethnic differences between Koreans, Korean-Chinese, and Han-Chinese. The managers' memory of the Korean War and radical Maoism, and their deep-rooted misgivings about historical Sino-centrism heavily affected their understanding. The actual managerial practices of Nawon indicate that MNCs' premise of their superiority and their resort to a universalist discourse are in fact heavily affected by their limited experience in their countries of origin and their own localized concepts and values.

Nawon management's particular view of the ethnic division between Han-Chinese and Korean-Chinese played a crucial role in shop-floor politics. The division was not an expression of any inherent ethnic differences. The management, with its essentializing ideas about the Korean nation and Korean culture, regarded Korean-Chinese as more reliable and obedient than Han-Chinese. The management made use of the alleged ethnic superiority of Korean-Chinese, the other side of the supposed ethnic inferiority of the Han-Chinese, to consolidate its control of local labor and expedite its adjustment to the new business situation in China. It was management's pronounced bias in favor of Korean-Chinese and against Han-Chinese that led to Korean-Chinese holding most of the prestigious white-collar jobs in the office and the intermediary managerial staff positions on the shop floor. The ethnic division of labor transformed the small group of Korean-Chinese employees into a wealthy ethnic minority who were strongly pro-management. This unique situation where the new post-socialist division between white- and blue-collar jobs closely overlapped with the ethnic division between Korean-Chinese and Han-Chinese created and perpetuated ethnic tensions on the shop floor and a deep schism among the Chinese employees.

Management's changing strategies of labor discipline and surveillance exemplified the influence of local politics and history. As management encountered unexpected problems in its "universal" methods of labor control and discipline, it increasingly resorted to its own experience and managerial know-how. The militarized work culture of South Korea and a plebeian version of Confucianism inspired management to introduce new principles and methods of labor discipline such as the morning drill and the writing exercise. It was management's "collective misrecognition," a local effect of globalization, that justified the introduction. Management believed that the Han-Chinese women workers at Nawon shared some key characteristics with the Korean women workers of the past. By introducing labor-controlling methods once widely used in South Korea, the managers argued that the similarities would guarantee the effectiveness of those methods when applied to the Han-Chinese workers.

In the multinational Nawon factory, personal memories, hopes for a better future, and expectations of "good" management contributed to a unique factory regime. In particular, under the charismatic-paternalist factory regime, plant manager Bak successfully administered the shop floor with the Han-Chinese workers' trust in his distinctive personal characteristics. On the one hand, his paternalistic concern for the Han-Chinese workers, mostly expressed in his effort to secure a large volume of subcontract orders, gained the workers' trust. His unusual concern originated from his personal memory of South Korean women workers and his sister, who had sacrificed her youth for the sake of their family. The plant manager saw the image of Korean women workers among the Han-Chinese workers. He believed that they shared with their Korean counterparts the virtue of filial obligation. On the other hand, the Han-Chinese workers acknowledged and followed the plant manager's charismatic leadership because they believed that he understood the importance of "decent" wages and treated them humanely. Some workers even found similarities between their fathers and Bak. None of them directly expressed this feeling, but the workers nonetheless thought that, like their fathers, Bak had a heartfelt concern for them. The interplay of memories and expectations created a subtle moral contract between management and labor. In this relationship, management attempted to secure "decent" wages and treat the workers in a "humane" way, while the workers followed management's orders, trusting in its ability and concern for them. The moral contract demonstrates how the transnational movement of a corporation can lead to unexpected local consequences in the tense situation of a sweatshop.

Post-socialist conditions of China also heavily affected the formation of management at Nawon and its factory regime. The secretive network of ties between village officials and the foreign management had a powerful labor-controlling effect. The network was also indirectly connected to the "merger of the black and white," the growing interpenetration of local government officials and criminal organizations. To ensure the success of its local operation, the Nawon management had relied on the village officials' support for the administration of the factory dormitories and a stable supply of cheap migrant labor. The deteriorating financial situation, aging facilities, and a tightening government's inspections of the factory led management to increasingly depend on the unofficial services provided by the village officials. Its growing reliance on the cozy relationship eventually gave birth to the tripartite collusion among the foreign management, the local government officials, and the village gang.

The deepening collaboration, however, eventually resulted in a violent collision between the foreign management and the local power holders. When management saw the increasingly negative effects of the local influence over the factory, it tried to reduce the local power holders' intervention. The attempt provoked a strong reaction from the local power holders that culminated in plant manager Bak's mysterious death. The aftermath of this incident revealed management's ultimate inability to check the intruding local influence, because it failed to prove the alleged local conspiracy behind Bak's death. Management's sense of being beleaguered by the local power holders demonstrates that the images of free-flowing transnational capital and multinational corporations are plainly wrong. The developments at Nawon suggest that multinational corporations may become vulnerable to local influence as they increasingly rely on the support of the local.

The process of globalization at Nawon made the Han-Chinese workers the most underprivileged of all the employees. On the sweaty shop floor, they endured the brunt of grueling sweatshop labor and the tight supervision of foreign management. The management's labor control was reinforced by the local surveillance of the village officials, local residents, and the village gang. Despite the hardships, however, most of the workers in the end could not escape from their fate as "daughters of poor peasants." By referring to their fate, I do not mean that the Han-Chinese workers were helpless victims of exploitative global capitalism and oppressive local politics. On the contrary, the workers at Nawon were conscious of the labor-controlling effects brought by the surveillance methods and tried to find loopholes in management's control of labor. They chose various tactics of resistance ranging from an open strike to more subtle forms of resistance that might be called "weapons of the weak" (Scott 1985: 29). Their resistance, however, did not bring them the expected results. As far as open resistance is concerned, the workers targeted the "global" management methods from Guatemala that were excessively exploitative and lacking any concern for them. They believed that replacing the "bad" management with a "good" one would resolve their grievances. However, they failed to see that the management they encountered on the shop floor was a local agent of the global garment industry, which was incessantly seeking to reduce lead time and production costs. The workers, therefore, were vulnerable to the structural changes in the global chain of garment industry, which could destroy whatever they achieved through resistance. The developments after the workers' successful strike against plant manager Jo, the topic of this chapter, reveal the fundamental limits of their resistance.

POST-FIELDWORK: THE CHINESE
GOVERNMENT'S POLICY CHANGES
AND THEIR IMPACT ON MNCS

Under Moon's supervision when he was the plant manager, Nawon restored its normal operations. The company statistics at Nawon Korea showed that the factory fulfilled every order that it received from the corporate headquarters on time. This was a fairly remarkable achievement for a factory that had recently experienced a strike. It was more remarkable because plant manager Moon had not always been successful in securing a sufficient volume of subcontract orders to guarantee "decent" wages. Sometimes Han-Chinese workers received wages that did not meet their expectations. They even experienced delayed pay at least twice. This, however, did not create any noticeable instability on the shop floor. The Han-Chinese workers still basically trusted that the new management was doing its best to guarantee them fair wages. Although the workers knew very well that the plant manager did not always meet their expectation for the on-time payment of a fair amount of wages, they thought that it was not entirely his fault: "We don't blame the plant manager for the small wages," a Han-Chinese worker said in her email correspondence with me. "We know that the plant manager does his best. . . . The problem is in the bad market situation, which he cannot control." The comment reflected the Han-Chinese workers' strong belief in the plant manager's effort to guarantee them "decent" wages and his personal concern for them.

The seemingly stable shop-floor situation, however, did not last for long. The factory regime under Moon was vulnerable to the changing situation outside the factory just as the preceding factory regimes were. Changes in the Chinese government's labor policy put management under mounting pressure. After 2000, the Chinese government started paying attention to the growing income gap in China and its potential negative effects on social stability and future economic growth. According to a report published by a government research institute, the average per capita disposable income of the richest 10 percent was more than eight times larger than that of the bottom 10 percent (CASS 2006). To check the growing inequality, the government launched a nationwide campaign for a "harmonious socialist society." The campaign aimed at building a society characterized by "socialist democracy, rule of law, equity, justice, sincerity, amity, vitality, stability and order, as well as the harmonious coexistence between man and nature" (Xin 2004; Xing 2005).

Under the slogan of "a harmonious society," the Chinese government vowed to improve the quality of life of low-income people by launching new polices and strictly enforcing existing laws. For example, the Standing Committee of the National People's Congress, one of the top state organizations, approved an amendment to the personal income tax law in 2005 that raised the threshold for monthly personal income tax from 800 yuan (about US$100 in 2005) to 1,600 yuan (about US$200 in 2005), thus increasing low-wage earners' actual income (Xinhua News Agency 2005b). The government also announced that it would strictly supervise corporate payments for employee benefits programs, such as retirement, health care, unemployment, education, and industrial-commercial insurance. For many MNCs in China, however, this policy change only meant a new burden of increased labor costs. If a firm fully complied with the strengthened requirements for insurance payments, it would have to bear up to a 30 percent increase in labor costs. The government also warned that the required monthly insurance payment would be increased if a firm failed to pay the obligated amount (Tak 2006a: 85–86).

What had the most direct impact on the MNCs was the Chinese government's new minimum wage guidelines. The guidelines had remained unchanged for almost ten years after their introduction in 1994. In March 2004, the government finally amended them in order to narrow the income gap. Under the new guidelines, local governments should make at least one upward adjustment to their local minimum wage within a two-year period. This policy change implied that the government had begun to change its initial laissez-fair attitude toward MNCs and take a more interventionist approach.

In addition to the changes in the minimum wage guidelines and the requirements regarding employee benefits, the central government announced a new plan to reduce the tax benefits enjoyed by MNCs, including the abolishment of the two-year basic tax exemption and a decrease in the preferred tax rates from 24 to 15 percent. The government made this decision in response to growing complaints from domestic firms about the tax benefits accorded to MNCs. They argued that the benefits were unfair and should be abolished in order to spur the growth of domestic businesses (Tak 2006b).

The central government's new policies and guidelines had an immediate effect on local governments. In 2005, the Shandong provincial government increased the local minimum wage by 29 percent, from 410 to 530 yuan. The Qingdao municipal government also urged corporations, including MNCs, to fully pay their share of the corporate benefits, especially insurance, for their employees (Tak 2006a: 86). In addition, local Chinese governments began to require MNCs to submit detailed reports about their imported and exported materials to the local customs office. Considering that many MNCs in China benefited from the local Chinese government's low tax rates and loose customs control, the changes in tax policies and supervision could be expected to further reduce MNCs' profits (Chen 2004; Tak 2006c; Tse and Zhou 2005; Xie 2006).

The Chinese government's revamped anticorruption drive also had an impact on the MNCs' business practices, because it targeted not only corrupt local officials but also businesses close to them. Since 2005, several key government reports and newspaper articles have severely criticized "corrupt elements" among party cadres and government officials as one of the key reasons of the growing income gap (Wu 2006).[1] For example, the Information Office of the State Council and the "internal reference" reports of the Xinhua News Agency warned of the growing numbers of local government officials "who do not believe in any socialist values but only pursue money and power" (*Guojia shiwu* 2006).

In fact, corruption in the CCP and various government bodies was not a new topic in Chinese media. Despite the government's repeated warnings about "bad elements" and periodic crackdowns on corrupt officials, the practice has remained widespread. A report of the Supreme People's Procuratorate shows that more than 32,000 officials were investigated in 2005 by public prosecutors for alleged corruption, and over a half of them were found guilty (Liu 2006).[2] Recognizing the growing scale of government corruption and its harmful impact on the people's faith in the government, the CCP finally took a series of comprehensive steps to prevent corruption and counteract the social instabilities caused by the unequal distribution of wealth (Xinhua News Agency 2006; Yan 2006).

The effects of the anticorruption campaign soon appeared in Qingdao. In 2005, the national media widely reported the public prosecutions of the former Qingdao vice-mayor Wang and the former director of the municipal planning department, Zhang (On 2005; Xie 2005). Court investigations revealed that, during their terms of office, Wang accepted twenty-four bribes from fourteen companies (amounting to 4.96 million yuan) while Zhang received ninety-six bribes from thirty-eight companies and individuals (amounting to 8.6 million yuan). Both were sentenced to death with a two-year reprieve and deprived of their political rights for life. The government confiscated all of their personal property. Local government's anticorruption campaigns also targeted foreign nationals. On February 25, 2005, the Shandong provincial bureau of public security announced that it had detained a South Korean on suspicion of running an underground bank in Qingdao. Using the underground bank, he allegedly transferred 240 million yuan in and out of China illegally. The municipal police arrested him together with seventeen local accomplices, and confiscated 1.35 million yuan in cash (Hu 2005).[3]

By weakening the existing cozy relationship between some local government officials and foreign management, the anticorruption campaign brought changes to the mode of global-local collaboration in China. It is difficult to judge exactly how much the recent anticorruption campaign has changed the collaborative relationship between MNCs and local government officials. As media reports have indicated, the campaign may have weakened the collaboration because it targeted both officials and foreign nationals. In email correspondence after my fieldwork, Korean-Chinese interpreters of Nawon testified that, at least in the factory, they rarely saw the president of Nawon Korea meeting local officials. They also maintained that the village officials stopped providing management with the schedule of the government's factory inspections. However, it is not clear whether these changes were directly related to the anticorruption campaign. Nawon's management and the officials might have been just waiting for the end of the campaign to resume their cozy relationship. Regardless of its long-term effects, however, the recent campaign clearly showed that Chinese government finally had begun to pay attention to the "special" relationship between its officials and MNCs. This suggests that the collaboration between the local and the global will not be the same as it has been.

KOREAN MNCS' RESPONSE
TO THE POLICY CHANGES

The management of many Korean MNCs in Qingdao took seriously the possible negative effects of the government's policy changes.[4] Especially for small- and medium-sized corporations in labor-intensive industries, it was clear that the changes would raise production costs, adding to the annual growth of labor costs.[5] Even before the policy changes, in the period from 1991 to 2002, the average wage in China multiplied by more than four times and the annual average increase was 16.3 percent (KITA 2003). So far, however, most corporations have been able to maintain their operations in China because the labor costs in China, even after the increases, are still lower than those of other countries. In 2002, the hourly compensation for workers in the manufacturing sector of China was only 3.3 percent of that of the United States. It was lower than those of South Korea (31 percent), Malaysia (12.3 percent), the Philippines (5.6 percent), and Thailand (8.7 percent) (KITA 2003). This difference explains why many Korean corporations in the labor-intensive, light industrial sectors have kept their businesses in China despite the double-digit wage increases each year.

The wage hike of close to 30 percent in the 2000s, however, made many Korean MNCs in labor-intensive industries feel the cost pressure to have been very serious indeed. They worried that another dramatic wage hike would bring their companies to a "deal-breaker" point, or make their business in the location virtually meaningless. In his email correspondence with me, a Korean expatriate manager of a nearby Korean shoe factory confirmed that many Korean MNCs thought business conditions in China were becoming unfavorable: "The golden age of labor-intensive industries in China," the manager said, "is nearing its end." With his long-term career as a senior manager both in South Korea and in China, he very well knew what the annual double-digit wage increases implied for the future of his company's business in China. Several Korean-Chinese interpreters in other Korean MNCs also said that many small-sized Korean MNCs already had begun calculating the relative advantages of relocating their business to places such as inland China and other foreign countries (Wang-Bae Kim 2004; Taehee Lee 2006; interview with a Korean manager 2003; online interviews with Korean-Chinese interpreters 2005).

The worrisome predictions of factory relocations soon became a harsh reality. Since early 2005, various news media started covering the possible massive relocation of MNCs from China to other countries such as India, Vietnam, and Bangladesh. According to the media reports, many MNCs began to arrange backup plans for relocation out of China, worrying that China's double-digit wage hike would soon substantially reduce their profits (Barboza 2006; BBC News 2005; Bonyeong Lee 2005b; Song 2006). Sometimes the relocation of MNCs was realized in a rather dramatic way. Korean national media reported stories of runaway Korean factory owners in China who had fled to Korea the night before their factories went bankrupt. Both South Korean and other foreign media reports pointed out that the rapidly growing labor costs in China would soon bring some MNCs in the labor-intensive industrial sector to the limit of what they could tolerate: "They went to China with the dream of a bonanza" a newspaper article wrote, "but what they eventually encountered was not a promised land but the harsh reality of rapidly increasing wages and strict government supervision" (Song 2006). This was, needless to say, a dramatic about-face from their overly positive view of MNCs in China during the pre-2004 period.

How, then, did the MNCs in China cope with all of the recent changes in government policies? What were their exact strategies to keep their businesses alive in the face of fast-growing operation costs? The developments at Nawon and Nawon Korea give us some hints about MNCs' responses to the changing business climate in China. Interestingly, the executives of Nawon Korea said that they were not that surprised by the big increase in the minimum wage. They acknowledged that it would certainly be a heavy burden on their business. At the same time, however, they argued that the wage hike was what they had expected: "There's nothing new in a double-digit increase in labor costs," an executive at Nawon Korea said. "What is important is exactly how we can cope with the change." He added that all the changes at Nawon, especially the constant shifts in the composition of the managerial staff, demonstrated how successfully they had responded to the rapidly growing labor costs "despite some glitches."[6] The executives at Nawon Korea seemed to believe that they could successfully deal with the wage hike and the enhanced government supervision, just as it had survived all the past challenges.

At this time, however, management's response was fundamentally different from before. Several months after the provincial government's decision to increase the minimum wage, Nawon Korea revealed a new plan of order outsourcing to "effectively cope with the rapidly changing market situation."[7] Nawon Korea began the practice of order outsourcing in a rather accidental way. During the brief but severe crisis caused by SARS (Severe Acute Respiratory Syndrome) in 2003, Nawon Korea happened to receive a rush order from one of its key buyers.[8] The executives at Nawon Korea soon realized that the rapidly spreading disease had caused lengthy delays in logistics and disrupted production, which made it nearly impossible for Nawon to fulfill the order in time. While desperately searching for a solution, Nawon Korea found a garment factory in Vietnam that offered a highly competitive per-unit price for the order. The executives at Nawon Korea finally signed a one-time production contract with the Vietnamese factory because the large profit that would be created by the low per-unit price in Vietnam was too attractive for them to decline. In fact, the decision reflected the big difference in the labor costs between the two countries. In 2006, the cost of labor in Vietnam was 25 to 30 percent lower than in China (Park 2006; Perlez 2006). This was a highly attractive condition for labor-intensive industries such as garments, toys, and shoes, which had been suffering from the rising labor costs in China.

The fortuitous contract with the Vietnamese garment factory led to a successful result for Nawon Korea. The product quality and the order fulfillment speed of the Vietnamese factory exceeded Nawon Korea's expectations and dissipated most of its doubt about the factory's reliability. The success also confirmed that Vietnam could be an alternative production site when Nawon Korea could not use Nawon as its primary production site. "It was our biggest harvest," a senior manager at Nawon Korea said, "finding such a reliable production site outside China." This successful outsourcing, however, did not lead to instant changes such as a new investment plan in Vietnam. Although quite successful, the Vietnamese deal was not large enough to convince Nawon Korea to take the risk of investing in Vietnam. As a medium-sized corporation that had suffered from steadily decreasing profits, Nawon Korea had every reason to be cautious when it came to large investments such as establishing a new production facility in another, remote place. Finally, after a long discussion, the executives at Nawon Korea decided to keep Nawon operating for the time being. They thought that it was still necessary to maintain production facilities in China at least until they recuperated their past capital investment in Nawon. Nawon Korea at the same time decided to use factories in Vietnam as secondary production sites.

The developments at Nawon Korea implied that the new practice of order outsourcing was a preparatory move for an ultimate relocation to Vietnam. The executives at Nawon Korea notified the two expatriate managers at Nawon of the order outsourcing after the decision was made. They asked the managers to keep the decision secret from other employees at Nawon because they were afraid it would disrupt the normal operation of the branch factory. Instead of making any public announcement of the outsourcing, the executives at Nawon Korea focused on retaining Moon as the plant manager. They believed that only he could maintain shop-floor stability during the critical period of relocation from China to Vietnam. Any disruption at Nawon, the executives believed, would delay their time-sensitive move to the next step of factory relocation. With this consideration, they gave the plant manager two promises that they thought would be enough to keep him in the factory. First, the executives assured him that his salary would be paid on time under any circumstances, even when the majority of employees at Nawon would not get their wages. Second, they also promised him that they would continue to give Nawon a certain amount of orders for quite a long period. Especially with the second promise, Nawon Korea guaranteed that there would be neither a big decrease in the volume of orders nor a sudden factory closure in the near future.

Nawon Korea's strategy for maintaining stability on the Nawon shop floor seemed to work. Company statistics show that, though Nawon Korea gradually decreased the volume of orders sent to Nawon, the factory continued to fulfill orders on time and kept its product quality above average. The same statistics also show the shop floor was fairly stable: despite the small volume of orders, there was no noticeable increase in the number of incidents of worker misconduct nor in the labor turnover rate. The executives at Nawon Korea believed that the retention of Moon as plant manager was responsible for the remarkable results. As mentioned in Chapter Seven, Moon sustained the normal operation of the shop floor by getting subcontract orders and building close ties with the Han-Chinese managerial staff. The unusual stability on the shop floor of Nawon may reflect that Moon had won the Han-Chinese workers' support of management.

Behind the seemingly stable workshop at Nawon, however, some signs of instability appeared. I observed the first sign among the expatriate Korean managers. Despite Nawon Korea's promise to maintain the production facilities at Nawon for "a certain period of time," the managers increasingly felt nervous about their job security. They suspected that Nawon Korea would break the promise whenever it concluded that it no longer needed to keep the aging production facilities at Nawon. With a deepening distrust of Nawon Korea, they began to search for new job opportunities mostly offered by Korean MNCs in other countries. Although the managers expected that the relocation to Vietnam would not happen in the near future, it still made sense to have some job information in hand. The two managers told me that they could find new jobs with no serious difficulties. "There are still many Korean garment factories," a Korean manager said in an email, "not only in China but also in Vietnam, Bangladesh, Indonesia . . . and even Ukraine." They argued that there were many "globalized" Korean garment factories in need of managers with experience and the know-how of supervising foreign workers. Whether those jobs would perfectly meet their needs was another issue.

The Korean managers' optimistic view of the job market, however, does not mean that their life in a multinational factory somewhere in the world would be stable and predictable. "Our life is not much different from that of nomads," plant manager Moon once cynically said, "because we have to constantly move from one place to another, searching for open managerial positions." They may enjoy the advantages created by "flexible citizenship" (Ong 1999: 6), which in this case meant the relative freedom to move beyond territorial barriers in search of bigger personal opportunities. This flexibility, however, does not grant the managers the freedom of "settling down." Except for those at the top of the corporate hierarchy, expatriate Korean managers did not receive corporate benefits when moving from one location to another with their families. Their homecoming was also difficult because, in Korea, they could hardly find factories that needed them. The expatriate managers' lives were tied to incessantly relocating multinational factories, which is hardly compatible with a stable life in a familiar place.

BRIEF HOPE, LONG DESPAIR:
CHINESE EMPLOYEES AT NAWON

Just like the expatriate Korean managers, the Chinese employees at
Nawon—the Korean-Chinese interpreters and the Han-Chinese workers—
increasingly felt uneasy about their job security at Nawon. The steadily
decreasing volume of orders made it difficult for the management at Nawon
to secure "decent" wages for the Han-Chinese workers. Although Nawon
Korea had promised to provide a sizeable volume of orders for Nawon, it
failed several times to keep its promise. Officially, Nawon Korea blamed a
bad market and intensifying competition for orders. Contrary to the official
explanation, however, at least one of the failures was related to its new
strategy of order outsourcing. As mentioned above, during the high-order
season of 2004, Nawon Korea made a short-term production contract with
a garment factory in Vietnam. The profit generated by the outsourcing well
exceeded the profit that could be generated by Nawon. The second order
outsourcing also proved successful: the profit that Nawon Korea gained
from the goods produced by the Vietnamese factory was more than 20
percent greater than it could have made at Nawon.[9] After the success of
the second outsourcing, the executives at Nawon Korea agreed that they
had to seriously consider if the timing was right for a relocation out of
China, which in fact would happen sooner than what they had originally
estimated.

The situation at Nawon further deteriorated because plant manager
Moon was not always successful in finding extra orders. That made the
Chinese employees' prospects for their future at Nawon bleak. With the
overall decrease in orders from Nawon Korea, Moon realized that he had
to aggressively seek extra orders. There was, however, no guarantee that he
could secure a large volume of subcontract orders. Such orders came onto
the local market irregularly and, once on the market, quickly became the
target of many local garment factories. Though his repeated failure to bring
"decent" wages to the factory did not lead to the Han-Chinese workers'
outright rejection of his leadership, it gradually undermined their trust in
his factory management.

Around the end of 2005, a rumor about the factory's possible shutdown
struck the final blow to the Han-Chinese workers' tenuous hope for "decent"
wages. Neither the Korean-Chinese interpreters nor the Han-Chinese

employees knew exactly how the rumor got started. Once the rumor began to spread, however, it quickly swept the entire shop floor.[10] Considering the deteriorating condition of the factory, many local employees, both the Korean-Chinese and the Han-Chinese, thought that the rumor was quite plausible. However, they responded to the same rumor in different ways, according to their individual situations.

First, the Korean-Chinese interpreters believed that they could find new jobs in case of a factory closedown. Their optimism was based on the fairly brisk Korean-Chinese job market in China. In 2006, there were still many Korean MNCs that had newly opened businesses in China and they needed Korean-Chinese as local business assistants. Thanks to the large number of Korean MNCs, there were more job openings than the instantly available number of Korean-Chinese interpreters. The large demand from the Korean MNCs allowed many Korean-Chinese to frequently change jobs, searching for higher wages and better corporate benefits (Taehee Lee 2006). The situation of the Korean-Chinese at Nawon was not much different from the overall job market situation of Korean-Chinese. Most of the Korean-Chinese employees in the factory believed that they would have no problem in finding a new job, especially thanks to their work experience at Nawon.

The Han-Chinese workers' responses were very different from those of the Korean-Chinese interpreters. According to employment statistics, more than forty Han-Chinese workers left Nawon during the first quarter of 2005. The statistics demonstrated that some important changes had occurred among the workers, including their growing disappointment with the low wages and their weakening confidence in management. Their wages actually decreased, because plant manager Moon often failed to fill the gap between the few orders from Nawon Korea and the "decent" wages that the workers expected to receive. The high turnover rate also reflected the Han-Chinese workers' weakening confidence in management. Even before the workers knew about the outsourcing plan, they had little hope for a recovery of business, which would once again assure them of "decent" wages. However, as the rumor about Nawon Korea's outsourcing plan spread over the entire shop floor, many Han-Chinese workers finally gave up all hope. Now with no prospect of "decent" wages, they simply terminated their contract with Nawon and left. "Management lost our trust," a Han-Chinese worker said in her email. "They had kept saying we should trust them . . . but they secretly decided to re-route orders from us to Vietnamese factories."

The Han-Chinese workers responded to the deteriorating conditions at Nawon in different ways depending on their individual situation. Factory records shows that most of the workers who resigned, thirty-five out of a total of forty-five, were relatively young and from the cutting or the finishing sections. "They simply went back to Pingshan," a Korean-Chinese interpreter said, "because they had virtually no skills and had little to lose." The workers in these two sections received the least in the way of corporate benefits because their jobs did not require particular skills. The meager benefits, together with their slight chance to go to Korea as industrial trainees, kept the turnover rate in the two sections higher than that of the sewing section. In fact, during my fieldwork, I often heard some young and unskilled workers say they were ready to leave at any time. "If I can find another job with better conditions," a young worker in the finishing section once said, "I'll quit this job without hesitation." The deteriorating situation at Nawon, together with the meager corporate benefits, made them the first to quit their jobs.[11]

The other group of workers who quit, thirteen in total, took a more successful path as they continued their career in other garment factories. This group of workers shared several things in common: they were machine operators in the sewing section, had worked at Nawon for five to six years, and had been to Korea as industrial trainees. Their high-level sewing skills and uncommon experience as industrial trainees in Korea helped them to make a smooth transfer. In fact, there had always been a high demand for machine operators, especially for young and highly skilled ones. During my fieldwork, I observed that garment factories in and around Qingdao actively recruited machine operators, luring them with better employment conditions.[12] During that time, however, aggressive recruitment campaigns did not create any serious problems at Nawon because the management could provide "decent" wages and continued to offer the industrial trainee program. Now the situation was quite different since management could neither guarantee "decent" wages nor promise to continue the trainee program. The resignation of the thirteen operators was a warning that Nawon might lose more skilled workers if its business continued to deteriorate.

Aside from the forty-five workers who quit, the remaining six hundred or so Han-Chinese workers at Nawon stayed on the job. At first, I felt it was hard to understand their decision to stay at Nawon despite the deteriorating situation and the rumor about the factory closing. The workers' trust in management could no longer explain why they continued to stay on, because the decrease in orders and the recent rumor dashed most of their hope for "decent" wages and with it their trust in management. The answer lies in Nawon's statistics. The records show that most of the remaining workers were "old"—in fact, they were in their late twenties or early thirties. Because of their long-term employment, many of them enjoyed several benefits based on seniority. These included a high basic salary and a high-rate of pay for overtime, which had increased yearly according to the length of their employment at Nawon. If they had quit their jobs at Nawon and moved to other factories, they would have lost these seniority-based benefits.

The most important reason for them staying on, however, was the bleak prospect for future jobs. Most Han-Chinese workers who remained in the factory believed that they were already too old to get new factory jobs. The volatile nature of the garment industry has made it a widespread practice of garment factories to require their workers to put in frequent overtime. In fact, overtime is the most arduous part of the garment manufacturing business, because, during the high-order seasons, workers often have to work for several days straight, or even an entire week, with only a few hours a day of sleep. For this reason, every management strongly prefers young workers who can put up with overtime with little sign of fatigue. "We are already old," a Han-Chinese worker said in her email. "What kind of companies would want to hire us, when they can find young girls who can easily endure endless overtime?" Many "old" workers' lack of technical skills further limited their chance to find a new job. With their low level of personal skills, they could only qualify for jobs in the same labor-intensive, light industrial sector. Again, most of the jobs in this sector come with low wages, long work hours, and frequent and irregular overtime. During my fieldwork, another senior worker in her late twenties said to me, "The factories [in the labor-intensive sector] will never hire old women like us because they believe old women who've already had experience with factory jobs can never be good workers. They suspect that old workers will easily get tired and always find loopholes in labor supervision." The "old" Han-Chinese workers who remained at Nawon worried that the impending shutdown of the factory would have a serious impact on their future. Before the recent crisis at Nawon, many of the senior workers believed that their factory jobs would still guarantee them a "good life" in the future. By a "good" life, they never meant that they expected to enjoy a comfortable life like that of the rising Chinese urban middle class. The life they envisioned was much humbler. Their future life, however, at least would be better than that of their parents, poor farmers in remote farming villages: with the money they made from their long-term jobs at Nawon, they believed they could arrange to marry men with backgrounds better than their parents and, therefore, could live the "good" life. They believed their jobs at Nawon could guarantee such a future, because Nawon was one of the few garment factories that had continued in business for more than a decade. Now with the rumor of the factory closing, many senior workers were afraid that all of their humble hopes would disappear forever. Without jobs, they thought, there would remain virtually nothing for them to do except to go back to their hometowns and resume "tedious and totally unprofitable" farm work.

CODA

Who should be blamed for all the feelings of uncertainty, anxiety, and betrayal that filled the workshop of Nawon? It seems easy to point to the Korean managers, and particularly the executives at Nawon Korea, as the cause of all the negative feelings. During my fieldwork, I repeatedly observed that the executives of Nawon Korea promised to make on-time payments of "decent" wages. Especially right after plant manager Jo's shameful resignation, the president of Nawon Korea visited Nawon and made a very personal promise to the local employees. In his address to the Han-Chinese managerial staff, the president vowed that he would do his best to secure enough orders and guarantee sizeable wage payments. However, Nawon Korea broke this promise by initiating the new outsourcing practice. During most of its decade of operation in China, management had boasted of its on-time payment of sizeable wages as the hallmark of the factory. It also had been the key to the Han-Chinese workers' trust in management. Management's promise of "decent" wages sounded increasingly empty, however, as its deteriorating financial condition and failed managerial strategies made it difficult to win the cut-throat competition for order contracts with other factories. The promise finally proved to be a managerial deceit foisted on the Han-Chinese workers when management began the outsourcing to Vietnamese factories.

It is important, however, to note that the practice of outsourcing was not a creation of Nawon Korea. It is a long tradition in the garment industry. As the literature on the globalizing history of the garment industry demonstrates, the initial formation of the global chain of production began when the large garment corporations in the United States adopted outsourcing (Bonacich et al. 1994; Howard 1999; Ross 1999). Breakthroughs in logistics and means of communication made outsourcing through the global chain increasingly manageable, highly effective, and cost-saving compared to conventional practices of domestic manufacturing. In addition, outsourcing orders to foreign contractors made it easy for corporations to evade government regulations and media criticism of poor working conditions in domestic workshops. It was the very practice of outsourcing that brought Nawon Korea into existence in South Korea during the 1970s, when buyers from the United States and Japan regarded the country as an ideal place for outsourcing garment production, mostly due to its vast reservoir of cheap and "docile" labor.[13]

Considering the historical origin of Nawon Korea as a contract factory, it is little wonder that Nawon Korea decided to outsource orders to Vietnamese factories. Beginning as a contract factory that fulfilled orders of foreign buyers, Nawon Korea was fully aware of the mechanism of global garment production and how buyers maintain or cut their contract relationship with factories based on their calculations of profit maximization. In retrospect, it was this very awareness that made Nawon Korea establish Nawon as its first overseas production site. When South Korea experienced an unprecedented wage hike during the late 1980s, Nawon Korea observed how the increased labor costs greatly reduced its production profits and thus threatened its relationship with its regular buyers. This prompted Nawon Korea to start searching for an alternative production site in China. Now experiencing sustained double-digit increases in Chinese labor costs, Nawon Korea began to consider relocation to countries that could offer it higher profits. With the sizeable profits offered by other production sites, the executives of Nawon Korea believed that they could keep their business alive.

Management's plan to relocate indicates how the factory regime at Nawon was vulnerable to changes in global garment production and the Chinese government's policies. Because the changes were so rapid and comprehensive, there was no room for the factory regime at Nawon to take the form of "hegemonic despotism." Under the factory regime that developed relatively recently in countries such as the United States, Great Britain, and Japan, management extracts concessions from workers on key issues, such as wages and welfare benefits. This factory regime is hegemonic, because management wins concessions through nonviolent processes such as collective negotiations. At the same time it is despotic, because management often exacts concessions by threatening workers with a possible relocation overseas and factory closures (Burawoy 1985: 150). The management at Nawon did not regard the time-consuming process of collective bargaining with its Chinese employees as a necessary step before its final decision to relocate. Because of the rapidly changing conditions in the global garment industry, together with the policy changes of the Chinese government, Nawon's management ignored the option of collective bargaining with its Chinese employees. The ever-growing market pressure to reduce production costs and the stiff competition among garment factories had greatly decreased Nawon's profit margins. The Chinese government's tightening supervision of the labor conditions and the business practices of the factory further worsened its business environment. The unprecedentedly rapid increase in labor costs since the mid-2000s was only a final blow to Nawon's management.

From the managerial point of view, the decision was completely rational since management put profit maximization and corporate survival at the very top of its priorities. The recent outsourcing was a part of Nawon Korea's continuing effort to survive the fierce competition with other factories. While the Han-Chinese workers struggled to stitch for "decent" wages that could change their fate, the executives at Nawon Korea struggled to keep their business alive. All the later developments at Nawon clearly indicate how the relocation of factories within the global chain of production constantly creates stories of runaway management and local employees' resentment over management's broken promises. Such stories are about management as well as about workers struggling to survive under the impersonal mechanism of global capitalism, which constantly seeks greater profitability.

Notes

The names of the factory and its headquarters are fictitious, as are the place-names (except for Chengyang, Qingdao, Seoul, Shenyang, Yanbian, Yanji, and the names of countries), and all personal names (except the name of the deputy-mayor of Qingdao). Following the practice of the factory, the managers of the Nawon factory are referred to by their surnames only. For the same reason, the Korean-Chinese and some of the Han-Chinese workers are referred to by their given names.

Chapter 1

1. Chengyang is one of the seven districts that make up the city of Qingdao; the others are Shinan, Shibei, Sifang, Licang, Laoshan, and Huangdao. Nawon Apparel was located in Chengyang.

2. *P'ali P'ali* (quickly, quickly) in Korean. Several Han-Chinese workers perfectly pronounced the Korean expression because they had heard it so often on the shop floor.

3. This reflects the larger investment trend of Korean enterprises in China. Korean enterprises' investments in China increased from US$1.2 billion in 1992 (the year Korea signed a treaty of amity with China) to more than US$62 billion in 2003, becoming the country with the largest investment in China (EIBK 2003, 2004; SERI 2004).

4. "Korean-Chinese" translates *Chaoxianzu* in Chinese, one of China's fifty-five ethnic minorities. The population was 1,920,597 in 2006 (NBSC 2007). Because Korean managers could not speak Chinese, they hired Korean-Chinese as interpreters to mediate between them and Han-Chinese workers. For more discussion of Korean-Chinese, see Chapters Three and Five.

5. A global commodity chain may be defined as a network of labor and production processes whose end result is a finished commodity (Hopkins and Wallerstein 1986: 159).

6. In 1979, the State Council of the PRC named Shenzhen, Zhuhai, and Shantou—all in Guangdong Province—as Special Export Zones (C. *chukou tequ*). In May 1980, the State Council added Xiamen, in Fujian Province, to the list and

changed the name of the regions to Special Economic Zones (C. *jingji tequ*). In August 1980, the Seventh Plenum decided to add Hainan Province to the category of Special Economic Zones. Serial legislation on local governments' jurisdiction in the Special Economic Zones has followed (Ota 2003: 1–20).

7. The patron-client relationship reflects the nature of "mono-organizational society," where most activities were directly managed by bureaucracies linked up in a single organizational system, the party-state (Rigby 1977: 59).

8. I use the term "post-socialist" or "post-socialism" following Dirlik (1989), who refers to a historical condition in which 1) the centrally planned economy no longer plays a dominant role in the production and redistribution of economic and social resources, and 2) the socialist state perceives a need to modify "actually existing socialism" to capitalism. The state's effort to transform itself is conditioned both by the social, economic, and cultural structures of its socialist past and by its attempt to overcome the deficiencies of capitalism (Dirlik 1989: 364).

9. Qingdao is one of China's fourteen coastal cities open to foreign investment. The others are Dalian, Qinhuangdao, Tianjin, Yantai, Lianyungang, Nantong, Shanghai, Ningbo, Wenzhou, Fuzhou, Guangzhou, Zhanjiang, and Beihai.

10. The workers' resistance and the subsequent changes in the management's labor strategies indicate that the creation of a factory regime is also conditioned by workers' reactions to the regime (Burawoy 1985: 36–40).

11. On Korea's industrialization since the Korean War (1950–1953), see Cumings (2005), Lie (2000), and Moon (2005).

12. The actual number of strikes could be higher if we include unreported strikes (CIFSJD 1987: 43–53; ICIME 1988: 24–30, 416–20).

13. In 1989, for example, the United States received 40.6 percent of Korea's garment exports while Japan received 33.8 percent (Lee and Song 1994: 149).

14. At the end of 2005, there were a total of 13,600 Korean direct investments in China, with a total investment of US$135.5 billion. The same year, the amount invested by small- and medium-sized enterprises comprised 49.7 percent of the total (Juyeong Kim 2006). In addition to China's cheap labor costs, its geographical proximity to Korea and the Chinese government's policy to attract FDI are additional factors that explain the rapid relocation of Korean enterprises to China (Tak 2006a).

15. In 2004, MNCs comprised 57.4 percent of China's total export trade (NBSC, *China Statistical Yearbook*, 2004).

16. For more information on the shop-floor organization and individual work positions, see Chapter Four.

17. On national and ethnic divisions, see Chapters Two and Three.

18. The term "Sino-centrism" refers to a hoary idea shared by many Han-Chinese. It assumes that the Han-Chinese, the ethnic majority of China, should occupy the center of China and the world in political, cultural, and geographical senses, because they are the most cultured and the most advanced in material and moral senses. The Sino-centric idea has been applied not only to the domestic relationship between Han-Chinese and other ethnic groups but also to the

international relationship between China and other countries, especially those close to China (Bilsky 1975; Fairbank 1968; Hsiao, 1967; Kang 2010; Thomas 1968).

Chapter 2

1. In addition, the interpreters had to serve themselves, while two Korean-Chinese women attendants (who also made food) served the Korean managerial staff.

2. All residents of the factory dormitories were young, unmarried Han-Chinese women currently working in the factory. Management did not accept male workers in the factory dormitories because it believed they were more inclined to be troublemakers. In addition, management believed that single-sex dormitories would be much easier to control. For this reason, the male Han-Chinese workers of Nawon individually rented rooms from private landlords near the factory.

3. In contrast, management allowed the Korean-Chinese interpreters to use the upper berth of each bunk bed for storing individual belongings.

4. Intriguingly, their view of Han-Chinese workers as backward and uncultured is quite similar to the Chinese urbanites' demeaning view of the migrants from the countryside (Jacka 2006: 215–17, 226–28; Ching Kwan Lee 1998a: 57; Pun 1999).

5. In 2003, Korean enterprises in Qingdao paid more than 10 billion yuan in income tax (SDBS 2003).

6. There is ample research on the discriminatory effects of the Chinese household registration system. For example, see Fan (2008).

7. There are some interesting studies about urban residents' prejudices against migrant workers. For example, see Chan (2001), Ching Kwan Lee (1998a), and Solinger (1999)

8. The gap is increasing year by year. For example, the difference in the mean household disposable per capita income was 2.83 (urban:rural ratio) in 1995 but increased to 3.18 in 2002 (Sicular et al. 2007).

9. Their self-depreciating views were shared not just among women workers. A male worker once said that he could not find anything attractive in the women workers at Nawon: "Although sometimes I could find pretty girls among them," he argued, "the very moment I saw their rough hands, I just gave up any idea of making their acquaintance."

Chapter 3

1. For more on their reaction to the shop-floor workers' body odor, see Chapter Two.

2. Because overtime was a factory routine, the regular closing time (5:00 p.m.) was meaningless for the shop-floor workers. In contrast, the office workers could

leave the office after 10:00 p.m. even if they were on overtime duty. For more details about the practices of overtime, see Chapters Four and Five.

3. Koreans who migrated to the north of the Yalu River in the region west of the Sino-Korean border numbered 98,657, while, to the east, 93,883 went to the area north of the Tumen River, making a total of 192,540 (Lim 2003). The total number of Korean-Chinese in 1920 was 459,000; in 1941, it had increased to 1,300,000 (Gwak 2008; Kang 2008).

4. China joined the Korean War as an ally of North Korea and fought against the Allied Forces of the UN, led by the United States. The official rhetoric commemorating the sixtieth anniversary of the war in 2010 provides the most recent example of the close relationship between the two countries. See Yu (2010).

5. This terminology is based on the literal translation of the two Chinese characters for "China," *zhong*, center or middle, and *guo*, country or kingdom.

6. There is an ongoing debate about the exact number of foreign invasions of Korea, most of which were from China. The fact that there were many invasions reminds Koreans of the potential vulnerability of their country to foreign aggression, and convinces them of the reality of the "China threat." See Wang (2005). During the Joseon dynasty (1392–1910), Korea assumed the status of a tributary state to two successive dynasties of China, the Ming (1368–1644) and the Qing (1636–1912). Joseon became a tributary state after it was defeated by Qing, which invaded the Korean Peninsula in 1637. The tributary relationship between the Qing and Joseon ended with the Sino-Japanese War (1894–1895), which resulted in the overwhelming victory of Japan.

7. Yanbian Korean-Chinese Autonomous Prefecture (C. *Yanbian Chaoxianzu zizhiqu*). The autonomous region—with a gross area of 43,474 sq km, and a population of 821,479—is located in Jilin Province, northeast China. Korean-Chinese comprise 40 percent of the population of the autonomous region (NBSC 1991).

8. For example, the *Manifesto of the Sixth CCP Congress* put forward a slogan proclaiming the equality of all ethnic groups (United Front Work Department of CCP 1991: 86–87). Mao Zedong also announced that Chinese ethnic minorities should enjoy equal rights. He even argued that the minorities should have their own committees at every level of local government (United Front Work Department of CCP 1991: 595).

9. A city in Liaoning Province, northeast China.

10. Before the mid-2000s, it was difficult for those with nonlocal residence status to purchase houses outside their hometown. This originated from the Chinese government's household registration system (C. *hukou*), introduced in the 1950s as a powerful administrative method to cut population movement from the countryside to the cities.

11. On this contrast, see Chapter Two.

Chapter 4

1. On the two production systems, see Hill (1994).

2. The problem of Chinese labor that the Korean management had to grapple with is similar to what the management of "new" socialist China experienced on the shop floor. Shortly after the "liberation" of China in 1949, the CCP sought fast industrialization that would quickly bring China out of its backwardness. However, the party cadres in the factories, the new managerial staff of socialist China, first had to overcome the overwhelming shortage of trained workers and their lack of labor discipline (Koo 2001; Priestley 1963; Walder 1986).

3. There are four countries in this category of newly industrializing economies: Korea, Taiwan, Hong Kong, and Singapore (see Bonacich et al. 1994; Lee and Song 1994).

4. Work diary entry for January 20, 1995.

5. Nawon's management was not alone in referring to "peasant nature" as a key obstacle to management's effective control of labor. Several researchers have reported that many Chinese managers working in factories owned and operated by Chinese also regard the supposed peasant nature as a key problem in their control of labor. "Peasant nature," in this context, meant some undesirable characteristics that were apparent among the workers fresh from the countryside, such as a low level of education, a lack of discipline, and uncouth language and behavior (Pun 2005; Rofel 1999; Zhang 2001). The wide economic and cultural gap between rural and urban China only strengthened such negative images of workers: with their own urban backgrounds, Chinese managers often exaggerated the rurality of the workers and thus justified extra measures of discipline and treatment. Ironically, Chinese managers believed that they could effectively control the workers because they shared the same nationality with the workers and thus understood their "deep-rooted" nature.

6. Memo of a managerial meeting, dated February 25, 1995.

7. The military service law of Korea stipulates that every male Korean above twenty must serve in the army. The length of service has changed over time from three to two years (Ministry of Government Legislation of Korea 2000). The managers at Nawon were in the army for three years.

8. About three U.S. dollars in 2003. The Han-Chinese workers felt the fine was too heavy because they could buy four big round flat cakes (C. *bing*) for one yuan.

9. As Gramsci pointed out, any form of domination will be costly if it only relies on external forces (Gramsci 1991; Williams 1978).

10. Confucian teaching has the implicit idea of the disciplinary effects of repetitive bodily movement. According to this idea, precise and repetitive bodily movements generate a particular moral orientation (Waley 1989 [1938]: 209, 225). Writing calligraphy, reading books, and even kowtowing with the right posture create disciplinary effects on one's mind and body. The human body functions as a mnemonic device reinforcing moral orientation (Brownell 1995: 125–26).

Chapter 5

1. On the just-in-time system, see Chapter Two.

2. In the late 1980s, to alleviate a labor shortage, the South Korean government permitted the employment of foreign workers as "trainees." With the exception of a small number of professionals, most trainees came from developing countries such as China, Indonesia, Bangladesh, the Philippines, Pakistan, Vietnam, and so on. They were mainly hired by small- and medium-sized firms in the textile, plastics, assembly, and auto-parts industries. Almost half of the foreign "trainees" came from China (Wang-Bae Kim 2004).

3. For further discussion on management's ideas of Korean-Chinese and how their ideas put Korean-Chinese in a difficult situation at Nawon, see Chapter Three.

4. For more on Sino-centrism, see Chapters One and Three.

5. For more on pattern templates, see Chapter Four.

6. On management's idea of "Han-Chinese defiance," see Chapters Three and Four.

7. Managerial meeting memo, September 15, 1997.

8. As of the year 2000, for example, the hourly wage of a Korean worker in the textile industry was US$5.32, while that of a Chinese worker in the same industry was only US$0.69 (Werner International 2001).

9. In 1998, a Han-Chinese industrial trainee earned about 20,000 yuan for twelve-months' work in the Korean mother factory.

10. Owing to the highly automated production facilities, there was little demand for overtime in the mother factory.

11. For example, among the third group of industrial trainees, 70 percent had worked in the factory for more than four years.

12. Management did not give Korean-Chinese interpreters a chance to go to Korea as industrial trainees. It was afraid that they could easily run away from the mother factory to find higher-paying jobs. During most of the 1990s, foreign workers with the status of industrial trainees could earn only about 50–60 percent of the full wages of Korean workers. Thus the trainees could make more money if they abandoned the jobs at the assigned factories and found jobs elsewhere as illegal workers. During this time, thanks to their Korean-language competence and cultural proximity to Korea, Korean-Chinese easily found illegal jobs in South Korea (Wang-Bae Kim 2004; Lim 2003). Nawon Korea preferred Han-Chinese as industrial trainees because it believed that they could not easily run away.

13. Nawon's management worried that the Korean-Chinese layoff might negatively affect its close relationship with its Korean-Chinese employees. In fact, many Korean managers who had worked with them since 1993 were personally concerned about the laid-off Korean-Chinese. Both practical managerial considerations and the Korean managers' personal concern explain why management helped the laid-off Korean-Chinese employees find new jobs. The situation at Nawon was much different from that of other Korean multinational corporations. Other corporations also reduced

the number of Korean-Chinese employees for the same reason: to cut labor costs. Unlike Nawon, however, only a few took care of their laid-off Korean-Chinese employees. Such managerial practices created and increased Korean-Chinese discontent with Korean multinational corporations. Thanks to the management's paternalistic concern, Nawon was largely exempt from the negative turn in the relationship between Korean management and Korean-Chinese employees.

14. See Chapter Four for more explanation about the plant manager's table on the shop floor and how it functioned as a powerful method of labor surveillance.

15. *Ta ganhuo, Wo fangxin* in Chinese. Han-Chinese workers expressed their belief in the plant manager by paraphrasing Mao Zedong's famous statement about Hua Guofeng, *Ni banshi, wo fangxin.*

16. What the plant manager said about the Han-Chinese workers' work motives corresponded to my own research results. During my fieldwork, I interviewed 31 workers about their work motives. More than 80 percent of them said that one of the key reasons for them to work was their concern for their family. The workers responded that they saved an average of 80 percent of their income and brought their savings home not only for their future use but also for the use of their families suffering from rural poverty.

17. His description of the South Korean women workers in the 1970s and the 1980s was similar to what labor studies reported on South Korean women workers. For example, see Hae-Min Kim (2009).

18. For more discussion of this culture-specific terminology, see Yunxiang Yan (2003).

19. For more discussion on paternalism and charismatic authority, see Dworkin (1972, 2005) and Kleinig (1983).

Chapter 6

1. Quoted from an interview with the village head.

2. The Labor Standards Act, promulgated by the Chinese government in 1995, has comprehensive lists of labor condition standards that every company, including foreign enterprises, must meet. Since the late 1990s the government has begun to more strictly enforce the law.

3. In 2003, the average monthly wage of the rank-and-file workers at Nawon was around 700 yuan.

4. The Nawon Korea president's gifts to the village head did not end with the car. At special times such as Chinese New Year and National Day, the president sent gifts to the village head's family. During my fieldwork, for example, I observed that the president even sent gifts to the village head's granddaughter, celebrating her entrance to elementary school.

5. A managerial meeting memo dated May 2002.

Chapter 7

1. Chapters Seven and Eight are based on my direct participant-observation of events in the factory.

2. Following the definition of culture offered in Chapter One, here I define the "culture" of labor as notions of time and punctuality, ideas of discipline, norms of desirable personhood, and beliefs in legitimate workshop authority.

3. From a managerial meeting memo in August 2002.

4. Ibid.

5. Ibid.

6. The first Korean factory had begun business in Guatemala in 1984, and by March 1992 fifty Korean garment factories were in operation, employing nearly twenty thousand Guatemalans. These factories accounted for nearly half of the *maquila* production at that time (Peterson 1994: 280–81).

7. Parts of the oppressive practices originated from the militarized work culture of South Korea. However, they were also widespread in other *maquila* factories regardless of the origin of their management. For more on *maquila* factories and their labor management, see Bonacich et al. (1994) and Chinchilla (1977).

8. In Guatemala, Mexico, and Nicaragua, *maquila* or *maquiladora* refers to garment factories specializing in outsourcing or contract production of garments (Grinspun and Cameron 1993; Mendez 2005; Petersen 1994; Sklair 1989).

9. For a more detailed explanation of the Han-Chinese workers' wage structure, see Chapter Five.

10. The low-water mark in wages in 1997 was caused by the economic crisis that hit hard many East and Southeast Asian countries at that time. Although China was not the hardest-hit country, Nawon's exports nosedived because of weak consumer demand in Japan.

11. I could observe management's reaction to the strike because, at the very moment, I happened to be in the office repairing one of the company's desktop computers. During my fieldwork, I spent most of my time on the shop floor as a novice worker. I was in the office for a while when management asked me to take care of computers with problems. Repairing computers is one of my hobbies.

12. *Wei renmen fuwu* in Chinese. This slogan was highly popular during the Cultural Revolution. At that time, Mao Zedong used it when he urged party and government officials to serve not their own interests but the needs of the people.

13. For a more detailed analysis of the charismatic-paternalist factory regime, see Chapter Five.

14. For example, while it was 5,786 yuan in 1996, it increased to 12,577 yuan in 2003, and to 16,581 yuan in 2005 (SDBS 2006).

Chapter 8

1. Almost ten years earlier, Deng Xiaoping, the late top leader of the CCP, emphasized the "buildup of a civilization with a high cultural and ideological level" as a preventive measure against slackened party discipline among party officials and government bureaucrats (Deng 1994: 367). To him, this was one of the two pillars that support "socialism with Chinese characteristics," which "would prevent the spread of unsound by-products of economic development, such as corruption and vulgar materialist thinking." He even warned that the CCP would lose the fruits of economic development and might not succeed in building a materially rich civilization "if it cannot check the harmful byproducts of economic development" (Deng 1993: 144, 154). Despite his repeated emphasis on building a "spiritual civilization" and its political significance, what has happened since the beginning of his economic reform program does not seem to have meet with his wishes.

2. Other government statistics also demonstrate the continuing trend of corruption among government and party officials, despite the CCP's nationwide anticorruption efforts. In 2004, for example, 35,031 government officials were investigated for alleged involvement in the crimes of corruption, bribe-taking, and embezzlement of public funds (Xinhua News Agency 2005a).

3. According to the police announcement, Kim's underground "exchange service" network reached into several other cities in Shandong Province, as well as Jilin Province and Shanghai. The network operated mainly for Korean enterprises and their Chinese business partners (Hu 2005).

4. This section of the book is based on the data I collected as part of my post-field research. After leaving Qingdao, I kept in contact with the employees at Nawon via email and occasional phone conversations. From them, I got information about the changing situation at Nawon even after my fieldwork. I also use data collected from internet bulletin boards of Korean managers and Korean-Chinese interpreters working in Korean MNCs in China. From the bulletin boards, I could get a broader picture of the changing business conditions of Korean MNCs in China and how Korean managers and Korean-Chinese interpreters in Korean MNCs felt about the changes. In addition, I used company statistics of Nawon, which I got from Nawon Korea, the corporate headquarters in South Korea.

5. In 2005, there were about seven thousand medium- and small-sized Korean enterprises in Qingdao.

6. By "glitches" he meant the death of plant manager Bak and the Han-Chinese workers' strike against plant manager Jo. For more on these two events, see Chapters Six and Seven.

7. From a managerial meeting memo at Nawon Korea in 2005.

8. The SARS epidemic started in Guangdong Province in November 2002. Most of the heavy local transmissions of SARS happened in China, in such places as Guangdong, Jilin, Hebei, Hubei, Shaanxi, Jiangsu, Shanxi, Tianjin, and Inner Mongolia. It made China the country with the largest number of cases (5,328) and

casualties (349 deaths) during the period between November 2002 and July 2003 (World Health Organization 2003).

9. From an internal managerial report of Nawon Korea.

10. From email correspondence and phone conversations with Korean-Chinese interpreters and Han-Chinese workers.

11. According to the testimony of Han-Chinese workers who were close to those who left Nawon, many of them found new jobs after they returned home, mostly thanks to their relatively young age.

12. During my fieldwork in 2003, eight operators of the sewing section quit their jobs and moved to a nearby garment factory, which offered them better employment conditions.

13. For more information about the foundation of the garment outsourcing industry in South Korea, see Chun (2003) and Moon (2005).

References

Abelmann, Nancy. 2007. How Do Youth Decide about Studying Abroad? A Case Study of Korean Students in a Small Town in the U.S. *Korean Journal of Youth Studies* 14: 115–43.

Abercrombie, Nicholas, and John Urry. 1983. *Capital, Labour, and the Middle Class.* New York: Unwin Hyman.

Agence France Presse. 2003. China Emerges as World's Workshop, to Consolidate Gains in 2004. December 22.

Amsden, Alice. 1989. *Asia's Next Giant: South Korea and Late Industrialization.* New York: Oxford University Press.

Anagnost, Ann. 2004. The Corporeal Politics of Quality (shuzhi). *Public Culture* 16.2: 189–208.

Appadurai, Arjun. 1996. *Modernity at Large: Cultural Dimensions of Globalization.* Minneapolis: University of Minnesota Press.

Appelbaum, Richard P., and Gary Gereffi. 1994. Power and Profits in the Apparel Commodity Chain. In Bonacich et al. 1994: 42–62.

Aronowitz, Stanley. 1992. *False Promises: The Shaping of American Working Class Consciousness.* Durham, NC: Duke University Press.

Ash, Lucy. 2002. Inside China's Sweatshops. *BBC News World Edition*, July 20. http://news.bbc.co.uk/2/hi/programmes/from_our_own_correspondent/2139401.stm.

Barber, Benjamin R. 1995. *Jihad vs. McWorld: How Globalism and Tribalism Are Reshaping the World.* New York: Times Books.

Barboza, David. 2006. Labor Shortage in China May Lead to Trade Shift. *New York Times*, April 3. www.nytimes.com/2006/04/03/business/03labor.html?pagewanted=all.

Barth, Fredrik. 1969. *Ethnic Groups and Boundaries: The Social Organization of Culture Difference.* Boston: Little, Brown.

Bartlett, Christopher A., and Sumantra Ghoshal. 1991. *Managing across Borders: The Transnational Solution.* Boston: Harvard Business School Press.

Bateson, Gregory. 1958 [1936]. *Naven: A Survey of the Problems Suggested by a Composite Picture of the Culture of a New Guinea Tribe Drawn from Three Points of View.* Stanford, CA: Stanford University Press.

BBC News. 2002. China: The World's Factory Floor. November 11. http://news
.bbc.co.uk/2/hi/business/2415241.stm.

———. 2005. China Tops India on Average Pay. November 14. http://news.bbc
.co.uk/go/pr/fr/-/1/hi/business/4436692.stm.

Berliner, Joseph S. 1957. *Factory and Manager in the USSR*. Cambridge, MA:
Harvard University Press.

Bian, Yanjie. 1994. *Work and Inequality in Urban China*. Albany: State University
of New York.

Bilsky, James L. 1975. *The State Religion of Ancient China*. Ann Arbor: University
of Michigan Press.

Black, J. T., and Joseph C. Chen. 1995. The Role of Decouplers in JIT Pull Apparel
Cells. *International Journal of Clothing and Technology* 7.1: 17–35.

Block, Fred. 1994. The Roles of the State in the Economy. In *The Handbook
of Economic Sociology*, ed. Neil J. Smelser and Richard Swedberg, 691–710.
Princeton, NJ: Princeton University Press.

Blumenberg, Eveln, and Paul Ong. 1994. Labor Squeeze and Ethnic/Racial
Recomposition in the U.S. Apparel Industry. In Bonacich et al. 1994: 309–27.

Bonacich, Edna, Lucie Cheng, and Norma Chinchilla (ed.). 1994. *Global Production:
The Apparel Industry in the Pacific Rim*. Philadelphia: Temple University Press.

Bourdieu, Pierre. 1970. The Berber House or the World Reversed. *Social Science
Information* 9.2: 151–70.

———. 1977. *Outline of a Theory of Practice*. Cambridge: Cambridge University
Press.

———. 1984. *Distinction: A Social Critique of the Judgment of Taste*. London:
Routledge & Kegan Paul.

Braudel, Fernand. 1992 [1979]. *Civilization and Capitalism, 15th–18th Century:
The Wheels of Commerce*. Trans. Sian Reynold. Berkeley: University of California Press.

Brenner, Neil. 1998. Global Cities, Glocal States: Global City Formation and
State Territorial Restructuring in Contemporary Europe. *Review of International Political Economy* 5: 1–37.

———. 1999. Beyond State-centrism? Space, Territoriality, and Geographical
Scale in Globalization Studies. *Theory and Society* 28: 39–78.

Brownell, Susan. 1995. *Training the Body for China: Sports in the Moral Order of
the People's Republic*. Chicago: University of Chicago Press.

Burawoy, Michael. 1985. *The Politics of Production: Factory Regimes under Capitalism and Socialism*. London: Verso.

CASS [Zhongguo shehui kexueyuan (Chinese Academy of Social Sciences)].
2006. *2005 shehui lanpishu: Zhongguo shehui xingshi fenxi yu yuci* (Social blue
book 2005: Analysis and forecasting of social conditions in China). Beijing:
Shehui kexue wenxian chubanshe.

Chae, Suhong. 2003. Spinning Work and Weaving Life: The Politics of Production in a Capitalistic Multinational Textile Factory in Vietnam. Ph.D. diss.,
City University of New York.

Chan, Anita. 1998a. The Conditions of Chinese Workers in East Asian Funded Enterprises. *Chinese Sociology and Anthropology* 30.4: 260–81.

———. 1998b. Labor Standards and Human Rights: Chinese Workers under Market Socialism. *Human Rights Quarterly* 20.4: 806–904.

———. 2001. *China's Workers Under Assault: The Exploitation of Labor in a Globalizing Economy.* Armonk, NY: M.E. Sharpe.

Chen, Yao. 2004. Evasion: A Taxing Problem. *China Business Weekly*, November 23.

Cheng, Lucie, and Gary Gereffi. 1994. U.S. Retailers and Asian Garment Production. In Bonacich et al. 1994: 63–79.

Chinchilla, Norma. 1977. Industrialization, Monopoly, Capitalism, and Women's Work in Guatemala. *Signs: Journal of Women in Culture and Society* 3.1: 38–56.

Cho, Joongsik. 2004. Qingdao e deuriun Hanguk ui myeongam (The dark and bright side of Korean enterprises in Qingdao). *Joseon ilbo* (Joseon Daily), July 8. http://news.chosun.com/svc/content_view/content_view.html?contid=2004070870400.

Choe, Minja, Sae-Kwon Kim, and Karen O. Mason. 1994. Korean Women's Labor Force Participation: Attitudes and Behavior. In *Korean Studies: New Pacific Currents*, ed. Dae-Sook Suh, 283–98. Honolulu: Center for Korean Studies, University of Hawaii.

Choe, Samryong. 1994. Joseon minjok ui jeontong munhwa wa Jungguk Joseonjok ui samui hyeonsang (Korean traditional culture and the current life style of Korean-Chinese). In *Joseonjok uyeolseong yeongu* (Research on the superiority and inferiority of Korean-Chinese), ed. Yeonbyeon University Editing Committee of Korean-Chinese toward the Twentieth Century (series), 58–68. Yeonbyeon: Yeonbyeon inmin chulpansa.

Choe, Seongjun. 1999. *Yanbian renmin kangri douzheng shi* (A history of fighting against the Japanese in Yanbian). Beijing: Minzu chubanshe.

Choi, Baegeun. 2004. Chaina dilemma: hwanyul (Chinese dilemma: money rates). *Hankyorae 21* (One Nation 21). September 2: 25.

Chun, Soonok. 2003. *They Are Not Machines: Korean Women Workers and Their Fight for Democratic Trade Unionism in the 1970s.* New York: Ashgate.

CIFSJD [Christian Institute for the Study of Justice and Development]. 1987. *Nodongja daetujaeng: 1987 nyeon chilwol, palwol* (Workers' general strike in July and August 1987). Seoul: Minjungsa.

Clark, Gregory. 2007. *A Farewell to Alms: A Brief Economic History of the World.* Princeton, NJ: Princeton University Press.

Clarke, Simon. 1992. The Quagmire of Privatization. *New Left Review* 196 (Nov.–Dec.): 3–28.

Classen, Constance. 1993. *Worlds of Sense: Exploring the Senses in History and across Cultures.* London: Routledge.

Classen, Constance, David Howes, and Anthony Synnot. 1994. *Aroma: The Cultural History of Smell.* London: Routledge.

Cohen, Abner. 1969. *Custom and Politics in Urban Africa: A Study of Hausa Migrants in Yoruba Towns.* London: Routledge.

Cohen, Anthony P. 1985 *The Symbolic Construction of Community.* London: Tavistock.

Corbin, Alan. 1986. *The Foul and the Fragrant: Odor and the French Social Imagination.* Trans. M. L. Kochan, R. Porter, C. Prendergast. Cambridge, MA: Harvard University Press.

Crang, Mike. 1998. *Cultural Geography.* London: Routledge.

Cumings, Bruce. 2005. *Korea's Place in the Sun: A Modern History.* New York: Norton.

Daegu Metropolitan Office of Education (Daegu si gyoyuk cheong). 2004. *Chodeunghakgyo haksaeng eul wihan gyeongpil daehoe jichim* (Guidelines on the beautiful calligraphy competition for elementary school students). Daegu, South Korea: Daegu Metropolitan Office of Education.

Dai, Xiahua. 2001. Life of a White Collar Lady Working in a Foreign Company. *Beijing Review Online.* www.bjreview.com.cn/2001/NationalIssues/China 200113c.htm.

DeAnda, Roberto M. 1996. Falling Back: Mexican-Origin Men and Women in the U.S. Economy. In *Chicanas and Chicanos in Contemporary Society,* ed. Roberto M. DeAnda, 41–50. Boston: Allyn and Bacon.

de Certeau, Michel. 1988 [1975]. *The Writing History.* Trans. Tom Conley. New York: Columbia University Press.

Deng, Xiaoping. 1993. *Selected Works of Deng Xiaoping* (III). *People's Daily Online.* www.people.com.cn/english/dengxp/contents3.html.

———. 1994. *Selected Works of Deng Xiaoping* (II). *People's Daily Online.* www .people.com.cn/english/dengxp/contents2.html.

Deyo, Frederic C. 1989. *Beneath the Miracle: Labor Subordination in the New Asian Industrialism.* Berkeley: University of California Press.

Ding, Xueling. 1999. Who Gets What, How? When Chinese State-Owned Enterprises Become Shareholding Companies. *Problems of Post-Communism* 46.3 (May–June): 32–41.

———. 2000. The Illicit Asset Stripping of Chinese State Firms. *China Journal* 43 (January): 1–28.

Dirlik, Arif. 1989. Postsocialism? Reflections on "Socialism with Chinese Characteristics." In *Marxism and the Chinese Experience,* ed. Arif Dirlik and Maurice Meisner, 362–85. Armonk, NY: M.E. Sharpe.

Doeringer, Peter B., Christine Evans-Klock, and David G. Terkla. 1998. Hybrids or Hodgepodges? Workplace Practices of Japanese and Domestic Startups in the United States. *Industrial and Labor Relations Review* 51.2: 171–86.

Doty, Richard. 1972. The Role of Olfaction in Man: Sense or Nonsense? In *Perception in Everyday Life,* ed. Samuel H. Bartley, 143–57. New York: Harper & Row.

Dreyfuss, Carl. 1977 [1938]. *Occupation and Ideology of the Salaried Employee.* Trans. Eva Abramovitch and Ernst E. Warburg. New York: Arno.

Drori, Israel. 2000. *The Seam Line: Arab Workers and Jewish Managers in the Israeli Textile Industry.* Stanford, CA: Stanford University Press.

Dworkin, Gerald. 1972. Paternalism. *The Monist* 56: 64–84.

———. 2005. Moral Paternalism. *Law and Philosophy* 24: 305–19.

Eckert, Carter J., Ki-baik Lee, Young-Ick Lew, Michael Robinson, and Edward W. Wagner. 1990. *Korea Old and New: A History.* Seoul: Ilchokak.

Editorial. 2003. Rencai qiangguo zhilu zenmezhuo? Renmin guandian (How to be a country with high-quality labor?) *Renmin ribao* (People's Daily), March 27. http://opinion.people.com.cn/GB/70241/4760331.html.

EIBK [Export-Import Bank of Korea]. 2003, 2004. *Hanguk yeongan suchulip bogo* (Annual report of Korean imports and exports). Seoul: Export-Import Bank of Korea.

Engels, Friedrich. 2009 [1887]. *The Condition of the Working Class in England.* London: Oxford University Press.

Escobar, Pepe. 2005. Sinoroving: Guangdong, the Unstoppable "World's Factory." *Asia Times,* January 25. www.atimes.com/atimes/China/GA25Ad05.html.

Fabian, Johannes. 1983. *Time and the Other: How Anthropology Makes Its Object.* New York: Columbia University Press.

Fairbank, John K. 1968. *The Chinese World Order: Traditional China's Foreign Relations.* Cambridge, MA: Harvard University Press.

Fan, C. Cindy. 2008. *China on the Move: Migration, the State, and the Household.* New York: Routledge.

Foucault, Michel. 1995. *Discipline and Punish: The Birth of the Prison.* New York: Vintage Books.

Fuller, Ellen V. 2009. *Going Global: Culture, Gender, and Authority in the Japanese Subsidiary of an American Corporation.* Philadelphia: Temple University Press.

Furnivall, J. S. 1948. *Colonial Policy and Practice.* London: Cambridge University Press.

Gereffi, Gary. 1994. The Organization of Buyer-Driven Global Commodity Chains: How U.S. Retailers Shape Overseas Production Networks. In *Commodity Chains and Global Capitalism*, ed. Gary Gereffi and Miguel Korzeniewicz, 95–112. Westport, CT: Greenwood.

Giddens, Anthony. 1991. *The Consequences of Modernity.* Cambridge: Polity.

Glazer, Nathan, and Daniel P. Moynihan. 1963. *Beyond the Melting Pot.* Cambridge, MA: MIT Press.

Goo, Ja-Ryong. 2009. Segye ui nuneul sarojapneun Jungguk (China attracts the world's eyes). *Sindonga* (New Dong-A) 600: 484–89.

Gottdiener, Mark. 1985. *The Social Production of Urban Space.* Austin: University of Texas Press.

———. 1987. Space as a Force of Production. *International Journal of Urban and Regional Research* 11.3: 405–17.

Gramsci, Antonio. 1991. *Prison Notebooks, Volume 1.* New York: Columbia University Press.

Green, Nancy L. 1997. *Ready-To-Wear, Ready-To-Work: A Century of Industry and Immigrants in Paris and New York.* Durham, NC: Duke University Press.

Grinspun, Ricardo, and Maxwell Cameron. 1993. *The Political Economy of North American Free Trade.* New York: St. Martin's.

Guojia shiwu (China Affairs). 2006. Hu Jintao jinggao wangdang weiji jiaju (Hu Jintao warns of threat to destroy the Communist Party). March 27.

Guthrie, Doug. 1999. *Dragon in a Three-Piece Suit: The Emergence of Capitalism in China.* Princeton, NJ: Princeton University Press.

Gwak, Seongji. 2008. *Dongbuk a sidae ui Yeonbyeon gwa Joseonjok* (Yeonbyeon and Korean-Chinese in the era of Northeast Asia). Seoul: Eyefield.

Hall, Stuart. 1997. The Local and the Global: Globalization and Ethnicity. In *Dangerous Liaisons: Gender, Nation, and Postcolonial Perspectives,* ed. Anne McClintock, Aamir Mufti, and Ella Shohat, 173–87. Minneapolis: University of Minnesota Press.

Hansen, Gary D., and Edward C. Prescott. 2002. Malthus to Solow. *American Economic Review* 92:4, 1205–17.

Hart-Landsberg, Martin. 1993. *The Rush to Development: Economic Change and Political Struggle in South Korea.* New York: Monthly Review Press.

Harvey, David. 1982. *The Limits to Capital.* Oxford: Blackwell.

———. 1985. The Geopolitics of Capitalism. In *Social Relations and Spatial Structures,* ed. Derek Gregory and John Urry, 128–63. London: Macmillan.

———. 1991. *The Condition of Postmodernity: An Enquiry into the Origins of Cultural Change.* Oxford: Wiley-Blackwell.

———. 1996. *Justice, Nature and the Geography of Difference.* London: Blackwell.

———. 2000. *Spaces of Hope.* Berkeley: University of California Press.

———. 2006. *Spaces of Global Capitalism: A Theory of Uneven Geographical Development.* London: Verso.

He, Qinglian. 1998. *Xiandaihua de xianjing: dangdai Zhongguo de jingji shehui wenti* (Pitfalls of modernization: Economic and social problems in contemporary China). Beijing: Jinri Zhongguo chubanshe.

Heintz, Monica. 2002. Changes in Work Ethic in Postsocialist Romania. Ph.D. diss., University of Cambridge.

Henderson, Gail, and Myron Cohen. 1984. *The Chinese Hospital: A Socialist Work Unit.* New Haven, CT: Yale University Press.

Heo, Myeoungcheol. 1994. Joseonjok jeontong munhwa ui wuyeolseong munje e daehan meot gaji saeng'gak (Several thoughts about the problem in the superiority and inferiority of Korean-Chinese traditional culture). In *Joseonjok uyeolseong yeongu* (Research on the superiority and inferiority of Korean-Chinese), ed. Yeonbyeon University Editing Committee of Korean-Chinese toward the Twentieth Century (series), 95–106. Yeonbyeon: Yeonbyeon inmin chulpansa.

Herzfeld, Michael. 2003. *The Body Impolitic: Artisans and Artifice in the Global Hierarchy of Value.* Chicago: University of Chicago Press.

Hill, James E. 1994. *A Study of the Cost and Benefits of a Unit Production System Versus the Progressive Bundle System.* Clemson, SC: Clemson Apparel Research, Clemson University.

Ho, Karen. 2009. *Liquidated: An Ethnography of Wall Street.* Durham, NC: Duke University Press.

Hong Kong Trade Development Council. 2003. *Foreign Direct Investment in China.* January 1.

Hopkins, Terence K., and Immanuel Wallerstein. 1986. Commodity Chains in the World Economy Prior to 1800. *Review* 10.1: 157–70.

Howard, Alan. 1999. Labor, History, and Sweatshops in the New Global Economy. In *No Sweat: Fashion, Free Trade, and the Rights of Garment Workers*, ed. Andrew Ross, 151–72. London: Verso.

Howell, John M. 1994. *Understanding Eastern Europe: The Context of Change.* London: Ernst and Young.

Hsiao, Kung-chuan. 1967. *A History of Chinese Political Thought.* Trans. F. W. Mote. Princeton, NJ: Princeton University Press.

Hu, Cong. 2005. South Korean Nabbed in Illegal Banking. *China Daily*, February 25: 1.

Humphrey, Caroline. 1995. Creating a Culture of Disillusionment: Consumption in Moscow, a Chronicle of Changing Times. In *Worlds Apart: Modernity through the Prism of the Local*, ed. Daniel Miller, 43–68. London: Routledge.

ICIME [Incheon Christian Institute for People's Education]. 1988. *1987nyeon nodongja daetujaeng: Incheon* (Workers' general strike in 1987: Cases in Incheon). Seoul: Poolbit.

Jacka, Tamara. 2006. *Rural Women in Urban China: Gender, Migration and Social Change.* Armonk, NY: M.E. Sharpe.

Janelli, Roger, and Dawnhee Yim Janelli. 1993. *Making Capitalism: The Social and Cultural Construction of a South Korean Conglomerate.* Stanford, CA: Stanford University Press.

Janelli, Roger, and Dawnhee Yim. 1999. The Mutual Constitution of Confucianism and Capitalism in South Korea. In *Culture and Economy*, ed. Timothy Brook and Hy V. Luong, 107–24. Ann Arbor: University of Michigan Press.

Jang, Segil. 2009. Jungguk saneop gujojojeong eu sahoe munhwajeok younghyang: Qingdao eu Hanguk jejoeop eu byeonhwa wa daeeung (The sociocultural impact of Chinese industrial restructuring: Change and response of Korean manufacturing industries in Qingdao). *Bigyomunhwayeongu* (Journal of Cross-cultural Studies) 15.1: 5–49.

Jang, Suhyeon. 2003. Jungguk nae Hanguk giup ui hyeonji jeogeng gwajeonggwa munhwajeok galdeung: Qingdao sojae han sinbalgongjang ae daehan inryuhakjeok yeongu (The localization process and cultural conflicts of Korean enterprises in China: An anthropological study of a shoe factory in Qingdao). *Hanguk munhwa inryuhak* (Korean Cultural Anthropology) 36.1: 83–118.

Jeon, Sungho. 1994. Joseonjok gwa Hanjok ui saenghwal munhwa bigyo (Comparison of living and culture between Korean-Chinese and Han-Chinese). In *Joseonjok uyeolseong yeongu* (Research on the superiority and inferiority of Korean-Chinese), ed. Yeonbyeon University Editing Committee of the

Korean-Chinese toward the Twentieth Century (series), 187–98. Yeonbyeon: Yeonbyeon inmin chulpansa.

Jing, Fu. 2006. Low Income Residents Face Growing Difficulties. *China Daily*, May 16: 2.

Jing, Jun. 1999. Villages Dammed, Villages Repossessed: A Memorial Movement in Northwest China. *American Ethnologist* 26.2: 324–43.

Kahn, Joseph. 2003. Foul Water and Air Part of Cost of the Boom in China's Exports. *New York Times*, November 4. www.nytimes.com/2003/11/04/international/asia/04CHIN.html.

Kang, David C. 2010. *East Asia before the West: Five Centuries of Trade and Tribute.* New York: Columbia University Press.

Kang, Wee-Won. 2008. *Joseonjok ui munhwa leul chajaseo* (A search for Korean-Chinese culture). Seoul: Yoksa gonggan.

Kawanishi, Masato. 2001. The Yen That Is Too Strong: A Note on Japanese Crisis. In *Global Financial Crisis and Reforms: Cases and Caveat*, ed. B. N. Ghosh, 284–94. London: Routledge.

Kessler, Dimitri. 2007. Nationalism, Theft, and Management Strategies in the Information Industry of Mainland China. In *Workings in China: Ethnographies of Labor and Workplace Transformation*, ed. Ching Kwan Lee, 209–28. London: Routledge.

Kikuchi, Takahiro. 2002. Offshore R&D Divisions Lured to China. June 2002. *Nikkei Electronics Asia*.

Kim, Choongsoon. 1992. *The Culture of Korean Industry: An Ethnography of Poongsan Corporation.* Tucson: University of Arizona Press.

Kim, Hae-Min. 2009. *Tteo' oreuneun paegwonja Junghwa sidae* (Emerging hegemonic power: The era of China). *Sisa Focus Online*, April 20. http://sisatoday.com/news/view.php?n=26929&p=1.

Kim, Hokyu. 2006a. Yeoksajeok hoego: 1987 nodongja daetujaeng eul ikkeun nodongja ui oechim I (Historical review: Outcry of the workers who led the 1987 general strike, I). *Huimang saesang*, July: 13–18.

———. 2006b. Yeoksajeok hoego: 1987 nodongja daetujaeng eul ikkeun nodongja ui oechim II (Historical review: Outcry of the workers who led the 1987 general strike, II). *Heemang saesang*, August: 2–8.

Kim, Il-Kweon. 1985. *Yugyo munhwa jiyeok ui jilseowa gyeongje* (Order and economy in the area of Confucian culture). Seoul: Korea Economic Daily Press.

Kim, Juyeong. 2006. *Saryae jungsim ui dongbuka jinchul jeonryak: Jungguk dongbuk jiyeok* (The strategy of investment in Northeast Asia based on case studies: China's northeast region). Seoul: Export-Import Bank of Korea.

Kim, Kyeong-Dong. 1994. Confucianism and Capitalist Development in East Asia. In *Capitalism and Development*, ed. Leslie Sklair, 87–106. New York: Routledge.

Kim, Seongcheol. 1992. Joseonjok yunli dodeok ui eoje wa oneul (The past and the present of Korean-Chinese ethics). In *Dangdae Jungguk Joseonjok yeongu* (Research on the Contemporary Korean-Chinese), ed. Yeonbyeon University

Editing Committee of the Korean-Chinese toward the Twentieth Century (series), 161–99. Yeonbyeon: Yeonbyeon inmin chulpansa.

Kim, Wang-Bae. 2004. Migration of Foreign Workers into South Korea: From Periphery to Semi-Periphery in the Global Labor Market. *Asian Survey* 44.2: 316–35.

Kim, Won. 2005. *Yeogong 1970: Gunyeodeul ui banyeoksa* (Yeogong 1970: Women's anti-history). Seoul: Imagine Context.

Kim, Yeonglim. 1994. Joseonjok ui gyoyuk'yeol e daehan sago (A consideration of the Korean-Chinese desire for higher education). In *Joseonjok uyeolseong yeongu* (Research on the superiority and inferiority of Korean-Chinese), ed. Yeonbyeon University Editing Committee of Korean-Chinese toward the Twentieth Century (series), 178–86. Yeonbyeon: Yeonbyeon inmin chulpansa.

Kipnis, Andrew. 2007. Neoliberalism Reified: *Suzhi* Discourse and Tropes of Neoliberalism in the People's Republic of China. *Journal of the Royal Anthropological Institute* 13: 383–400.

KITA [Korea International Trade Association, Beijing Branch]. 2003. Jungguk teukjip: Jungguk nodongryeok eun ssanga? (China special: Is Chinese labor cheap?). *Metalnet Korea*, December. ftp://www.metalnet.co.kr/Press/CHINA_News/CHINA-1.html.

Kleinig, John. 1983. *Paternalism*. Towata, NJ: Rowman and Allenheld.

Klubock, Thomas M. 1996. Working-Class Masculinity, Middle-Class Morality, and Labor Politics in the Chilean Copper Mines. *Journal of Social History* 30.2: 435–63.

Ko, Kyeong-sim. 1988. Hanguk yeoseong nodongja ui geon'gang munje (Korean female workers' health problems). *Yeoseong* (Women) 3: 50–68.

KOFOTI [Korean Federation of Textile Industries]. 1988, 1990, 1992. *Seomyu saneop yeongan bogo* (Annual report on the textile industry). Seoul: Korean Federation of Textile Industries.

———. 2003, 2005. *Haeoe tuja yeongan tonggye* (Annual statistics of overseas investment). Seoul: Korea Federation of Textile Industries.

Koo, Hagen. 1993. *State and Society in Contemporary Korea*. Ithaca, NY: Cornell University Press.

———. 2001. *Korean Workers: The Culture and Politics of Class Formation*. Ithaca, NY: Cornell University Press.

Kondo, Dorinne K. 1990. *Crafting Selves: Power, Gender, and Discourses of Identity in a Japanese Workplace*. Chicago: University of Chicago Press.

Kong, Qingtong. 2005. Current Situations and Prospects of Korean Enterprises in Qingdao, China. presented at the 10th Memorial International Conference for City Friendship between Incheon and Qingdao. October 18. Incheon, South Korea.

KPMG. 2006. KPMG in China Expands into Qingdao. Qingdao: KPMG Financial Advisory Services (China) Ltd (October): 1-4.

———. 2007. Qingdao Shinan District Investment Environment Study 2007. Qingdao: KPMG Advisory (China) Ltd.

Kubicek, Paul. 2004. *Organized Labor in Post-Communist States: From Solidarity to Infirmity*. Pittsburgh: University of Pittsburgh Press.

Kuttner, Kenneth N., and Adam S. Posen. 2001. The Great Recession: Lessons for Macroeconomic Policy from Japan. *Brookings Papers on Economic Activity* 2: 93–160.

Kwon, Oh-Hong. 2008. Bukgyeong Olimpik ihu ui Jungguk (China after the Beijing Olympics). *Sindonga* (New Dong-A) 588: 336–45.

Kwong, Julia. 1997. *The Political Economy of Corruption in China*. New York: M.E. Sharpe.

Lamphere, Louise. 1992. *Structuring Diversity: Ethnographic Perspectives on the New Immigration*. Chicago: University of Chicago Press.

Lane, Jan-Erik. 2006. *Globalization and Politics: Promises and Dangers*. Burlington, VT: Ashgate.

Largey, Gale P., and David R. Watson. 1972. The Sociology of Odors. *American Journal of Sociology* 77: 1021–34.

Lawrence, John J., and Rhy-song Yeh. 1994. The Influence of Mexican Culture on the Use of Japanese Manufacturing Techniques in Mexico. *Management International Review* 34.1: 49–66.

Ledeneva, Alena V. 1998. *Russia's Economy of Favours: Blat, Networking, and Informal Exchange*. Cambridge: Cambridge University Press.

Lee, Bonyeong. 2005a. Chingdao, Hanguk, Daryeon, Ilbon (Qingdao, Korea, Dalian, Japan?). *Hankyeorae sinmun* (One Nation Daily), January 16. http://legacy.www.hani.co.kr/ection-004000000/2005/01/00400000020050116175 1032.html.

———. 2005b. Sarajineun ssan nodongryeok—naesu sijang eul yeoleora! (Disappearing cheap labor—Open up domestic markets!). *Hankyeorae sinmun* (One Nation Daily), January 16: 7.

Lee, Buhyong. 2005. Jeongbu ui jeongchek silpae ro choraedoen Ilbon ui janggi bulhwang (Japanese long-term recession caused by the failure of government policy). *Hanguk gyeongje joopyeong* (Korea Economy Weekly), June 22: 1–10. Seoul: Hyundai Research Institute.

Lee, Ching Kwan. 1998a. *Gender and the South China Miracle: Two Worlds of Factory Women*. Berkeley: University of California Press.

———. 1998b. The Labor Politics of Market Socialism: Collective Inaction and Class Experiences among State Workers in Guangzhou. *Modern China* 24.1: 3–33.

———. 1999. From Organized Dependence to Disorganized Despotism: Changing Labour Regimes in Chinese Factories. *China Quarterly* 157 (March): 44–71.

———. 2000a. The "Revenge of History": Collective Memories and Labor Protests in Northeastern China. *Ethnography* 1.2: 217–37.

———. 2000b. Pathways of Labor Insurgency. In *Chinese Society: Change, Conflict and Resistance*, ed. Elizabeth Perry and Mark Selden, 41–61. London: Routledge.

Lee, Hongwoo. 1994. Jagi banseong jungeseo ui Joseon minjok ui baljeon (Korean-Chinese development through self-reflection). In *Joseonjok uyeolseong yeongu* (Research on the superiority and inferiority of Korean-Chinese), ed. Yeonbyeon University Editing Committee of Korean-Chinese toward the Twentieth Century (series), 33–48. Yeonbyeon: Yeonbyeon inmin chulpansa.

Lee, Kyeong. 2004. Ilbon janggi bulhwanggi wa guknae gyeongje yeogeon (The Japanese long-term recession and the economic situation of Korea). *Jugan Hanguk gyeongjae* (Korea Economy Weekly), June 12: 1-4. Seoul: Hyundai Research Institute

Lee, Ok-jie. 1990. *Labor Control and Labor Protest in the South Korean Textile Industry, 1945–1985.* Madison: University of Wisconsin-Madison.

Lee, Seung Hoon, and Ho Keun Song. 1994. The Korean Garment Industry: From Authoritarian Patriarchism to Industrial Paternalism. In Bonacich et al. 1994: 147–61.

Lee, Taehee. 2006. Byeonhwa haneun Jungguk nodong jeongchaek gwa Hanguk gyeongyeongjin ui daeeung jeonryak (Changing conditions of Chinese labor policies and Korean managements' responding strategies). Paper presented at the conference of the Current Conditions of Chinese Labor Management and Our Response. Korea Chamber of Commerce and Industry (KORCHAM), April 13. Seoul.

Lefebvre Henri. 1976. *De l'Etat: L'Etat dans le monde moderne.* Volume 1. Paris: Union Générale d'Editions.

———. 1991. *The Production of Space.* Translated by D. Nicholson-Smith. Oxford: Blackwell.

Levy, Richard. 1995. Corruption, Economic Crime and Social Transformation since the Reforms: The Debate in China. *Australian Journal of Chinese Affairs* 33: 1–25.

Lie, John. 2000. *Han Unbound: The Political Economy of South Korea.* Stanford, CA: Stanford University Press.

Lim, Geumsook. 1992. Gaehyeok gaebang irae Joseonjok ui gaein gyeongjae wa sayeong giup ui baljeon (The development of Korean-Chinese individual business and private enterprises since the economic reform). In *Dangdae Jungguk Joseonjok yeongu* (Research on contemporary Korean-Chinese), ed. Yeonbyeon University Editing Committee of Korean-Chinese toward the Twentieth Century (series), 104–27. Yeonbyeon: Yeonbyeon inmin chulpansa.

Lim, Gyesoon. 2003. *Uri ege dagaon Joseonjok eun nugu'inga* (Who are the Korean-Chinese?). Seoul: Heonamsa.

Lin, Gang. 2003. *Crisis in the Hinterland: Rural Discontent in China.* Introduction. Special Report No. 108. Woodrow Wilson International Center, Washington, D.C.

Liu, Alan P. L. 1983. The Politics of Corruption in the People's Republic of China. *American Political Science Review* 77.3: 602–23.

Liu, Chang. 2006. 32,000 Investigated for Corruption. *China Daily*, January 20: 2.

Liu, Xin. 2000. *In One's Own Shadow: An Ethnographic Account of the Condition of Post-Reform Rural China.* Berkeley: University of California Press.

Lucas, Robert E. 2002. *Lectures on Economic Growth.* Cambridge, MA: Harvard University Press.

Luo, Peng. 2008. Analysis of Cultural Differences between West and East in International Business Negotiation. *International Journal of Business and Management* 3.11: 103–6.

Mackerras, Colin. 2003. *China's Ethnic Minorities and Globalisation.* London: Routledge Curzon.

Management of Nawon. 1994. Nawon Apparel: hoesa sogae (Introduction to Nawon Apparel). Qingdao: Nawon Apparel. Internal document; not available to the public.

———. 2002. Weolbyeol bosu jigeuppyo (Monthly report about the wage payments of employees). Qingdao: Nawon Apparel. Internal document; not available to the public.

Marx, Karl, and Frederick Engels. 1992 [1848]. *The Communist Manifesto.* New York: Bantam Books.

Mauss, Marcel. 1990 [1922]. *The Gift: Forms and Functions of Exchange in Archaic Societies.* London: Routledge.

Mendez, J. B. 2005. *From the Revolution to the Maquiladoras: Gender, Labor, and Globalization in Nicaragua.* Durham, NC: Duke University Press.

Mills, C. Wright. 1956. *White Collar: The American Middle Classes.* New York: Oxford University Press.

Ministry of Government Legislation of Korea (Daehan minguk beopjaecheo). 2000. *Byeong yeok bup* (The military service law). Seoul: Ministry of Government Legislation.

Ministry of National Defense of Korea (Daehan minguk gukbangbu). 1996. *Gukgun jeongsin gyoyuk gyobon* (Textbook for the education of mental discipline in the military). Daejeon, South Korea: Ministry of National Defense.

Mokyr, Joel. 1990. *The Lever of Riches: Technological Creativity and Economic Progress.* New York: Oxford University Press.

Moon, Byeonghoon. 2002. Jungguk ui Hanguk bongjae hoesa—bulhwang eul ijeora (Korean garment corporations in China—forget economic recession). *Apparel News Korea*, November 22: 1.

Moon, Seungsook. 2005. *Militarized Modernity and Gendered Citizenship in South Korea.* Durham, NC: Duke University Press.

Mulvenon, James. 2006. So Crooked They Have to Screw Their Pants On: New Trends in Chinese Military Corruption. *China Leadership Monitor* 19: 1–8.

NBSC [Zhongguo guojia tongjiju (National Bureau of Statistics of China)]. 1991. *Zhongguo 1990 nian renkou pucha ziliao* (Databook of China's 1990 census). Beijing: China Statistics Press.

———. 2007. *Zhongguo 2006 nian renkou pucha ziliao* (Databook of China's 2006 census). Beijing: China Statistics Press.

————. Various years. *Zhongguo tongji nianjian* (China statistical yearbook). Beijing: China Statistics Press.

Nike, Howard J. De, Uwe Ewald, and Christopher J. Nowilin (ed.). 1995. *Crime in East Europe: Recent Reflections from the Eastern Academy.* Bonn: Forum-Verl. Godesberg.

North, Douglass C., and Barry Weingast. 1989. Constitution and Commitment: The Evolution of Institutional Governing Public Choice in Seventeenth-Century England. *Journal of Economic History* 49.4: 803–32.

O'Brien, Kevin J. 1996. Rightful Resistance. *World Politics* 49.1: 31–55.

————. 2006. *Rightful Resistance in Rural China.* Cambridge: Cambridge University Press.

O'Rourke, Kevin H., and Jeffery G. Williamson. 2002. From Malthus to Ohlin: Trade, Growth, and Distribution since 1500. *Trinity Economics Papers* 2002. Dublin: Trinity College.

Oh, Sun Joo. 1983. The Living Conditions of Female Workers in Korea. *Korea Observer* 14: 185–200.

On, Kihong. 2005. Bupaehan jeongbu gwanryodeul ege sahyeong seongo (Death sentence to corrupt government officials). *Media Daum,* August 30. http://news .media.daum.net/snews/foreign/others/200508/30/m_daum/v10029726.html.

Ong, Aihwa. 1987. *Spirits of Resistance and Capitalist Discipline: Factory Women in Malaysia.* Albany: State University of New York Press.

————. 1999. *Flexible Citizenship: The Cultural Logics of Transnationality.* Durham, NC: Duke University Press.

Oppenheimer, M. 1973. The Proletarianization of the Professional. *Sociological Review Monography* 20: 213–27.

Orwell, George. 1937. *The Road to Wigan Pier.* London: Victor Gollancz.

Ota, Tatsuyuki. 2003. The Role of Special Economic Zones in China's Economic Development as Compared with Asian Export Processing Zones: 1979–1995. *Asia in Extenso,* March: 1–28.

Park, Deok Jae, and Ki Seong Park. 1989. *Hanguk ui nodong johap* (Labor unions in Korea). Seoul: Korean Labor Institute.

Park, Kyeonghwi. 1994. Joseonjok mipung yangsok ui gyeseung gwa jegeohaeyahal myeotgaji pungseup (On the inheritance of superior customs and the elimination of several bad customs). In *Joseonjok uyeolseong yeongu* (Research on the superiority and inferiority of Korean-Chinese), ed. Yeonbyeon University Editing Committee of Korean-Chinese toward the Twentieth Century (series), 217–34. Yeonbyeon: Yeonbyeon inmin chulpansa.

Park, Minhui. 2006. Baeteunam, nae chingu: Baeteunam eul dugo gyeongjaeng haneun Miguk gwa Jungguk (Vietnam, my friend: U.S. and China compete over China). *Hankyeorae shinmun* (One Nation Daily), June 21: 7.

Park, So Jin, and Nancy Abelmann. 2004. Class and Cosmopolitan Striving: Mother's Management of English Education in South Korea. *Anthropological Quarterly* 77: 645–72.

Parker, P., and P. Aggleton. 2003. HIV and AIDS-related Stigma and

Discrimination: A Conceptual Framework and Implications for Action. *Social Science and Medicine* 57: 13–24.

Perlez, Jane. 2006. U.S. Competes with China for Vietnam's allegiance. *New York Times*, June 19: section A, page 3, column 1.

Personnel Department, Nawon Apparel. 1995. *Singyu jikgong jidoseo* (Workshop manual for new workers). Qingdao: Nawon.

———. 2003. *Yeongan sa'eop bogoseo* (Annual report of factory operations). January 2003. Internal document.

Personnel Department, Nawon Korea. 1997. Saneup yeonsusaeng ui seonbal e gwanhayeo (Concerning the selection of foreign apprentices). Seoul: Nawon Korea. Internal document.

Peterson, Kurt. 1992. *The Maquiladora Revolution in Guatemala.* Center for International Human Rights at the Yale Law School. New Haven, CT: Yale Law School.

———. 1994. The *Maquila* Revolution in Guatemala. In Bonacich et al. 1994: 268–86.

Pine, Frances. 1996. Redefining Women's Work in Rural Poland. In *After Socialism: Land Reform and Social Change in Eastern Europe*, ed. Ray Abrahams, 133–56. Oxford: Berghahn.

Pine, Frances, and Sue Bridger. 1998. Introduction: Transitions to Post-Socialism and Cultures of Survival. In *Surviving Post-Socialism: Local Strategies and Regional Responses in Eastern Europe and the Former Soviet Union*, ed. Frances Pine and Sue Bridger, 1–15. London: Routledge.

Plywaczewski, Emil W., and Wieslaw Plywaczewski. 2005. The Threat of Corruption in Poland with Particular Reference to Public Servants. In *Policing Corruption: International Perspectives*, ed. Rick Sarre, Dilip K. Das, and H. J. Albrecht, 129–36. Lanham, MD: Lexington Books.

Pomeranz, Kenneth. 2000. *The Great Divergence: China, Europe, and the Making of the Modern World Economy.* Princeton, NJ: Princeton University Press.

Porter, Michael, Takeuchi Hirotaka, and Mariko Sakakibara. 2000. *Can Japan Compete?* London: Basic Books.

Priestley, K. E. 1963. *Workers of China.* London: Holywell.

Pun, Ngai. 1999. Becoming Dagongmei (Working Girls): The Politics of Identity and Difference in Reform China. *The China Journal* 42 (July): 1–18.

———. 2004. Women Workers and Precarious Employment in Shenzhen Special Economic Zone, China. *Gender and Development* 12.2: 29–36.

———. 2005. *Made in China: Women Factory Workers in a Global Workplace.* Durham, NC: Duke University Press.

Pun, Ngai, and Chris Smith. 2007. Putting Transnational Labour Process in Its Place: The Dormitory Labour Regime in Post-socialist China. *Work, Employment & Society* 21.1: 27–45.

Qingdao ribao (Qingdao Daily). 2003. Qingdao shizhengfu de yufang SARS de gongzuo yanhuan Hanguoren (Efforts of the Qingdao city government to prevent SARS reassure the Korean people). May 1: 1.

Reich, Robert B. 2007. *Supercapitalism: The Transformation of Business, Democracy, and Everyday Life*. New York: Knopf.

Riain, Seán Ó. 2000. States and Markets in an Era of Globalization. *Annual Review of Sociology* 26: 187–213.

Rigby, Harry T. 1977. Stalinism and the Mono-Organizational Society. In *Stalinism: Essays in Historical Interpretation*, ed. Robert C. Tucker, 53–76. New York: W.W. Norton.

Rofel, Lisa. 1999. *Other Modernities: Gendered Yearnings in China after Socialism*. Berkeley: University of California Press.

Rohlen, Thomas P. 1974. Sponsorship of Cultural Continuity in Japan: A Company Training Program. In *Japanese Culture and Behavior*, ed. Takie Sugiyama Lebra and William P. Lebra, 332–41. Honolulu: University Press of Hawaii.

Ross, Andrew. 1999. Introduction. In *No Sweat: Fashion, Free Trade, and the Rights of Garment Workers,* ed. Andrew Ross, 9–38. London: Verso

Saich, Tony. 2007. China in 2006: Focus on Social Development. *Asian Survey* 47.1: 32–43.

Salinas, R., and Paldan, L. 1979. Culture in the Process of Dependent Development: Theoretical Perspectives. In *National Sovereignty and International Communication*, ed. Kaarle Nordenstreng and Herbert I. Schiller, 82–98. Norwood, NJ: Ablex.

Sassen, Saskia. 2000. Spatialities and Temporalities of the Global: Elements for a Theorization. *Public Culture* 12: 215–32.

SCC [State Council of China]. 1986. *Provisions of the State Council on the Encouragement of Foreign Investment*. Beijing: State Council of China.

Schaeffer, Robert K. 1997. *Understanding Globalization: The Social Consequences of Political, Economic, and Environmental Change*. Lanham, MD: Rowman and Littlefield.

Schiller, Herbert I. 1976. *Communication and Cultural Domination*. New York: M.E. Sharpe.

Scott, James C. 1985. *Weapons of the Weak: Everyday Forms of Peasant Resistance*. New Haven, CT: Yale University Press.

SDBFT [Shandong Bureau of Financial Trade]. 2005. Benefits to foreign direct investment in Shandong. In *Guidebook of Foreign Investment in Shandong*. Ji'nan: Shandong People's Government.

SDBS [Shandong sheng tongjiju (Shandong Bureau of Statistics)]. 2003, 2005, 2006, 2008, 2009. *Shandong tongji nianjian* (Statistical yearbook of Shandong). Ji'nan: Shandong tongji chubanshe.

Sen, K. Amartya. 2006. *Identity and Violence: The Illusion of Destiny*. New Delhi: Penguin.

SERI [Samsung Economic Research Institute]. 2004. *Jungguk naesu sijang gaecheok ui seonggong jogeon* (Conditions of success in developing the Chinese domestic market). November 24.

Shaiken, Harley. 1990. *Mexico in the Global Economy: High Technology and Work*

Organization in Export Industries. La Jolla: Center for U.S.-Mexican Studies, University of California, San Diego.

Shanghai Asset Inc. 2005. Jungguk eseoui seonggong iyu: LG ui sarye (The reason for success in China: The case of LG). Data Room. http://shanghaiasset .com/info/view.asp?idx=550&search1=&search2=&news_type=.

Shelley, Louise I. 1997. Post-Soviet Organized Crime: A New Form of Authoritarianism. In *Russian Organized Crime: The New Threat?* ed. Phil Williams, 122–38. London: Frank Cass.

Shin, Yunhwan. 1993. Hanguk ui jesam segye gukga tuja (Korean investment in third world countries: A critique of the "mean" management of Korean enterprises in these countries). *Changjak gwa bipyeong* (Creation and Critique) 21.3: 303–23.

Sicular, Terry, Yue Ximing, Bjorn Gustafsson, and Li Shi. 2007. The Urban-Rural Income Gap and Inequality in China. *Review of Income and Wealth* 53.1: 93–126

Sklair, Leslie. 1989. *Assembling for Development: The Maquiladora Industry in the U.S. and Mexico.* London: Unwin Hyman.

Snyder, Carl D. 1973. *White-Collar Workers and the UAW.* Chicago: University of Illinois Press.

Solinger, Dorothy J. 1992. Urban Entrepreneurs and the State: The Merger of State and Society. In *State and Society in China: The Consequences of Reform,* ed. Arthur L. Rosenbaum, 121–41. Boulder, CO: Westview.

———. 1995. The Floating Population in Cities: Chances for Assimilation? In *Urban Spaces in Contemporary China: The Potential for Autonomy and Community in Post-Mao China,* ed. Deborah S. Davis, Richard Kraus, Barry Naughton, and Elizabeth J. Perry, 113–42. Washington, D.C.: Woodrow Wilson Center Press.

———. 1999. *Contesting Citizenship in Urban China: Peasant Migrants, the State, and the Logic of the Market.* Berkeley: University of California Press.

Song, Eudal. 2006. Jungguk eseo jjotgyeo naneun Hanguk gieopdeul (Korean enterprises expelled from China). *Joseon ilbo* (Joseon Daily), January 22: 7.

Song, Ho Keun. 1989. The State against Labor Segmentation: Union Wage Effects in the Manufacturing Industries. *Korean Journal of Labor Economics* 12: 121–38

Sun, Yuandong. 1999. Lun xiangcun dipi dui jiceng xingzheng de yingxiang (The influence of local bullies on basic-level administration). *Kaifang shidai* (Open Age) 3: 38–41.

Swain, Nigel. 1996. Getting Land in Central Europe. In *After Socialism: Land Reform and Social Change in Eastern Europe,* ed. Ray Abrahams, 193–216. Oxford: Berghahn.

Swyngedouw Erik. 1992. Territorial Organization and the Space/Technology Nexus. *Transactions of the Institute of British Geographers: New Series* 17: 417–33.

———. 1997. Neither Global Nor Local: "Glocalization" and the Politics of Scale. In *Spaces of Globalization,* ed. Kevin Cox, 137–66. New York: Guilford.

Synnott, Anthony. 1993. *The Body Social: Symbolism, Self and Society*. London: Routledge.

Tak, Sereong. 2006a. Jungguk oeja gieop ui nodong gwanli e yesang doeneun munjae (Expected troubles in labor management of foreign enterprises in China). *Haeoe gyeongje* (Foreign Economy), March: 82–86. Seoul: Export-Import Bank of Korea.

———. 2006b. Tuja hwangyeong byeonhwa e dahae jeungga haneun uryeo (Increasing worries about recent changes in the investment environment). *Haeoe gyeongje* (Foreign Economy), September: 57–60. Seoul: Export-Import Bank of Korea.

———. 2006c. Jungguk jeongbu ui ganghwa deon josae jeongchaek (Reinforced tax surveillance by the Chinese government). *Haeoe gyeongje* (Foreign Economy), December: 70–73. Seoul: Export-Import Bank of Korea.

Taylor, Frederick W. 1947 [1911]. *Scientific Management*. New York: Harper & Row.

Taylor, Peter J. 1995. World Cities and Territorial States: The Rise and Fall of Their Mutuality. In *World Cities in a World-System,* ed. Paul Knox and Peter Taylor, 48–62. New York: Cambridge University Press.

Thomas, Elbert D. 1968. *Chinese Political Thought*. New York: Greenwood.

Thompson, Edward P. 1966. *The Making of the English Working Class*. New York: Vintage Books.

Tse, Constant, and Elizabeth Zhou. 2005. New Tax Rules Are Aimed at Full Reporting of Individual Incomes. *China Daily*, September 28: 4.

United Front Work Department of the CCP (Zhonggong zhongyang tongyi zhanxian gongzuobu). 1991. *Diliujie quanguo renmin daibiao dahui de shengming* (Manifesto of the sixth CCP Congress). Beijing: United Front Work Department of CCP.

van Gennep, Arnold. 1961. *The Rites of Passage*. Chicago: University of Chicago Press.

Varese, Federico. 2001. *The Russian Mafia: Private Protection in a New Market Economy*. Oxford: Oxford University Press.

Voronin, Yuriy A. 1997. The Emerging Criminal State: Economic and Political Aspects of Organized Crime in Russia. In *Russian Organized Crime: The New Threat?* ed. Phil Williams, 53–62. London: Frank Cass.

Walder, Andrew G. 1986. *Communist Neo-Traditionalism: Work and Authority in Chinese Industry*. Berkeley: University of California Press.

Waley, Arthur. 1989 [1938]. *The Analects of Confucius*. New York: Vintage Books.

Wang, Ren Min. 2004. Fifty-Five Economic Terms since Founding of People's Republic of China—Part One. *People's Daily Online*. http://english.people.com.cn/200411/15/eng20041114_163921.html.

Wang, Seon-Taek. 2005. Gubaek guship sam charye ui oechim: sasil inga? (Nine hundred and ninety-three foreign invasions: Is it true?). www.ytn.co.kr/news/clmn_view.php?idx=292&s_mcd=0612&s_hcd=01&page=8.

Wang, Tongxun, and Guo Yangdao. 2002. Miandui WTO: renli shi ziyuan geng shi ziben (Encountering WTO: Labor power is a resource that surpasses capital). *Renmin ribao* (People's Daily), April 27. http://opinion.people.com.cn/GB/70241/4760547.html.

Wank, David L. 1995. Civil Society in Communist China? Private Business and Political Alliance, 1989. In *Civil Society: Theory, History, Comparison*, ed. John A. Hall, 56–79. London: Polity.

Weber, Max. 1968 [1956]. *Economy and Society*, ed. Guenther Ross and Claus Wittich. New York: Bedminster.

———. 1986 [1921]. *The City*. Trans. Don Martindale. Glencoe, IL: Free Press.

———. 2001 [1930]. *The Protestant Ethic and the Spirit of Capitalism*. London: Routledge.

Wei, Zhe. 2006. Woguo lingshouye fazhanmianlin de tiaozhan yu duice (Challenges and countermeasures of developing Chinese retail business). *Journal of Contemporary Business* 5. http://business.sohu.com/20060620/n244711091.shtml.

Weiss, Michael J. 1988. *The Clustering of America*. New York: Harper & Row.

Werner International. 2001. *Spinning and Weaving Labor Cost Comparisons 2000*. Reston, VA: Werner International Management Consultants.

Williams, Raymond. 1978. *Marxism and Literature*. London: Oxford University Press.

Willis, Paul. 1981 [1977]. *Learning to Labor: How Working Class Kids Get Working Class Jobs*. Reprint, Morningside Books. New York: Columbia University Press.

World Health Organization. 2003. Global Alert and Response: Summary Table of SARS Cases by Country, 1 November 2002–7 August 2003. August 15. Geneva.

Wu, Jinglian. 2006. Keynote Speech. *Chang'an Forum of Chinese Economists 50*. Beijing, June 25.

Wu, Ximing, and Jeffrey M. Perloff. 2005. China's Income Distribution, 1985–2001. *Review of Economics and Statistics* 87.4: 763–75.

Xie, Chuanjiao. 2005. Vice-Mayor Sentenced to Death for Bribes. *China Daily*, January 14: 3.

Xie, Xuren. 2006. A Report on the State Tax Reform: A Report Presented by the State Administration of Taxation at the Joint Conference of the Six Ministries on the Current Situation. March 14.

Xin, Bei. 2004. Striking a Chord for Social Harmony. *China Daily*, September 24: 6.

Xin, Meng, Ron Duncan, Maree Tait, Ross Garnaut, Reuven Glick, Enzo R. Grilli, and Mario B. Lamberte. 2000. *Labour Market Reform in China*. Cambridge: Cambridge University Press.

Xing, Zhigang. 2005. Experts Discuss a Harmonious Society. *China Daily*, March 4: 4.

Xinhua News Agency. 2005a. China Prosecutes 30,788 Officials in 2004. March 9.

———. 2005b. China Cuts Income Tax for Low Wage Earners. October 23.

———. 2006. President Hu Jintao Calls for Corruption Fight. January 8.

Yan, Hairong. 2003. Neoliberal Governmentality and Neohumanism: Organizing Suzhi/Value Flow through Labor Recruitment Networks. *Cultural Anthropology* 18.4: 493–523.

Yan, Yangtze. 2006. CPC Promotes "Core Value System" to Lay Moral Foundation for Social Harmony. Xinhua News Agency, October 18.

Yan, Yunxiang. 2000. Of Hamburger and Social Space: Consuming McDonald's in Beijing. In *The Consumer Revolution in Urban China*, ed. Deborah Davis, 201–25. Berkeley: University of California Press.

———. 2003. *Private Life under Socialism*. Stanford, CA: Stanford University Press.

Yang, Lawrence H., S. H. Cho, and Arthur Kleinman. 2008. Stigma of Mental Illness. *International Encyclopedia of Public Health* 6: 219–30.

Yang, Mayfair Mei-hui. 1989. Between State and Society: The Construction of Corporateness in a Chinese Socialist Factory. *Australian Journal of Chinese Affairs* 22 (July): 31–60.

Yu, Feng. 2010. Xi Jinping: zai jinian Zhongguo renmin zhiyuanjun kangmei yuanchao chuguo zuozhan liushizhounian zhuotanhuishang de tanhua (Xi Jinping: An address at a symposium commemorating the 60th anniversary of the Korean War). Xinhua News Agency, October 25. www.360doc.com/content/10/1026/20/2275617_64255262.shtml.

Zhang, Li. 2001. *Strangers in the City: Reconfigurations of Space, Power, and Social Networks within China's Floating Population*. Stanford, CA: Stanford University Press.

———. 2008. Private Homes, Distinct Lifestyles: Performing a New Middle Class. In *Privatizing China: Socialism from Afar*, ed. Li Zhang and Aihwa Ong, 23–40. Ithaca, NY: Cornell University Press.

Zhang, Wei-Wei. 2000. *Transforming China: Economic Reform and Its Political Implications*. New York: St. Martin's.

Index